RFID Toys

Cool Projects for Home, Office, and Entertainment

Amal Graafstra

WILEY

Wiley Publishing, Inc.

RFID Toys: Cool Projects for Home, Office, and Entertainment

Published by
Wiley Publishing, Inc.
10475 Crosspoint Boulevard
Indianapolis, IN 46256
www.wiley.com

Published simultaneously in Canada

ISBN-13: 978-0-471-77196-8
ISBN-10: 0-471-77196-1

Manufactured in the United States of America

10 9 8 7 6 5 4 3 2

1B/TR/QR/QW/IN

For general information on our other products and services or to obtain technical support, please contact our Customer Care Department within the U.S. at (800) 762-2974, outside the U.S. at (317) 572-3993 or fax (317) 572-4002.

Library of Congress Control Number: 2005034027

Wiley also publishes its books in a variety of electronic formats. Some content that appears in print may not be available in electronic books.

About the Author

Amal Graafstra is an entrepreneur and jack-of-many-trades. Currently involved in no less than three different companies, he still finds time to think up interesting ways to apply various technologies in his daily life and wield a soldering iron from time to time. Amal is CEO of Morpheus Inc., a computer and networking company that specializes in supplying managed terminal environments to the medical industry.

He is also president of txtGroups Inc. (`www.txtgroups.com`), an SMS text messaging company soon to launch group messaging services across Canada, with plans for expansion to the US, UK, and Australia.

Since learning about the contactless RFID technology used in cats and dogs for identification, Amal wanted to leverage that technology himself. Getting an implant meant there was no need to carry an RFID access card around and he could implement his own RFID access control systems instead of buying expensive off-the-shelf products. Soon after getting his first implant (`www.amal.net/rfid.html`) and posting some pictures of the process for a few friends, word quickly spread over the Internet and soon he found himself talking to everyone from industry players to clergy to book publishers about RFID technology and its possibilities.

Amal Graafstra can be reached at `amal@amal.net`.

Credits

Executive Editor
Chris Webb

Development Editor
Rosanne Koneval

Technical Editor
Nathan Yocom

Production Editor
Michael Koch

Copy Editor
Kathryn Duggan

Editorial Manager
Mary Beth Wakefield

Production Manager
Tim Tate

Vice President and Executive Group Publisher
Richard Swadley

Vice President and Executive Publisher
Joseph B. Wikert

Project Coordinator
Michael Kruzil

Graphics and Production Specialists
Denny Hager
Stephanie D. Jumper
Barbara Moore
Lynsey Osborn
Alicia B. South

Quality Control Technicians
John Greenough
Brian H. Walls

Proofreading and Indexing
TECHBOOKS Production Services

Cover Design
Anthony Bunyan

Contents at a Glance

Contents

• •

Acknowledgments

Always there for me, my companion Jenny gives me constant and unwavering support. During the entire writing process, I had to deal with selling my house, moving to a new country, disassembling a company, and launching a new business. Jenny was always patient and helpful, encouraging me while at the same time ensuring I wouldn't go off the deep end by wrenching me out of my cave/office for fun breaks and fresh air.

I'd also like to thank hardware vendors like Matt Trossen of Phidgets USA (www.phidgets usa.com) who took an interest in my RFID projects and contributed hardware for the book. Special thanks also goes out to Tony Anast of SkyeTek (www.skyetek.com) who was easy to work with and very helpful.

Thanks goes out to Nathan Yocom, author of the open source pGina project (http://pgina.xpasystems.com). Working with him to develop some of the code used in Chapter 4 was both fun and enlightening.

I'd also like to thank everyone who has contributed over the past 20–30 years to producing such an amazing thing as the Internet. Without leaving my home office, I was able to gather information, contact people, experience my 15 minutes of fame (Google for "Amal Graafstra"), and write a book. The Internet and all the people who contribute to its contents are truly amazing.

Thank you all for picking up this book. Writing it has been a great experience for me, and I hope after reading it, you have some inspiration to create some of your own RFID-enabled projects.

Introduction

Until the day technology is at a level where an item, person, or object can be automatically scanned at the molecular level from a distance with some kind of "Star Trek"–like device to determine its unique identity, RFID will play a major role in object identification. The contactless nature of RFID enables just about anything to be tagged and identified, even if it's inside a drawer or moving through an assembly line or wrapped in packing paper.

Consider for a moment a simple access-control scenario at any business. A single employee has to pass through a secure door twice a day. Using a traditional key to pass through the door would require time to fumble with a key ring to find the key, time to get the key into the lock and unlock the door, and still more time to push the door open, remove the key, and maybe even lock the door. Using RFID, that same person with a contactless RFID access card in a wallet or purse simply has to wave their wallet or purse in front of the RFID reader and walk through the door. Multiply that time savings by several hundred employees and perhaps several secure doors and you've just saved a huge amount productivity time.

Consider also the idea that each RFID tag has a unique identification number. Unlike UPC barcodes, RFID tags can identify the exact item it's affixed to. With that level of detail, supply chain managers, storefront managers, and even consumers would be able to know much more detail about a particular item. Consider the use of RFID labels on milk cartons. By employing a smart-shelf in the storefront, a manager could see instantly what his milk inventory is and even what milk cartons will go bad within the next week, possibly prompting a sale on that overstock of 2 percent. This could all be done without any floor clerks so much as opening a cooler door. For the consumer, a smart refrigerator could easily identify that same milk carton and know that it will go bad soon and remind the people in the house that breakfast cereal is a good way to start the day.

If read/write RFID tags were used on those milk cartons, they could easily store the manufacture date as well as the sell-by date the milk would go bad, enabling every step of the chain from manufacture to end-consumer to know the details without needing to access a central database to get information for that tag ID. This could easily leverage RFID technology without raising privacy concerns about a person's refrigerator contents.

Whom This Book Is For

People who love learning concepts rather than steps will get the most out of this book. If you want to get into RFID but need to see a few practical examples and solid implementations first, then you're in luck. I hope by building the projects presented in this book you will learn important concepts, explore new technologies, and be inspired to design and create your own unique and creative RFID based projects and solutions.

Even though RFID has been around a long time, only recently has it seen widespread use in many different markets on many different levels. The record-breaking pace at which it's being implemented, and the new technologies evolving, suggests RFID may make the leap from factories and warehouses to becoming a common household technology. Imagine having smart shelves in your home that can tell you where you car keys are and what drawer or closet that favorite sweatshirt of yours is in. Get a head start and trick out your life with RFID today!

What This Book Covers

The projects in this book cover different RFID technologies using various frequency ranges and power levels. The book features both passive and active RFID systems, as well as the different kinds of antenna systems each type of technology uses.

Most of the projects deal with passive RFID. The reason for this is that low-frequency and high-frequency passive RFID systems are both cheap and intriguing. Because passive RFID transponders, or tags, do not require a battery or internal power source, they do not have a finite lifespan. The contactless nature of RFID enables you to use it when direct contact or even line-of-sight is not possible.

Access control is one of the most common applications that RFID is used for today. By identifying authorized personnel via RFID, people don't even have to remove the RFID access card from their purses or wallets; they can just wave it in front of the sensor and gain entry. This book contains several RFID-based solutions for various types of access control situations.

Passive systems are also used to help manage supply chains and inventory. Many businesses employ RFID in what are known as smart shelves. These are shelves that contain reader hardware that can take a real-time inventory of tagged items resting on, or sometimes in, the smart shelf. These shelves can also actively monitor these items to initiate a business process when the inventory gets too low, like a restocking order for example. I'll show you how to build your own smart shelf that you can use to keep an eye on any tagged items you want, including your DVD collection.

Active RFID systems use powered tags that contain an internal power source or battery. Because these tags have a battery, they also have a limited lifespan. Generally, tags are designed to have a 3- to 5-year useful life before they need to be replaced. The advantage of active RFID, however, is the extremely long range these systems are capable of when compared to passive RFID systems. Active RFID can be used to monitor and track personnel and/or objects that are either difficult to control (stand here while we scan you), or aren't practically accessible (boxes stacked in a shipping truck). Because active tags transmit their information constantly, they can also be employed by high-end asset monitoring solutions that require flexible but rock-solid detection of missing assets. I've dedicated a couple chapters to active RFID, showing you how you can use it to track people and monitor assets.

There are some types of active and passive RFID tags that can be used to store data as well. Expanding their usefulness beyond simple identification, writable tags enhance the spectrum of possible applications by allowing applicable data to move with the tag. A normal, read-only RFID tag affixed to a pair of white gym socks in a storefront fulfills its purpose by providing a unique identification number to the reader, thereby identifying itself. If the application reading the tag needs to know that this tag represents white gym socks, it has to access some form of centralized database where the RFID tag identification number is linked to the information "white gym socks." But what if the application reading the RFID tag doesn't have access to that centralized database? What if there is no database at all? Writeable tags allow data like "white gym socks" to be written directly to the tag, letting any application reading the tag know more about the item the tag is affixed to without access to any external data source. You'll learn how to leverage this data storage capability to get more functionality out of your RFID applications for less money.

The world of RFID is a rapidly growing realm of possibilities. Businesses, organizations, and everyday people are making use of RFID in unique and amazing ways. In an effort to get you thinking creatively about RFID, the final chapter in this book covers some interesting ways people are using RFID in their homes and businesses.

What You Need to Use This Book

To build the projects in this book, you'll need to know how to handle a soldering iron and have plenty of spare wire around. Some imagination and patience won't hurt either, as you might not have access to exactly the same hardware and equipment shown in this book.

Access to the Internet is a must because you'll need to order parts and visit www.`rfidtoys`.`net` to download software and/or source code. You can also access the forums on www.`rfidtoys`.`net` to get help building your projects, post your own project suggestions, and exchange information and ideas with others.

Other than that, some imagination and a lot of enthusiasm is all you need.

Getting Started with RFID

*R*FID or *Radio Frequency Identification* is used throughout the world. It's mostly leveraged by big business, but that's changing. It's becoming a technology well within reach of the everyday hobbyist. Unfortunately, the majority of RFID books you'll find on shelves today mostly deal with the process of implementing RFID throughout businesses large and small, for the purpose of inventory management, personnel management, and supply chain automation. Other books about RFID contain every piece of technical information you could ever want to know regarding radio energy theory and signal propagation. This book is not about either of these things.

The purpose of this book is to introduce enthusiastic, project-hungry gadgetiers everywhere to the concepts of RFID and make the point that this technology isn't just for big business — you can build great projects on a hobbyist's budget.

The approach taken with this book is one based on concepts and components. You may notice several projects centered on the same basic idea of access control, but the point of each project is to present solutions using different available components, or show different ways to overcome project-specific challenges. The idea is to give a good selection of RFID based projects you can build, while at the same time conveying the concepts involved so you can choose to either duplicate the projects shown in this book, or come up with your own RFID solutions.

in this chapter

- ☑ Introducing RFID
- ☑ Using RFID
- ☑ Understanding RFID basics

What Is RFID?

As mentioned at the beginning of this chapter, RFID stands for Radio Frequency Identification. The name perfectly describes the purpose of this technology: to identify something using radio signals.

Early RFID — IFF

One of the first widespread systems to use radio signals for identification was the *IFF* (Identification Friend or Foe) system first developed and used by the British during World War II. From there it was further developed into the RFID-based technology currently used by air traffic controllers everywhere. Its design was developed around radar signals, so the IFF system was easily adapted and integrated with aircraft track control systems. The IFF system went through several generations, but each generation used radar signals to interrogate an aircraft and receive identifying information back from that aircraft.

RFID Tags and Interrogators

RFID is a two-part system including interrogators and tags. The interrogators are the "readers" and the tags are the pieces that store the information. Compared to a barcode system, the barcode scanner is like the reader and the barcode label itself is like the RFID tag.

RFID tags come in a variety of shapes, styles, and sizes designed to suit a particular need. Figure 1-1 shows some of the different types of tags available, including access cards, printed labels with embedded RFID tags, RFID key chains (sometimes called *keyfobs*), and so on.

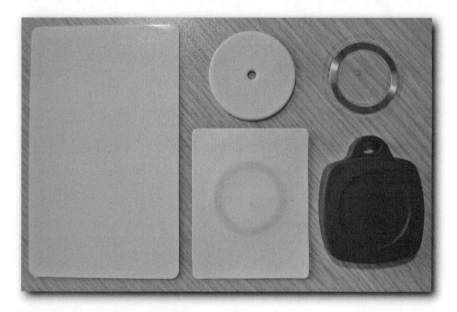

FIGURE 1-1: Various types of RFID tags

Contemporary Uses of RFID

Since the IFF system, RFID has slowly crept into society, seemingly undetected. Many people don't realize that the anti-theft systems that now guard many storefront entryways and exits use RFID technology, or that the access cards people pass over sensors to get in and out of security doors everyday are RFID devices.

The *EAS* or *Electronic Article Surveillance* systems seen in stores typically use a simple bit tag like the one shown in Figure 1-2, which can only represent two states: 1 or 0, on or off. So really, the EAS system is basically looking for presence. The system is asking, "Is there a tag present in my field that has not been switched off by the counter clerk?" If so, an alarm sounds.

FIGURE 1-2: EAS label type RFID tag

A much more complicated system employs RFID tags to track inventory, the scope of which could range all the way from the manufacturer, through the shipping and distribution process, right down to retail shelves. Unlike barcodes and UPC codes, which label only a type of inventory with a specific number (like 1234 for oranges and 5678 for apples), RFID can assign each item (each orange and each apple) its own serial number, and track each item.

Let's take a look at a piece of clothing—a sweatshirt, for example. The idea is that supply chains and inventory could be tracked and managed from the moment the shirt was sewn together, through shipment to a distribution house, to resellers, and all the way to sitting on the shelf in some storefront. With the advent of "smart shelves," real-time inventory tracking is now possible. A simple query can actively scan the store that instant to reveal the exact number of blue sweatshirts sitting on shelf B254 in store 19301. With that kind of visibility, region managers could shuffle inventory around between stores according to demand in an area instead of simply ordering more sweatshirts while a store 5 miles away has plenty sitting on the shelf.

The idea of tracking people has been around a long time, but until recently there just wasn't enough social tolerance or technical capability to implement these types of systems. People viewed the possibility of being tracked as an egregious and oppressive intrusion into their personal privacy, even on the job. Over the last decade or so, privacy concerns have waned and RFID has been used to track employees via RFID-enabled badges, implement access control and personnel tracking for Mexican government officials implanted with RFID transponders, and track prisoners wearing RFID tracking bracelets throughout prison complexes. This type of technology is on a rapid ascent. It's being used to track the attendance and, in some cases, the location and movement of people, animals, and things.

Some rather interesting and innovative uses for RFID have been creeping into the mainstream lately. Casinos now use the same RFID technology in their betting tables that stores use to track inventory on their shelves. With betting chips that contain RFID tags, casinos now have unprecedented visibility of the floor. For instance, the dealer can know exactly what amount is on the table and where the bets are placed. The table itself knows automatically if more bets are placed after being waved off, or if chips are removed or stolen. This information is relayed back up to the security room to be combined with camera information so a security officer watching a table can see what's happening and get backup data from the RFID system in the table to confirm his or her observations.

Medical schools and universities are now tagging, of all things, cadavers. Apparently, cadaver theft is a big problem and by tagging cadavers in random places, unauthorized removal of the cadaver is immediately caught and reported.

RFID Basics

A few basic things can define RFID: standards; data access, encoding, and transmission (air interface protocol); power source; and frequency.

RFID Standards

There are several RFID standards in place, covering many different aspects like frequencies and data-encoding methods as well as specific uses of RFID technology such as animal tracking (ISO 11784/11785). There are also countless proprietary implementations of RFID systems (tags, readers, and software) used for various purposes, including pet "chipping" and registration. While there are ISO standards-based solutions intended for animal identification, there are three or four proprietary systems made by companies like AVID, Destron, Trovan, and others. These proprietary chips all use their own air interface (method for communicating between tag and reader) and require special reader hardware made by the same company as the tag. But, it may be possible to find hardware made by other manufacturers that has the ability to read these proprietary tags. Just don't count on it being cheap.

At first, there was no set of rules in place that standardized on a frequency that was internationally friendly and a data encoding and transmission method (called the *air interface*) for RFID that was compatible across various tags and readers. RFID systems were all based on the same basic ideas and concepts, but manufacturers were creating their own reader and tags that were essentially proprietary. Eventually some tag standards came along, but they only governed certain aspects like frequency or air interface, leaving manufacturers to continue to create their own proprietary tags and readers. On one hand, this allowed manufacturers to innovate and give their products a competitive edge. On the other hand, it created an RFID industry filled with incompatible devices and tags that used frequencies that were not permissible in other countries.

In December 2004, the non-profit group EPCglobal Inc. submitted the high frequency (UHF) RFID Generation 2.0, or "RFID Gen 2" standard to the ISO standards committee. If it's approved, it would mean UHF tags and readers using Gen 2 would be cross compatible, and the frequency used would not break regulatory law in the various countries around the world using RFID Gen 2. The end result is that an RFID tag affixed to a shipping crate in the United States will work properly with readers when it gets to the United Kingdom, regardless of tag and reader manufacturer. Lack of international standards has been a major roadblock to smooth global deployment and intercontinental use of RFID technology thus far.

Data Encoding and Transmission

Tags are the heart of RFID systems. They store the data, which enables the entire point of the system: identification. How this data is stored, accessed, changed, and transmitted over the air is different based on the maker of the tag. There are a few standards in place, but the fact is that many manufacturers of RFID equipment have come up with their own methods of storing data on RFID tags and developed their own protocols for reading, writing, and transmitting that data. There are several types of data encoding and access methods out there such as EM4102 from EM Microelectronic, ISO 14443, ISO 15693, HiTag from Philips, and many others. Some support security measures, while others are open to any reader within range.

Table 1-1 shows a quick cross-section of the types of RFID technologies out there, their uses, and their typical read ranges.

Table 1-1	RFID Frequencies, Uses, and Typical Range		
Frequency	*Use*	*Pros and Cons*	*Range*
125 KHz – 148 KHz			
Type: Passive	Animal tracking (ISO 11784/ 11785), access control, and OEM applications.	Signal negotiates liquids and metals fairly well. Higher tag cost due to long length solid copper antennas.	½" to 4" is typical. 6" to 12" or more may be possible with specialized equipment.

Continued

Table 1-1 *(continued)*

Frequency	Use	Pros and Cons	Range
13.56 MHz			
Type: Passive	EAS (anti-theft), book and document management, access control, and OEM applications.	Antennas can be printed on substrate or labels, lowering tag costs. Serious interference from metals.	Can range from inches to several feet depending on reader hardware and tag type.
433 MHz (and 2.5 GHz)			
Type: Active	Highway toll payment systems, vehicle/fleet management, asset tracking, and so on.	Very long range. Very high tag cost. Uses a battery, so tags have a finite lifespan (typically 5 years).	Typically around 30 feet, but can range up to hundreds of feet.
915 MHz			
Type: Passive	Supply chain tracking and OEM applications.	Very low cost tag. Long range. Anti-collision capabilities allow simultaneous tag reads. Serious interference from liquids and the human body.	About 10' from a single antenna and 20' between two antennas. Longer ranges can be realized with special hardware.

Project Preparations

Before you begin the projects in this book, you should be aware of the security and safety issues involved.

Security

The projects in this book are meant to be cheap, easy, and fun. But they use tags and readers that are open format. There are inherent security risks involved as these tags can be read by anyone with the right reader. The IDs stored on each tag are unique, but can be duplicated onto another tag, or an entire tag can be spoofed as well, given the right kind of equipment and software. Keep this in mind when implementing your own RFID projects and solutions.

There are secure RFID options available, but it costs quite a bit more for this kind of hardware. However, even secure tags like the ones used for Exxon Mobile's SpeedPass quick payment system have already been easily compromised, as shown at www.rfidanalysis.org.

While the RFID projects in this book may not seem secure to some readers, you may want to think about your security concerns in a different context. If you build an RFID-enabled front door for your home, consider what a person who wanted to break in would rather do. Would they want to sneak up on you, get a reader within 2" of your RFID tag, duplicate your RFID tag ID and break in that way, or would they rather just walk up and break your window?

Safety

There will be a lot of cutting and soldering and other various activities that could potentially harm you in some manner or fashion. Please use common sense, and if you're unable to handle hot soldering irons or sharp cutting implements without cutting yourself or burning your house down, get someone who can handle these kinds of things to help you out.

Getting in the Front Door

RFID has many uses, such as pet identification and supply chain management, but access control is one of the most prevalent applications for personal use. Many people use RFID access cards to get into buildings, use elevators, or even open the doors to those special penthouse-type hotel suites. Setting up your own front door (or any door for that matter) with an RFID-enabled access mechanism is fun and easy.

Electronic Strike

Most access-control solutions use an electronic door strike, which gives way when activated so you don't have to unlock or turn the doorknob; you just push (or pull) the door open. This is exactly what's used to "buzz" someone in a door. That buzzing sound is AC power rushing through the magnetic coil windings in the door strike, pulling up and vibrating the pin that normally keeps the strike in the closed and locked position. You're going to use DC power to operate your electronic strike, so all you should hear is a slight click.

There are many different kinds of strikes out there. Figure 2-1 shows a couple of different products from two different manufacturers. Some are small and expensive, and some are larger and fairly cheap. The important thing is that it fits your doorframe, and uses DC power between 5 and 12 volts to activate.

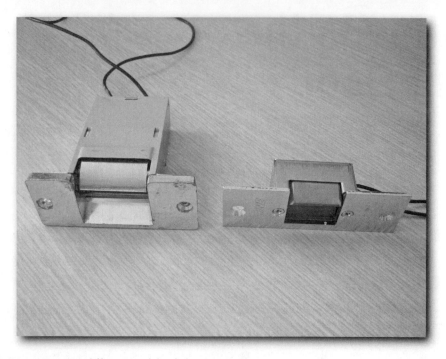

FIGURE 2-1: Two different models of electronic strikes

Electronic Deadbolt

If you use a deadbolt to secure your front door, the electronic strike isn't the best solution. The strike is designed so that you can push the door open without needing to retract the door latch. But when the door closes, the latch in the door is designed to push inward and snap back into place behind the strike. A deadbolt won't retract when the door closes — it will smash loudly against the strike and possibly damage the door, the strike, the doorframe, or any combination of the three. It would be the same result as if you opened your door, locked the deadbolt with the door open, and then tried to slam the door closed.

One solution to the deadbolt problem involves getting one of those keypad deadbolts like the one shown in Figure 2-2. It's a deadbolt that lets you use a standard door key or a number combination entered on a front keypad to retract the deadbolt and unlock the door. If you have a deadbolt in your front door and want to use RFID to get inside, you need to get an electronic strike and hack up one of these keypad deadbolts as well.

There are actual electronic deadbolts available that function like the electronic strike. They retract when power is applied, but they don't have the option of unlocking with a standard key. You don't want to be stuck outside because of a power outage or some other kind of Murphy's Law–type problem, so that kind of electronic deadbolt is out.

FIGURE 2-2: Powerbolt 1000 electronic deadbolt with a keypad made by Kwikset

Parts and Tools

You need the following parts for this project:

- Two general purpose circuit boards, Radio Shack part number 276-148a
- A 5V reed relay, Radio Shack part number 275-232
- A 5V DPST or DPDT relay from www.digikey.com

- An electronic door strike that fits your doorframe from www.nokey.com
- Phidgets USB RFID Reader from www.phidgetsusa.com
- Plastic project box from www.web-tronics.com, part number PB-3P
- A Kwikset Powerbolt 1000 electronic keypad deadbolt

And here are the tools you need:

- Small flat-blade screwdriver
- Soldering iron and solder
- Desoldering wick or solder vacuum
- Hot glue gun and glue
- Drill and drill bits both large and small

Get Started

The first thing you're going to do is build the RFID control box that will go on the outside of your door. If you have thin walls or a thin wooden door, you may be able to mount the RFID control box inside and use an ISO access card to get in. The passive 125 KHz RFID clamshell and credit-card type ISO cards have very long range because they have good-sized coil-wound antennas inside them.

Step 1: Build the RFID Control Box

There are many RFID reader options for use in the control box, but for this project you're going to use a USB-based Phidgets RFID reader (see Figure 2-3). While this reader does require a PC to function, having one increases the list of possible features and options almost limitlessly. For example, with a PC you could allow certain tags access only during specific hours of the day, get e-mail notifications when a tag is presented, and so on.

Note If you want to build a standalone RFID control box that does not require a PC, read through Chapter 5 to get ideas, and then apply those ideas to this project.

When you are finished with this project, the control box will contain the USB reader board, an indicator LED, and a DPDT relay used to activate the electronic strike and keypad deadbolt. Figure 2-4 shows a simple circuit diagram detailing what you'll be doing.

FIGURE 2-3: Phidgets RFID reader

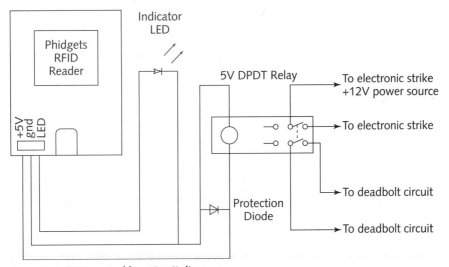

FIGURE 2-4: RFID control box circuit diagram

Building the control box is easy. The RFID reader board rests snug in the bottom of a plastic project box. Go ahead and take the reader board and drop it down in the plastic box to get a feel for how it will fit inside. You'll want it resting flat against the bottom of the project box. There's no extra room for the USB cable to plug into the connector on the board, so depending on how you want the cables to run, you may need to desolder and remove the USB connector from the board.

A Word on Desoldering

If you're not sure how to desolder components, it's really quite easy if you have the correct tools. You'll need a soldering iron and a solder wick, which looks just like a thick candlewick, only made of copper. The basic idea is, you just heat up the solder points on the board holding the component in place and the wick will soak up the solder, leaving the solder point on the board devoid of solder. The component should lift right out. To do it, you just place the wick over the solder point you wish to desolder, and then press it down into the solder point with the soldering iron. The heat transfers through the wick and heats the solder until it flows to the wick. Because solder only flows to unused portions of the wick, keep trimming off the solder-soaked end of the wick as you move from point to point.

If you have a solder vacuum, then chances are you know all about desoldering.

Prepare the Phidgets Reader

Normally, you mount the control box outside, and there is a hole behind the control box for cables. You never want an access control system to show any cabling because exposed cabling is the security equivalent to showing an arsonist a pile of gasoline soaked rags. It means trouble. You want the USB cable and additional control cables to run out the backside of the control box, into a hole drilled into the wall directly behind to hide the cables. To do that, you have to reposition the USB connector on the reader board so it points backward instead of down.

Desolder the USB type B port and remove it from the Phidgets reader board. The best way to desolder these types of components is to start with the solder mount points of the outer casing. Once those are free, focus on the four data and power pins. Be sure to work the connector out gently.

Now simply solder four short jumper wires from the solder points on the board to the pins on the connector. Be sure to jumper the correct pins to the correct points on the board, which should be easy enough to figure out. Just hover the connector over where it used to be on the board to get an idea of which pin goes to which solder point. Once you have the jumper wires in place, you should have something that looks like Figure 2-5. If you want, you can also solder an additional wire from the USB connector's external casing to one of the corresponding solder points on the board. That should help shield line noise.

Grab four more jumper wires about 6" long. These will go into the output connector block on the reader board, as shown in Figure 2-6. The connector block is nice because you can just use a small flat-blade screwdriver to synch down the wires — no soldering necessary! Strip the ends and twist ends of two of the jumper wires together. Connect the end of this twisted pair to the ground output of the output connector block on the Phidgets reader board. Strip the ends of the other two jumper wires and connect them to the +5V output and the LED output.

FIGURE 2-5: Reader with an extended USB port

FIGURE 2-6: Jumper wires connected to output connector block

Test the Phidgets Reader

Now that you've extended the USB port on the reader, it's time to test it to make sure everything still works. If you haven't loaded the Phidgets RFID driver package on your PC yet, download it from www.phidgetsusa.com or www.rfidtoys.net and install it. Once that's done, download the RFIDTest software from www.rfidtoys.net and run it. No installation is required; just run the software as soon as you download it.

Connect the Phidgets USB reader to the PC. The RFIDTest software should detect it and start listening for tags (see Figure 2-7). Wave a tag over the reader to confirm that it's working.

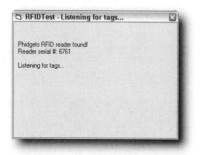

FIGURE 2-7: RFIDTest software listening for tags

Build the Relay Board

You can easily build this simple relay circuit without even using a circuit board, but since there is enough room for it in the control box, it makes sense to secure things a little bit by using one. Grab one of your general-purpose circuit boards and solder the relay to it. Make sure to keep the relay near the edges so you can easily trim off the excess circuit board when you're done.

Now solder the +5V jumper wire from the Phidgets reader board to one of the relay's coil leads. Solder one of the ground jumper wires to the other relay coil lead. Once you've got the relay connected to the reader board, you'll have to get a hold of some very long wires to connect to the strike and the deadbolt circuitry. These wires have to be long enough to run from the control box to each device, so take that into consideration before soldering them. Or, you could easily add a connector of some kind so the wires from the control box don't have to lead nonstop from the relay to each device. You'll need four wires, or two sets of two-conductor wire. Radio Shack sells coils of two-conductor speaker wire that works well. Solder one pair of wires to one of the switched lead pairs on the relay and solder the other pair of wires to the other pair of switched leads, as shown in Figure 2-8.

FIGURE 2-8: Leads soldered to the relay

Usually when you are working with relays, you add diodes across the relay's coil pins to sink the high voltage currents generated when the relay is switched off. When a relay is switched off, the electromagnetic field collapses through the relay's coil windings and generates a high voltage spike. This voltage usually has no place to go except through the circuit the relay is connected to and can end up damaging sensitive components like transistors and ICs.

You'll want to solder a protection diode across the relay coils so that the anode (the side opposite the end with the colored band around it) is soldered to the coil lead connected to the Phidgets ground output. Solder the other diode lead to the other relay coil pin. This lets the induced voltage generated by the relay's coil flow from one side of the coil to the other, through the diode, without damaging the Phidgets reader the relay is connected to. If you connect the diode in the wrong direction, the current meant to switch on the relay flows through the diode instead, possibly damaging the Phidgets reader.

Trim the Relay Board

Now that the board is finished, you'll want to trim it down so it fits in the project box comfortably. Put the Phidgets reader in the box along with the board to see what kind of trimming you'll have to do. After you've trimmed the board, you should end up with something like Figure 2-9.

FIGURE 2-9: Trimmed relay board

Prepare the Project Box

The only preparation you have to do to the project box is drill a hole big enough for the indicator LED. You can also get little LED holding clips that look a little fancier from places like Radio Shack. You can put this LED indicator (shown in Figure 2-10) pretty much anywhere you want, but as Figure 2-11 shows, I've decided to put it on the top of the box. The only place you can't put it is facing outward, unless you want to drill a hole through the Phidgets reader and the project box. Placing the LED in the middle of the reader coil would probably negatively affect the read range of the RFID board, so choose an adequate place on one of the four sides of the box. When you drill, make sure to place the LED close to the open edge of the box, keeping it reasonably far away from the RFID reader coil.

Just solder the LED to the two remaining jumper wires from the Phidgets reader connector block to the LED and trim the extra LED leads down to size. Put the LED into the hole you drilled and you're done with the project box preparation.

FIGURE 2-10: LED in a fancy plastic LED holder

FIGURE 2-11: Indicator LED in project box

Secure Everything in the Project Box

Hot glue is one of my favorite project adhesives. It's strong enough for most jobs, but if you really mess something up, you can usually get it all apart and cleaned up again. Before you get to gluing, position everything where you want it and put the project box cover on to make sure everything fits right.

Use some hot glue to secure the reader board to the bottom of the project box. Press it down as flat as you can before the glue cools. Now secure the extended USB port to the project box and reader board. Finally, secure the relay board and you should have something like Figure 2-12.

FIGURE 2-12: Everything glued into the project box

Prepare the Project Box Cover

The project box cover is going to get a lot of holes drilled into it. You're going to need a hole for the cables, as well as holes for hanging the box on the wall.

Start out by measuring the right place for the cables using a ruler as shown in Figure 2-13. Place the cover on the project box and mark the correct place on the cover to drill. The hole has to be quite large, so make sure you have your USB cable and additional relay wires handy to test the size. Figure 2-14 shows what things should look like once you're finished.

Figure 2-13: Finding the right spot to drill

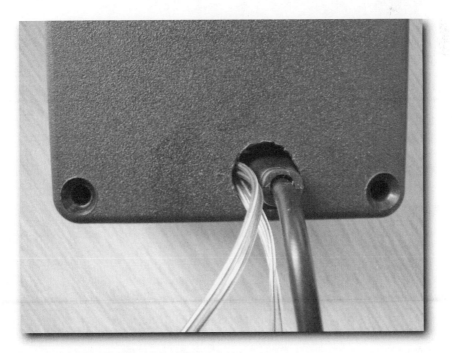

Figure 2-14: Hole drilled for USB cable and relay wires

With that out of the way, you have to drill a couple screw hang slots. You do this with two different drill bit sizes: one small and one larger. First, use the ruler to find the center of the cover. Since the box is 3" across, the center is 1.5" from the side. Mark the cover at the point that the box will be hanging on the screw. This will be the top of the screw slot. Move down maybe $^3/_8$" and mark the cover again. This marking will be the bottom of the same screw slot. Now move down about $1^1/_4$" or $1^1/_2$" and mark a place for the top of the second screw slot. Move down another $^3/_8$" and mark again.

Now that you have four markings on the cover, drill small holes at each marking. The holes should be the same diameter as the shaft size of the screws you'll be mounting the control box with. You should have four holes drilled, so now you need to make two neat slots as shown in Figure 2-15. You can do this by drilling a series of holes between the two you wish to slot out, or you can use an Exacto knife or other cutting tool. I drilled a series of holes then smoothed it out with an Exacto knife.

FIGURE 2-15: Two screw slots in the project box cover

Now get a large drill bit — something larger than the heads on the screws you'll be using to mount the control box with. When you drill these holes, place the drill bit at the bottom of the screw slots and drill with firm pressure, slightly angling the bit so it's drilling downward, away from the top of the screw slot. If you drill straight in, the bit could walk up and down the slot, tearing up the plastic. When you've finished, your control box cover should look similar to Figure 2-16.

FIGURE 2-16: Finished screw slots

Put the cables through the cable hole, put the cover into place, and screw the cover down with the screws included with the project box.

If you feel like weatherproofing your box, get some caulking and seal up the LED indicator hole and the entire seam around the project box before you put the cover on. After you've run wires and secured the cover, load up the cable hole with lots of gooey calk so water and vermin don't get inside your control box.

Step 2: Prepare the Keypad Deadbolt

I thought it might be an interesting and difficult challenge to hack a keypad deadbolt to work with this RFID control box project. For one, the motor inside the deadbolt works both ways, so you can't just apply power to it because the circuit design used in these deadbolts won't play nice with that plan. Both conductors of the motor show continuity to ground when the motor isn't actually doing any work, which could cause a short through the control circuit if you tried to directly power the motor. But as luck would have it, the Kwikset Powerbolt 1000 that I picked up at the local hardware store (shown in Figure 2-17) had a little extra inside that worked like a charm. I would suggest getting the same model deadbolt I was able to pick up; otherwise, you'll have to figure out your own hack.

Like any other typical keyless entry deadbolt, the Kwikset Powerbolt 1000 consists of two parts. The first part is the external keypad and standard keyhole, while the other part is a large control box that sits on the inside of the door. The part you'll be hacking is the control box, not the keypad. In fact, you can leave the keypad disconnected and uninstalled if you want to — it won't be required to unlock the door using RFID. But it might be nice to have a lock button you can press when standing outside, rather than having to use a regular key to lock your door.

FIGURE 2-17: Keypad deadbolt control box

Inside the Control Box

Remove the top cover of the control box by just pulling on it. It's designed to come apart so you can easily replace the batteries (which are not included). Figure 2-18 shows the inside, where you will find a battery pack, a simple circuit board, and a motor.

FIGURE 2-18: Inside the electronic deadbolt control box

On the circuit board, there are two silk-screened words that almost brought tears to my eyes: OPEN and CLOSE. The board was designed to have two switches you could press to open and close the lock from the inside. Even the top cover shown in Figure 2-17 has a design that lends itself to the idea that the buttons were meant to be included, but it appears the idea was scrapped before final production. Hacking this thing is easy as pie.

The OPEN Button Problem

There is one little catch about this open-button windfall. Speaking as if the open button were actually there, it was designed so the deadbolt would open after the button is released, not as soon as it is pressed. That means our RFID control box relay will not open the deadbolt until the relay is switched back off, which means the deadbolt will unlock but the strike will be locked again.

At first, the thought of using some kind of LM555-based timer circuit came to mind, but there is a much simpler solution. The goal is to allow the relay contacts in the RFID control box to close and somehow get the open button circuit to momentarily close and open again very quickly while the RFID control box relay contacts are still closed. Accomplishing that will allow the deadbolt to unlock while keeping the electronic strike unlocked so you can walk through the door.

An easy way to do this involves a 5V reed relay, a capacitor, and a resistor. Check out the circuit diagram in Figure 2-19 to get an idea of how to put it together.

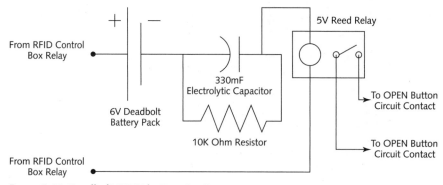

FIGURE 2-19: Deadbolt OPEN button circuit

How It Works

When the RFID relay contacts close to unlock the strike and open the deadbolt, power from the deadbolt battery pack flows through the RFID relay's switched contacts, through the capacitor, and through the 5V reed relay. That activates the reed relay and closes the connection for the deadbolt OPEN button circuit. The capacitor is quickly saturated and current stops flowing. At that point, the reed relay opens, the deadbolt control board thinks the OPEN button has been released, and the deadbolt retracts. When the RFID control relay contacts finally do go back to their open state, the electronic strike locks again and the circuit powering the reed relay is broken. The 10K resistor has too high a resistance to keep the relay active once the capacitor reaches full saturation, but will allow the capacitor to discharge once the power is cut from the circuit. If the resistor was not there, the capacitor could not discharge and would remain saturated for quite a long time, which means you could only unlock the deadbolt once every 5–10 minutes.

Note   I know some capacitor fans out there might be annoyed. Very technically speaking, current doesn't actually flow through the capacitor, but logically speaking it does. If you want to find out more about how capacitors work, there's tons of information on the Internet about these fascinating little devices.

Build the OPEN Button Control Circuit

First you'll need to solder jumper wires to the OPEN button circuit contacts on the deadbolt control board as shown in Figure 2-20. There are four solder pads, but only the two on the left side are used.

FIGURE 2-20: Jumper wires connected to the OPEN button solder pads

Because of the limited space inside the deadbolt control box, I opted not to use any circuit board for mounting. The tips of the coil leads on these Radio Shack reed relays stick out the top, so you can simply trim off the coil leads from the bottom of the relay. Then bend up the switched contact leads, making the bottom of the reed relay completely flat and void of any metal or leads.

Use some hot glue to stick components onto the reed relay, like a sort of component pack mule. Solder the positive lead from the capacitor to one of the reed relay coil post tops. Solder the resistor across the two capacitor leads. Now you should have something you can glue on to the deadbolt control board. Use hot glue to create an insulating pad on the control board and gently press the bottom of the relay down into it. That will keep the components in place while you solder up connecting wires. See Figure 2-22 for an ideal place to put the relay and accompanying components.

To get the relay connected to the deadbolt control circuit, solder the OPEN button jumper wires to the reed relay's switched contact leads. When the reed relay closes, it appears to the control board that the OPEN button is being pressed. Now solder a jumper wire from the other relay coil post to the deadbolt battery pack's negative terminal.

The only two wires left to connect are the relay contact wires coming from the RFID control box. You can drill a hole in the deadbolt control box housing for these wires as shown in Figure 2-21.

FIGURE 2-21: Drilling a hole for RFID control box relay wires

You're probably going to have to use a connector of some kind between the RFID control box relay wires and the deadbolt control box. It's just impractical to try and string a continuous run of wire from the RFID control box to both the strike and deadbolt. It doesn't have to be a heavy-duty connector; any two conductor connector will do since there will only be about 20mA passing through these relay wires.

To finish the deadbolt, solder one of the RFID control box relay wires to the positive terminal on the deadbolt battery pack. Solder the other to the negative lead on the capacitor. Secure the wires with some hot glue and you should have something like Figure 2-22.

FIGURE 2-22: Finished OPEN button circuit

Step 3: Install the RFID Control Box

This step is a big step, involving a lot of work. Because this book is about RFID and not carpentry, and everyone's doors, frames, and walls are different, it covers this step only in a generalized fashion. The basic goals that you achieve in this step are as follows:

1. Find a suitable place to put the control box.

2. Drill a hole for cabling.

3. Mount the RFID control box.

4. Connect the control box to your PC.

Install the RFID Control Box

The first thing you have to do is figure out where you want to mount the control box. This is entirely up to you. Because every house and wall is different, the only thing I can tell you is to keep in mind that connecting wire has to run from the control box to the electric strike and to the deadbolt control box on the inside of the door (if you are installing a keypad deadbolt). The other thing to keep in mind is that you have to run external power to the strike, through the RFID control box. (Check the circuit diagram in Figure 2-29 to get a sneak peak at how things are connected.)

After you have a hole drilled for the cables and mount screws installed for the RFID control box to hang on, you can add some large rubber feet for the back of the box. Adding those little feet gives just a bit of flexible pressure so the box sits snugly and doesn't jiggle around on the mount screws.

Note Just before this book went to production, I found out that Phidgets has changed the form factor of their reader boards and now they are slightly larger. The older boards that fit perfectly into the project box may still be in stock when you go to purchase one, so your board may fit. If your board doesn't sit perfectly at the bottom of the project box, you will need to trim the edges of the Phidgets RFID board. Or you could trim off the plastic guides on the inside of the project box instead.

The USB Cable Length Issue

The USB connection to your PC will probably be one of the most difficult things you'll have to deal with when installing the control box. Standard USB cables have an absolute maximum length of 16' before signal degrades and the device as well as the entire USB bus the cable connects to become unreliable. There are special powered repeater cables you can buy that can extend the USB connection another 15' or so, but typically you can only extend a USB cable once. Extending twice or more can cause signal noise and other problems to crop up.

One solution would be to get ahold of a very cheap laptop that can run at least Windows 2000 Professional. If the laptop has a USB port, you can set it up as a dedicated access control server for your front door. If it also has a network card, you could enable other interesting capabilities like remote control of the access server.

Another possible solution involves using a very nifty little device. Keyspan (www.keyspan .com) makes a device called a USB Server. It's a tiny box (shown in Figure 2-23) that allows up to four USB devices to be virtually connected to one or more computers over a network. You load special drivers on your Windows 2000 or Windows XP computer and the devices connected to the Keyspan USB Server act as if they are connected directly to your PC. The implications of this are amazing given the global reach of networks like the Internet. Imagine a USB scanner connected to a USB Server sitting in Japan, but your PC in New York sees it as a local device — or maybe a USB printer sitting in Australia that you can directly print to while working on a PC in Seattle.

For this project, the idea is that you can use the Keyspan box to virtually connect your USB-based Phidgets RFID reader in the front door RFID control box to any PC on your home network. Since Ethernet cable has a maximum length of 100 meters (about 329'), it would be quite easy to run a network cable to the USB Server your RFID control box would be connected to.

If the idea of using the USB Server intrigues you and you have a wireless network setup in your home, you might consider also picking up a Netgear WGE111 wireless bridge (see Figure 2-24). It's a device that was designed to be used to wirelessly connect network-aware game consoles, but it can turn any single-wired Ethernet device into a wireless network node. You could connect the USB Server directly to the WGE111 box and you'd have a wireless virtual USB connection to your RFID control box.

FIGURE 2-23: Keyspan USB Server

FIGURE 2-24: Netgear WGE111 wireless bridge

Note   I know some of you might be excited about the prospect of connecting a hub to the WGE111 bridge, but calm down. Something about the firmware in the device limits the number of connected devices to just one. Don't ask me why they would limit it, but if you connect two or more wired devices to the WGE111 via a hub or switch, neither one will work reliably.

A Word about Electronic Strikes

There are a few different kinds of strikes, as shown in Figure 2-25. The two security distinctions are fail-safe and fail-secure. Most strikes are *fail-secure*, meaning if the system controlling the strike fails; the strike is left in the secure configuration and will not give way. Because doors are built to function with a regular strike installed, there is usually no safety reason to let the strike open in the event of a failure. People inside a burning house for example, could always just open the door to get out, like they would any other normal door.

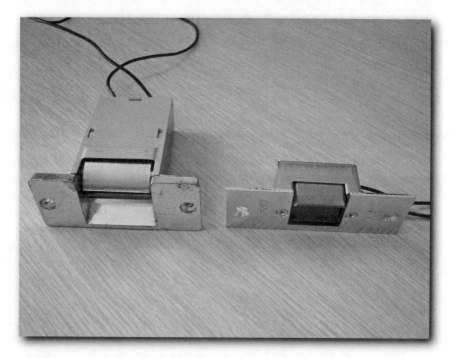

FIGURE 2-25: Different kinds of strikes

However, there are some rare instances where a *fail-safe* strike might be preferable. The system controlling the strike actively holds fail-safe strikes in the secure configuration. If power to the system fails, the strike gives way, allowing the door to open even if the doorknob or latch is locked.

Another difference in strikes is the type of power used. Many can function off AC power directly from the power utility or "wall socket." Others are powered from DC voltages that can range from 3 volts up to 24 volts DC. Because these strikes function as simple electromagnets, polarity usually does not matter.

Finally, strikes have different dimensions. Some are meant for metal doorframes while others are meant for wood. Some have a very long base, while others are very short and compact. Another thing to keep an eye on is where the wiring comes out of the strike. The Trine strike I'm using to demonstrate has wires that come out perpendicular to the strike, so they point up or down when the strike is installed. Others have wiring that comes straight out of the back. Keep all this in mind when you select the correct strike for your doorframe.

Step 4: Install the Electronic Strike and Deadbolt

I got a pre-hung door to show how an installation might go. I also got a friend of mine who is more carpentry savvy than I am to help. Here are the basic steps, which are explained in detail in the following sections:

1. Install the electronic strike.

2. Run the connecting wire as covertly as possible.

3. Find suitable power for the electronic strike.

4. Install the keypad deadbolt and connect it to RFID control box.

Make a Hole

The doorframe I picked up has a space for a standard door strike, but no strike installed. The doorframe you plan to modify should already have one, which you need to remove. You can see in Figure 2-26 that the electronic strike is much larger than the pre-drilled hole that the door latch normally clicks into. You'll have to route it out with a drill, roto-zip, or some other tool so the strike will fit.

Before you start drilling or routing, make sure you take into consideration the business end of the strike. Be sure the back edge of the strike that the door latch clicks into when the door is closed is in the same place the back edge of your old strike was. If it's too far back, the door will butt up against the frame before the latch can snap into the strike and your door won't latch closed. If it's too far forward, the door will sit loose in the frame, and both you and your power bill won't like that.

After finding the right place, use a pencil to trace the edges of the strike on the doorframe. You'll have to route out the doorframe for all three dimensions: height, width, and depth of the strike. If you've got a strike with wiring coming out of the back, you'll have to make the depth a bit deeper to accommodate. If your wires are coming out of the top or bottom, make the hole a bit taller. You'll want the strike to fit in the hole nicely, but it doesn't have to be absolutely snug. Now drill (see Figure 2-27).

FIGURE 2-26: Sizing up the necessary hole size for the electronic strike

FIGURE 2-27: Drilling out the doorframe

After you've drilled the hole, you may also have to remove some additional material from area where the door latch meets the doorframe and strike (see Figure 2-28). Because an electric strike doesn't have a large ledge out in front of it like a standard strike, the door latch may catch on this extra material when you open the door and either damage the frame or simply keep you locked out.

FIGURE 2-28: Hole for strike

You may also need to do some additional routing around the strike hole so the larger mounting plate sits flush with rest of the doorframe.

Figure Out a Wiring Method

There are two ways to run wires to the strike. First, you can drill a deep hole directly through the back of the doorframe into the wall space and fish the wires through the wall, or you can route a notch out of the doorframe and run them up or down the inside of the frame, sealing them in with wood epoxy.

If you drill into the wall space behind the doorframe, you must have a very long drill bit meant for that purpose. Doorframes usually have several 2×4 boards surrounding them for additional strength, so you'll probably have to drill through about three or four of them before you get to the wall space behind.

Wire the Strike for Power

An external power source powers the electronic strike. The RFID control box relay contacts simply allow that power to flow and activate the strike; it does not power the strike itself. The easiest way to power the strike is to use a typical wall socket transformer with a long power wire.

If your wall transformer is the typical type, the power wire consists of two wires with the housing connected together, just like speaker wire. Cut the tip off the end of the power wire and split the positive and negative leads into two separate wires. You're going to be dealing with six wires: two from the power source, two from the RFID control box relay, and two from the strike. You're going to want to wire them up like the wiring diagram shown in Figure 2-29.

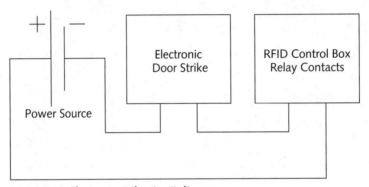

FIGURE 2-29: Electronic strike circuit diagram

Since polarity doesn't necessarily matter on this one, you don't have to fret about which power source wire to connect where. Just connect one of them directly to the strike. Connect the other power source wire to one of the RFID control box relay wires. Connect the other relay wire to the remaining strike wire and you're in business.

Install the Deadbolt

Ok, again, I'm no carpenter so I'll just state the obvious here. If you are replacing a deadbolt you already have, it couldn't be easier. Just remove the old one and install the new one in its place. If you have to drill a new hole in your door to install the deadbolt, there are handy instructions that come with the deadbolt detailing how to do just that.

Once the deadbolt is in place, connect the relay wires from the RFID control box to the OPEN button circuit in the deadbolt control box and you're done. If you feel the need to be fancy, you can get some of that plastic wire-guide stuff to run up the door so the bare wires don't show (see Figure 2-30).

FIGURE 2-30: Deadbolt installed with RFID control box relay wires connected

Step 5: Set Up the Software

Software is the brain of the RFID door project. It authenticates tag IDs and actuates the relay that opens the deadbolt and strike. Most importantly, it also makes the little LED indicator light blink. Get online and download the DooRFID software from www.rfidtoys.net.

Note Like most pieces of software written for the projects in this book, DooRFID serves as a simple example of how you might implement your own software solutions. The source code is available for download and you are encouraged to update, change, and modify it to your heart's content.

Install Software

The first thing you need to do is ensure you have the Phidgets hardware drivers installed. You can download them from www.phidgetsusa.com or from www.rfidtoys.net.

Jordan Russell's amazing and free software package installer called Inno Setup handles the DooRFID software installation (see Figure 2-31). If you're a software developer and interested in this nifty installer, you can download Inno Setup from www.jrsoftware.org, but it's not required to install DooRFID.

FIGURE 2-31: Installing DooRFID

If you get an ActiveX error when you try to run DooRFID, make sure your Phidgets drivers are installed properly. If you've already installed the Phidgets drivers, uninstall them, reboot, and try to re-install. After you re-install the drivers, try running DooRFID again. If you still run into trouble, check the www.rfidtoys.net site to get a better idea about what the problem might be.

Note   DooRFID uses a Microsoft JET database to keep track of authorized RFID tag IDs as well as store an event log. You can use Microsoft Access to view and update the DooRFID.mdb database file. If you want to create queries or generate reports, you can do so with Microsoft Access or even fancier software like Crystal Reports. FYI: the database file does not exist upon software installation. You have to run DooRFID first. It's created on-the-fly in the same folder DooRFID.exe resides in.

Configure DooRFID

When you first start DooRFID, it detects the Phidgets reader and starts listening for tags. You should see something like Figure 2-32.

If you pass a tag over the RFID control box, you get an Access Denied message and the LED indicator light should stay solid for 5 seconds. During this time, the control box cannot read any tags (see Figure 2-33).

Now click the Manage Tags button. You should see the Tag Management screen, as shown in Figure 2-34. This is where you can add, remove, and update the list of tags authorized for access. You can even restrict the times between which they are allowed access. If a tag with time restrictions is presented to the control box outside the allowed time limits, it will be denied access, as shown in Figure 2-35.

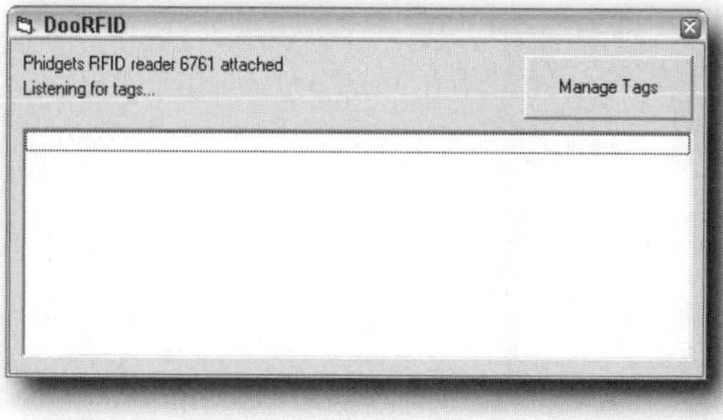

FIGURE 2-32: Running DooRFID

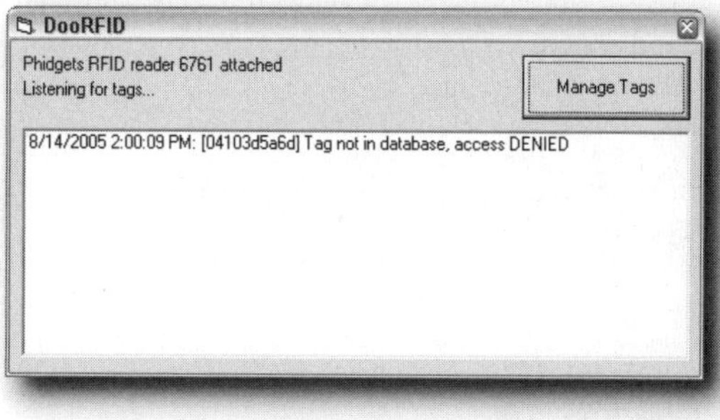

FIGURE 2-33: Access denied

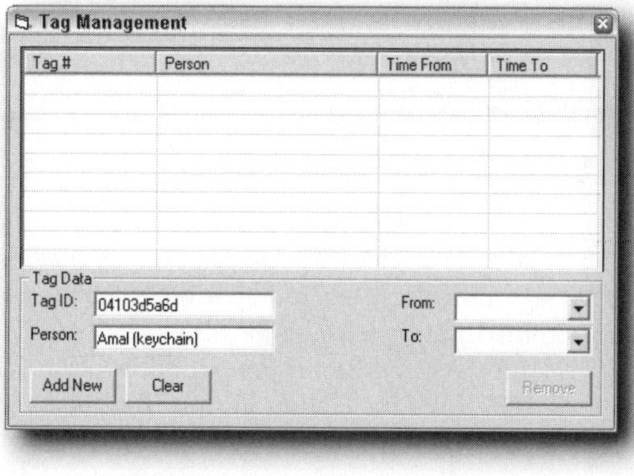

FIGURE 2-34: Adding tags in the Tag Management screen

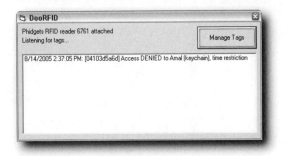

FIGURE 2-35: Access now denied due to time restrictions

To add tags, simply fill out the Tag ID field and, optionally, the name of the person who has the tag. Click the Add New button and the system inserts the tag data into the database. You will see the list update as well, showing the new tag.

Now pass the tag over the RFID control box and the system grants you access (Figure 2-36). The electronic strike unlocks, the deadbolt retracts, and the LED indicator flashes for about 7 seconds. After 7 seconds, the strike locks again and the LED indicator stops flashing.

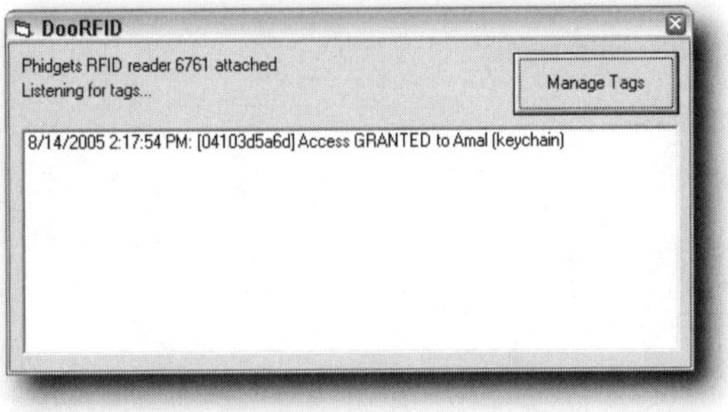

FIGURE 2-36: Access now granted

You can update the tag data by clicking the tag in the list. The Add New button changes to an Update button and the data from the tag automatically appears, as shown in Figure 2-37. You can change the person's name and modify the time restrictions for the tag, but you can't change the tag ID itself. When you've made your changes, click the Update button. To cancel the update, click Clear.

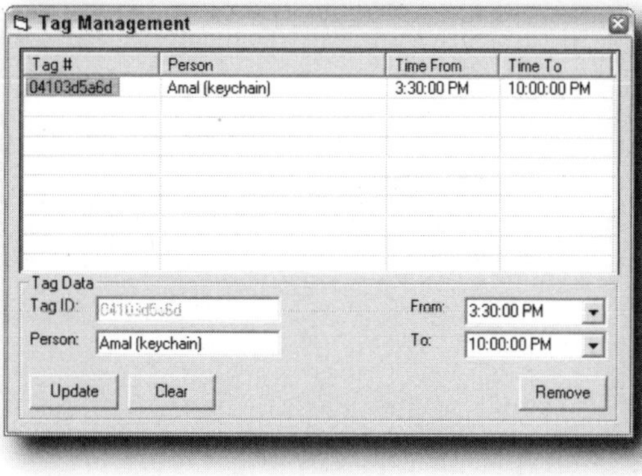

FIGURE 2-37: Updating tag data with time restrictions

Beyond DooRFID

DooRFID is one example of how you might implement an access-control software solution. If you so desire, you can add many more features, like e-mail notifications and support for multiple control boxes on multiple doors. Changes to the database structure could allow certain tags through only certain doors at certain times. If you wanted to, you could create a crazy maze of doors with readers and time restrictions for certain tags so that a maze-runner has to not only make their way through the maze, but also try doors at the right time. They may or may not be allowed back through the same door they just came from. It could be great RFID fun!

Check the forums at www.rfidtoys.net for more ideas, and to possibly get help from other software programmers on how to implement your own DooRFID access control software options.

Stepping into Your Car

The most common keyless entry system for vehicles is a radio transmitter that sends a special code to the car to unlock the door. In a way, this could be considered an active RFID system. The remote sends radio signals to the car, which identifies it as an authorized transmitter, and the car unlocks the door.

You're going to set up a keyless entry system for your vehicle that doesn't require pressing any buttons. With your keys in your pocket, you could bump your hip up to the reader to unlock the door — great for when you're carrying a bag of groceries or even a child. For those of you who've ever locked your keys inside your car, you might want to keep an authorized RFID access card in your wallet or purse.

If your car already has a typical keyless entry system, no need to worry. You can interface with it easily enough using the car's built-in system to do the hard work. If your car has a car alarm coupled with the keyless entry system, you're still in luck. You'll be able to deactivate the alarm and unlock your door using RFID.

If your car doesn't have any keyless entry system installed yet, no problem. You can build your own from scratch using a power door lock actuator, available for most vehicle models. Even if you can't find a specific power door lock actuator for your car, there are several generic actuators available that work just fine. These actuators are unbelievably cheap, too, costing anywhere from $5 to about $20 for model-specific units.

Note The parts list calls for a cheap pre-packaged RFID solution, but you could build one yourself using a BASIC Stamp microcontroller based solution like the one featured in Chapter 5. Even the code shown in Chapter 5 would be the same for this project.

Parts and Tools

You need the following parts for this project:

- If you have a pre-existing keyless entry system, get an additional remote.
- No keyless entry system? Get a high-power, two-wire power door lock actuator, available at www.parts-express.com, part number 330-010.
- A pre-packaged RFID access solution kit from www.qkits.com, part number KL042.
- A 9V–12V center positive 2.1mm AC to DC wall jack power adaptor for testing.
- Optional: 125 KHz keychain tag from www.qkits.com, part number SK0102.
- Pre-punched perfboard, Radio Shack part number 276-1394.
- An "M" size coaxial DC power plug, Radio Shack part number 274-1569.
- 6' RG-58 50 ohm coax cable, Radio Shack part number 278-964.
- Plastic project box 4" × 3" × 1.6" from www.web-tronics.com, part number PB-3P.
- Plenty of automotive connecting wire (at least 18 gauge).
- Wire connectors (ring, bullet, blade).

And here are the tools you need:

- Screwdrivers
- Drill and drill bits for the power lock actuator version
- Wire crimpers
- Soldering iron and solder

Get Started

The KL042 kit from www.qkits.com is a cheap and simple access control solution that can store up to 42 different RFID tags in memory. Any stored tag will activate the onboard relay, allowing access to the vehicle. You can clear the stored tags and assign a "master tag," which is used to put the reader into "update mode." In update mode, you can present new tags to the reader to add them to the access list, or hold a listed tag for 3 to 5 seconds to remove it from the access list. With audible alerts and colored LEDs, using the module is a snap.

If you are using an extra remote for your pre-existing keyless entry system, the KL042 onboard relay will activate your keyless remote switch. If you are building your own keyless entry system from scratch, the onboard relay will power up the door lock actuator to unlock your door.

Step 1: Solder Together the KL042 Circuit

Soldering the circuit together is pretty straightforward. Figure 3-1 shows the contents of the kit. Take all the stuff out of the package and lay it out in front of you. The kit contains the circuit board, components, an antenna, and two 125 KHz access cards.

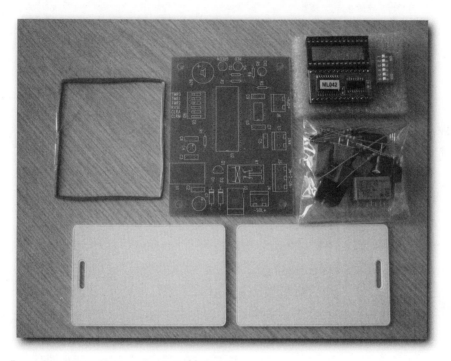

FIGURE 3-1: KL042 RFID access control kit parts

Build It

Follow the included instructions and simply place components on the board, solder them, and then trim the excess from the component leads. You may notice the board has spaces for components not included in the kit. The board is used for multiple kits and those components are not part of this kit, so don't worry about those extra spaces. When you're done, you should have something like Figure 3-2.

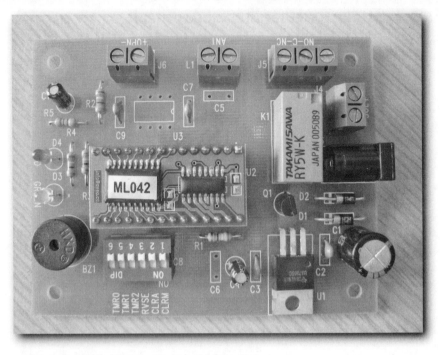

FIGURE 3-2: Assembled KL042 access control circuit

This little circuit is great as a standalone solution because of its many options. You can set the relay close times between 1 and 100 seconds, or even set it to toggled operation.

Note The only difficulty I've had with this kit is the included antenna. The included antenna is very fragile and has no connection cable. I've also had problems getting good read range using other external antenna alternatives, so be very careful with the supplied antenna. If you need to replace it, you can order part number AN0301 from www.qkits.com.

Program It

Carefully connect the ends of the antenna wires that have not been coated with resin to the ANT connector block, as shown in Figure 3-3. Don't tighten down the screws too hard as this will pinch and cut the fragile antenna wire leads, and you don't want that.

Note If you break an end off an antenna wire lead and need to clear some more resin off, use a cigarette lighter or hot soldering iron to burn it off. Wire strippers won't do the job when it comes to resin-coated wire this small. Just slowly heat up the wire until the resin burns off. Be careful, as too much heat will melt the wire.

FIGURE 3-3: Antenna connected to KL042 circuit

When you have connected the antenna, connect a center positive 9V to 12V DC plug-in power pack that fits the 2.1mm DC power jack and connect it to the KL042 board. Before you power up the board, move the DIP switch marked CLRA to the ON position. This will clear out all previously stored access cards and set the unit into learn mode so you can designate the master access card. Power up the circuit and run the access card you want to use as the master over the antenna. The board should beep and you should see the green LED flash. Power down the board and set the CLRA switch back to the OFF position.

Now you'll want to program the system to grant the other access card entry. To do that, power up the unit and hold the master card over the antenna for about 5 seconds, or until the green LED stops flashing and goes solid. Remove the master card and run any additional RFID tags you want to have access to your car over the antenna. The KL024 will beep for each card that's read into the system. If the unit beeps twice, that means the tag has been removed from the access list.

Note

You can use the master access card to activate the relay, but it's a good idea to add the other keycard to the access list, and then store your master card in a safe place. With a normal access card, the system activates the relay as soon as the card is read. If you use the master card as an access card, the system activates the relay only after a card is read and removed again. Also, you have to remove the card from the RFID antenna in less than 5 seconds; otherwise the unit will go into programming mode.

Step 2: Secure the RFID Antenna

Now that you've built, tested, and programmed the KL042 kit, carefully disconnect the antenna. You'll be separating it from the reader hardware, which will allow you to mount the antenna in an easy to access location and secure the reader hardware under the dashboard.

The RFID antenna that ships with the KL042 is very delicate, so you need to secure it to a rigid surface. The leads are very fragile, so you need to secure them to a sturdy cable suitable for 125 KHz signal propagation. The prepunched perfboard will serve as a rigid surface and the RG-58 50 ohm coax will be your antenna cable.

Reinforce the RFID Antenna

Now take the RFID antenna and place it in the upper left corner of the perfboard. You're going to secure the antenna to the perfboard using any non-metallic method you can think of (see Figure 3-4). Hot glue will work, or even a needle and thread. I used thread because, well, it was lying on the floor next to my workbench and the hot glue gun was downstairs. The only things you need to be sure of are that the antenna stays square shaped, it stays flat against the perfboard, and you don't squish or pinch the windings. Make sure you orient the antenna lead wires toward the bottom, where there's plenty of extra perfboard space.

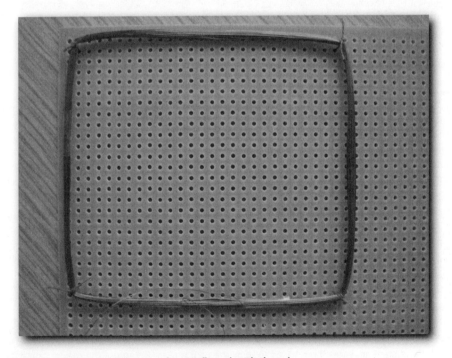

FIGURE 3-4: RFID antenna secured to perfboard with thread

Prepare the Coax Cable

Take the coax cable out and cut the BNC connectors off both ends. Strip off about an inch of housing from one end to expose the outer shielding. Peel back the shielding, unweaving and separating it as you go. Bring it all together on one side and twist it all together so it resembles a twisted multistoried wire. Strip about ¼" of housing off the center conductor, leaving you with something like Figure 3-5. Now do that to the other end of the cable as well.

FIGURE 3-5: Prepared end of RG-58 Coax cableConnect the Cable

Place the cable on the perfboard under the RFID antenna, near the lead wires. This will give you a good idea of where the cable will rest when finished. Mark some spaces between the holes in the perfboard as shown in Figure 3-6. This is where securing wire or cable-tie will hold the coax securely to the perfboard. Put the cable aside and use an Exacto knife or some other cutting implement to cut the marked space between the perforation holes. You're going to need enough of a slot to fit a cable-tie through on both sides of the cable.

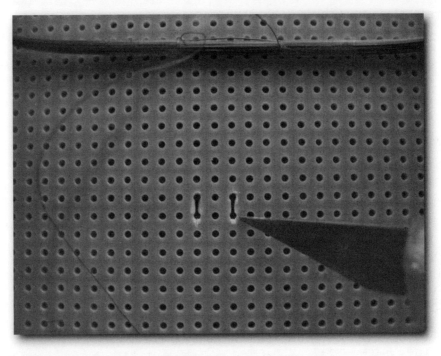

FIGURE 3-6: Cut slots between perforation holes for cable-tie

Count a couple holes down from the slots you just cut and cut a couple more. You're going to secure the cable with two cable-ties so it doesn't move around and stress the fragile RFID antenna lead wires. After you've cut the two additional slots, lay the cable down on the perfboard and secure it with cable-ties so the conductors are relatively close to the RFID antenna.

Take the antenna lead wires and wrap them around the coax conductors, as shown in Figure 3-7.

You can trim off any extra lead wire after you've made a few winds around the coax conductors. Solder the lead wires to the coax conductors using a relatively hot soldering iron. The resin on the lead wires will not burn off that easily due to heat traveling up the coax conductors. Use a lot of solder and bathe the lead wires in hot solder, using the tip of the hot soldering iron to lightly scrape the lead wires. That will help remove resin from the wires and allow the solder to flow on to them. When you're done, trim off any extra lengths of coax conductor.

You might want to further secure the coax cable using hot glue, just to make sure the cable will not stress, stretch, or break the RFID antenna leads. Figure 3-8 shows the coax cable secured with light and dark colored cable ties as well as glued down to the perf board with hot glue.

Trim off any extra perfboard, leaving a nice rectangular shape as shown in Figure 3-9.

FIGURE 3-7: Antenna lead wires wrapped around coax conductors

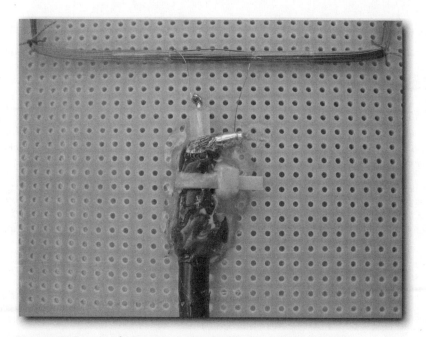

FIGURE 3-8: Coax conductors trimmed and cable secured with hot glue

FIGURE 3-9: Trimmed perfboard

Encase the Antenna

This antenna will be in your car, probably smashed up against one of the windows. Depending on what kind of person you are, you may want it to look a bit nicer, but I do know some people who would proudly display their handiwork and leave the antenna as-is.

There are many options for encasing the antenna, ranging from simple painted cardboard to a custom sized plastic case. No matter what you choose to use, remember that you have to secure this antenna to a nonmetallic surface on the vehicle in a location you can access from outside the car. Mounting near antenna cable or power-door-lock wiring will not be a problem, as long as you don't mount the RFID antenna on top or behind a large metal surface.

No matter what you use, remember that metal will degrade the performance of the RFID antenna. If you choose to encase the antenna in a plastic case, try to find plastic screws to hold the case together, or just use a dab or two of hot glue and leave the screws out. The low 125 KHz frequency of this RFID project is the best frequency to use when it comes to mitigating interference caused by metal, but in this case, the read range of the antenna needs every single millimeter it can get. Higher frequency RFID systems that use VHF and UHF are very susceptible to interference and signal degradation caused by metallic surfaces and even liquids. The solution I've decided to go with is a spray-on rubber coating (see Figure 3-10). It protects the antenna and keeps it sealed tight, and the black color matches the car's interior. It didn't turn out very nice though, so if you plan to go the rubber-coating route, try getting the kind you dip things into as opposed to the spray-on kind. Plasti-Dip makes a coating you can just dip things into and they come out nicely coated with rubber.

FIGURE 3-10: Rubber-coated RFID antenna

Connect and Test

Take the other end of the coax cable and connect it to the KL042 unit, as shown in Figure 3-11. Then power up the unit and run an access card over it to see if the unit can read the card. A successful read produces a beep tone and the green LED lights momentarily.

FIGURE 3-11: Coax cable connected to the KL042 board

Step 3-A: Prepare the Keyless Entry Remote

What you're going to do here is wire up the keyless remote so the RFID control circuit can fool the remote into thinking someone is pressing the unlock button. When the KL042 onboard relay closes, current will flow between the two normally open circuit paths which the unlock button normally closes when it's being pushed.

Note If you don't have a keyless entry system already and are building the power actuator version, skip to step 3-B.

My car is a VW, and the spare remotes are rather expensive. For many cars, you might be able use a cheaper kind of universal remote replacement, which learns your remote code and mimics it. However, if you are forced to go to your dealer to get an additional remote, make sure you only get the remote portion and not the extra key section as well. That should save you about half the cost right there. The dealer will also make sure your remote is programmed for your car for you before you leave, which is a plus. Figure 3-12 shows the spare remote for my car, minus the key section, which is usually attached.

FIGURE 3-12: Additional keyless entry remote

If you also have a VW remote like the one in Figure 3-12, you can just pull it apart. There are no screws or anything holding it together. You will have two cover sections and an internal circuit board that looks like the one in Figure 3-13.

If you get an additional remote from your dealer, ask them how to replace the batteries and they should show you how it comes apart. If you are using a generic universal remote, check the instructions on battery replacement to see how to get it apart.

Note From here on, I'll just be showing the process using a VW remote, but the concept is the same for any remote. Just keep that in mind and modify the process to suit your own unit.

When the remote is apart, take the bottom piece with the battery in it and set it aside. You'll be working with the circuit board and the top cover with the button faces in it. Flip the circuit board over so you can see the actual buttons, as shown in Figure 3-14. Lay the board next to the casing with the button faces on it so you can figure out which button is the unlock button.

FIGURE 3-13: Remote casing and circuit board

FIGURE 3-14: Casing with button faces and the button side of the remote board

This remote board uses surface mount buttons. There are four leads, but a couple of them are redundant. You only need two connections, but the designers added an extra two to secure the button itself to the circuit board. Otherwise, it might easily break off when used. Test the button for resistance across leads to find out which two leads represent the switched connections. Hold your meter leads across a couple connections and press the button. The reading should go to 0 (zero). The other approach would be to just short the button leads until your car door unlocks. There's no danger shorting this lead because that's what the button is designed to do — just make sure you're shorting the button leads and not two other leads.

When you find the correct leads, solder a couple 6" wires to them. Make sure you use very thin wire and choose button leads that allow you to run these wires as flat as possible against the board. You may want to put the remote casing back together later to protect the circuit board, and the board has to fit back into the casing without the wires pinching or getting in the way of proper circuit board seating. You could optionally leave the remote circuit board out of the original casing and just mount it in a project box with the RFID reader hardware, but keeping the casing provides short protection as well as allows you to use the remote later if you decide to disassemble your RFID project.

Figure 3-15 shows the two lead wires soldered and run flat and tight against the remote circuit board.

FIGURE 3-15: External switch wires soldered to surface mount button

Test the connections by stripping the tips of the wires you just soldered and touch them together. The remote should react as if you'd just pressed the unlock button and your car door should unlock. If you have an integrated alarm system, it should also disarm at this point.

Now take the top casing of the remote (the one with the button faces in it), and locate a suitable drill-hole point for your external switch wires to fit through. Check both the inside and front face of the remote casing for fit, function, and fashion before drilling. When you're sure the wires will fit through correctly, the circuit board will seat properly, and the hole won't mess up any of the remote button faces, carefully drill the hole.

Now just run the wires through the hole and set the circuit board back in place. Press the back casing and top cover back together and you're done. Figure 3-16 shows a finished product, with the button extension wires coming through the newly drilled hole.

FIGURE 3-16: Remote with external switch wires

Step 3-B: Prepare Power Lock Actuator

There isn't really anything to do to prepare the actuator. It's ready to go out of the package. Figure 3-17 shows what should be included in the package. You should have the actuator itself, a pack of mounting screws, a coupling block, a connecting rod, and a mounting bracket.

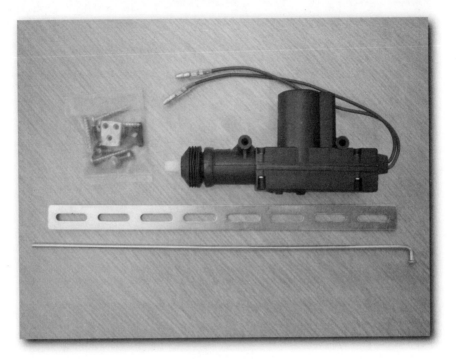

FIGURE 3-17: Power lock actuator package contents

When power is applied to the actuator, it will push outward or pull inward, depending on polarity. The actuator requires just about 1 amp to operate, which is the maximum capacity of the KL042 onboard relay.

In an effort to keep the project cheap and simple, the actuator only unlocks your car door; it does not lock it. If you can think up a cheap and easy way to enable door locking, by all means, go for it and share your experiences in the www.rfidtoys.net project forum.

Step 4: Wire Up and Encase the KL042

The KL042 board is just a hair too big to fit inside the project box, so the first thing you need to do is trim it down a slight bit.

Prepare the KL042 Board

Use side cutters, an Exacto knife, or other cutting tool to trim off the corners of the KL042 board as shown in Figure 3-18.

Now place the KL042 board inside the plastic project box cover to make sure it fits.

FIGURE 3-18: KL042 board with trimmed corners set in the plastic cover

Place the project box over the cover to make sure it all fits together. Take the box back off and use hot glue to secure the KL042 board to the project box cover.

Prepare the Project Box

With the board secured, place the box back over the cover. Hold it up slightly so you can see where the power connector is situated. Take a ruler and place it next to the power connector as shown in Figure 3-19 to measure how far up from the work surface the center rod in the power connector is.

Drop the project box down so it fits in place, then mark it with a marker or scar it with an Exacto knife directly over where the center rod in the power connector should be. Take the project box back off and drill a hole big enough to let a power cable plug into the power connector through the project box wall as shown in Figure 3-20.

FIGURE 3-19: Measuring the distance from the desktop to the power rod

FIGURE 3-20: Hole drilled for power connector

Now do the same thing for the antenna connector block. Measure and mark the box the same way you did for the power connector. The hole for the antenna cable should be just big enough for the coax cable to fit through. The hole for the relay wiring can be about the same size, unless you plan on using huge cables.

Trim down the conductors on the coax cable so you can get the coax housing as close as possible to the antenna connector block on the KL042 board. Figure 3-21 shows just how close you'll want the coax cable's outer shielding to be to the connector block. Keeping the leads short ensures the coax cable housing protects the conductors and does not leave anything exposed outside the project box wall.

FIGURE 3-21: Coax conductors trimmed tight to connector block

Don't bother pushing the antenna wire through the hole in the project box yet. You might need to snake the wire through some tight spaces when you install everything in the vehicle.

Note Be sure to read the following portions of this step carefully as the instructions differ based on which type of project you're building.

Additional Preparation for the Power Lock Actuator

If you are installing a power lock actuator for your door, you need to drill an additional hole for the wires that will connect to the onboard relay. Measure and drill a hole as you did for the power connector so you can easily connect wires to the NO and C connectors on the relay connector block.

Run two good-sized connecting wires through the hole in the project box and connect them to the NO and C connectors on the relay connector block as shown in Figure 3-22. Make sure the wires are long enough. One will connect to +12V from the vehicle's battery, and the other will connect to the power lock actuator inside the door panel.

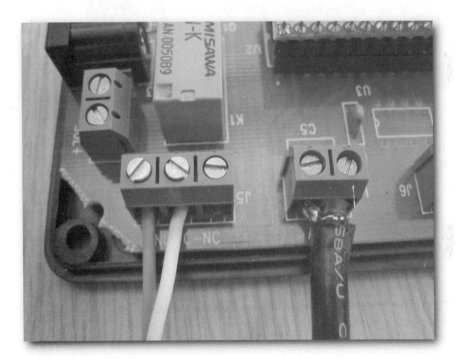

FIGURE 3-22: Antenna and connecting wire set in connecting blocks

Additional Preparation for the Keyless Entry Remote Interface

If you are using an additional keyless entry remote, the remote will sit inside the project box with the KL042 board, so you don't need to drill additional holes.

Connect the two wires coming from the keyless remote to the NO and C connectors on the relay connector block as shown in Figure 3-23. When the relay on the KL042 closes, the keyless remote thinks the unlock button has been pressed and unlocks your car door. If your alarm system is coupled with the keyless entry system, your alarm should disarm and your door should unlock.

FIGURE 3-23: Keyless remote connected to KL042 board

If your alarm system requires a separate remote, you've got some more work to do before you can continue. You have to hack up and wire the additional remote the same way you did the door remote. Connect the additional alarm remote wires to the same relay connections on the RFID control board the car door remote wires are connected to.

Make sure there's no chance the remote could short anything on the KL042 board. If there is a metal screw for example, cover it with electrical tape. Place the remote inside the project box. You could secure it with hot glue or even electrical tape, or just let it sit inside.

Step 5: Mount the Antenna

Locating an appropriate place for the RFID antenna might be difficult considering you cannot place it directly on or near any metal surface. One option might be to place the antenna far up on the dashboard of the car where the windshield meets the dashboard. This would be a great out-of-the-way spot for an antenna that wouldn't make using an emergency access card that difficult. If you have a two-door car with backseat windows that don't roll down, you could situate the antenna closer to the door-handle by placing it in a rear window. If you're some kind of racecar driver, your car door might be made out of composite or fiberglass, and you could mount the antenna inside the door panel near the door handle.

In my friend's white 1990 Honda Civic, the best place we could find was right up on the dash, where the windshield meets the dashboard. Figure 3-24 shows the antenna mounted on the driver's side, in the lower corner of the windshield. No adhesive was necessary—we just wedged the antenna board between the sidebar, windshield, and dashboard. If you do need to secure the antenna to glass in some way, use hot glue or silicone. Both are easy to remove from glass if need be.

FIGURE 3-24: Antenna mounted in the windshield

Step 6: Install the RFID Control Box

First find a spot for the RFID control box in your car. When you have a place for the box, you can snake the antenna wire through the car innards to the box. Run it through the hole you drilled, and then connect it to the ANT connector block on the KL042 board.

Now you have to find power for your RFID control box. You'll have to run a ground wire and a +12V power wire to your control box. Make sure you're using automotive grade connecting wire of at least 18 gauge, especially if you're building the power door lock actuator version. Generally speaking, automotive wire has slightly tougher housing and can withstand higher currents.

For ground, you can just connect to any available chassis ground. Make sure your +12V power wire connects directly to the battery, or to a lead from the fuse box that is not an ACC or accessory supply. Accessory wires only supply power when you turn the key, which would make an RFID keyless entry system rather pointless.

When you have your power wires run, connect them to the RFID control box. To do that, solder two short lead wires to your "M" sized 2.1mm DC power plug, taking note which wire is connected to the center conductor. Now you can use crimp-style butt connectors to connect the +12V power wire to the center conductor wire on the power plug. Connect the ground wire to the DC plug's outer conductor. Now insert the DC power plug into the DC power jack in the control box and you've got power.

Keyless Remote Version

If you are using the keyless entry remote in your RFID solution and not building the power-door-lock-actuator version, you can close up the RFID control box and mount it. You're done with your RFID keyless entry project.

Power Door Lock Version

If you are building the power-door-lock-actuator version, don't bother putting together the RFID control box quite yet. You still need to connect wires to NO and C on the relay connection block. You can start by connecting a wire from a suitable +12V power source in the car to NO on the connection block. The power door actuator can draw over 1 amp of current, so make sure your lead wires are large enough to handle the current. Using 18-gauge wire should suffice for this project. You can choose to either connect to another 12V power source or just splice into the RFID hardware power supply line.

Connect another long wire to C on the connection block. This wire will run out to the lock actuator in the car door, so make sure it's long enough to snake through the car's interior and dashboard, and out to the door.

Step 7: Install the Door Lock Actuator

I used a 1990 Honda Civic shown in Figure 3-25 for the power-lock-actuator version of this project. You'll be taking apart the door, mounting the door lock actuator, and wiring it up.

The actuator works by moving a connecting rod a short distance up or down, based on the polarity of the power that runs through the actuator motor. The connecting rod is coupled to the locking rod inside the door, moving it up or down as if someone had used the door lock on the inside of the car.

Take Apart the Door

Most car doors are easy to take apart if you know where all the screws are hidden.

Unless you're working on a 1990 Honda Civic, it would be best to get a repair manual for your car. Getting one that details how to take apart the door would probably be a good idea. You can get repair manuals from www.books4cars.com for just about any car. Even local libraries sometimes have repair manuals for cars, but they usually have them for older cars only.

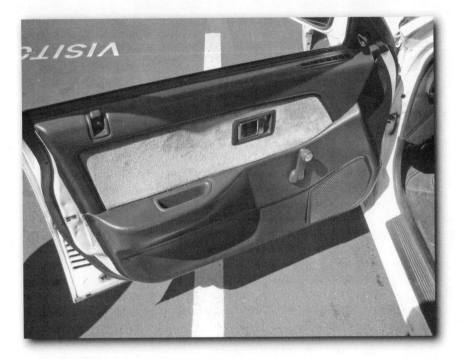

FIGURE 3-25: 1990 Honda Civic driver's-side car door

On this car door, there are mount screws hidden at the bottom of the armrest storage compartment, behind the inside door handle, and along the outside perimeter of the door panel. After you have the screws out, you can pull off the interior door panel. Tension posts that flare out hold the panelon. These posts are on the door panel and fit into holes in the car door — you can just pull the panel off. Under the panel is a protective plastic sheet, shown in Figure 3-26.

The protective plastic sheet seals the doorframe. Carefully pull it off. The factory didn't use regular glue to hold this plastic sheet on; they used white gummy glue. If you're careful, you will be able to just press the plastic back in place and the glue will hold it in place, just like it was before. If the factory glue is dried and brittle, or doesn't want to hold the plastic up when putting the door back together, you can use silicone adhesive or caulking to glue the plastic sheet to the doorframe.

With the plastic sheet off, you should be able to see the locking mechanism and associated rods, which lead to the door handle and manual lock plunger. Figure 3-27 shows these rods in the Civic's door panel.

Figure 3-26: The door panel removed and set aside

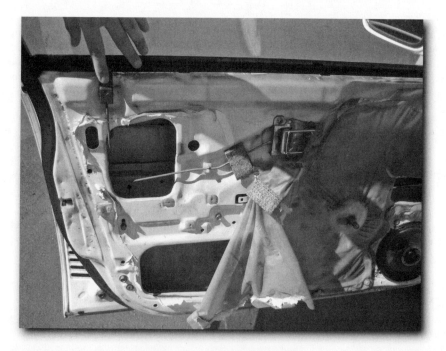

Figure 3-27: Plastic sheet peeled back to reveal locking rods

Mount the Power Lock Actuator

Because the locking mechanism in this door is situated toward the back of the door, near the door latch, the locking rod inside the door runs vertically. Doors with locks that are situated toward the front of the door, near the hinge, usually have locking rods that run horizontally, from the front of the door toward the back where the latch is. Because the Civic has a vertical locking rod, I installed the actuator vertically as well.

Figure 3-28 shows how a typical manual locking system works inside the car's door panel. You press the manual lock down to lock the door, and pull it up to unlock the door. This motion is vertical in this case, but inside some car doors, the locking rod moves horizontally.

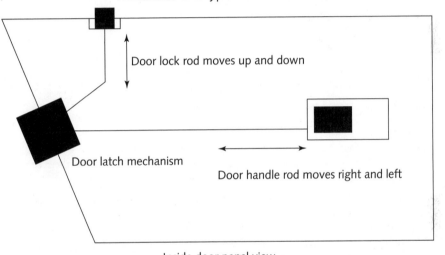

Mechanics of a typical car door lock

Door lock rod moves up and down

Door latch mechanism

Door handle rod moves right and left

Inside door panel view

FIGURE 3-28: Locking rod moves up and down vertically

You need to couple the power door lock actuator rod with the manual locking rod so the actuator rod moves in the same direction as the locking rod, as shown in Figure 3-29.

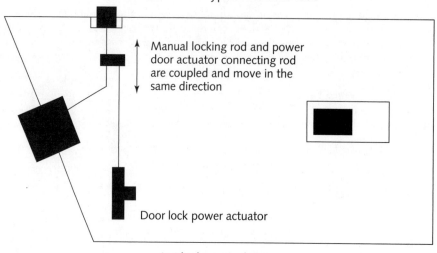

Mechanics of a typical car door lock

Manual locking rod and power door actuator connecting rod are coupled and move in the same direction

Door lock power actuator

Inside door panel view

FIGURE 3-29: Actuator rod moves in the same direction as the locking rod

Locate a place to put the mounting bracket. In the bag of parts, you'll notice two black snap-on screw nuts. These are flat U shaped black metal plates with a special hole in them so you can drive the provided screws into them to hold the bracket to the doorframe.

Put the bracket inside the doorframe and try out different positions until you find a spot you can drill holes safely and mount the bracket. Try to place the bracket as parallel as you can to the locking rod inside the doorframe. The connecting rod that couples the actuator to the locking rod needs to be as straight and in-line with the locking rod as possible. Also make sure there is room inside the doorframe for mounting the actuator itself before you start drilling holes.

When you find a good spot, drill holes in the doorframe. The holes only have to be large enough for the mount screws provided with the lock actuator. However, you should make the holes slightly smaller so the mounting screws used have to thread themselves through. This ensures that the mounting bracket is well-grounded to the metal doorframe. Figure 3-30 shows a good place to drill the Civic's doorframe.

Slip the U-shaped screw nuts on to the mounting bracket and adjust them so the holes you drilled in the doorframe line up with the screw nuts. Screw the mounting bracket in place as shown in Figure 3-31.

You're going to have to do some testing and checking before you mount the actuator to the mounting bracket. Put the connecting rod through the actuator. Slip the rod through the actuator all the way through to the 90-degree end with the lip, as shown in Figure 3-32.

FIGURE 3-30: Drilling holes in the doorframe for the mounting bracket

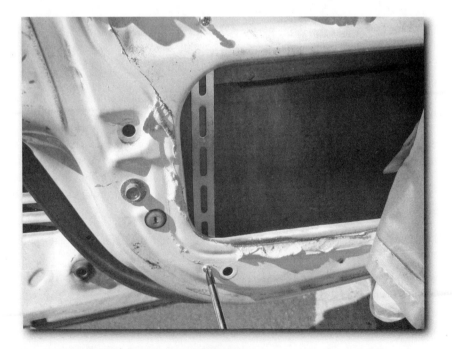

FIGURE 3-31: Screwing down the mounting bracket

FIGURE 3-32: Connecting the rod and actuator

Hold the rod and actuator up to the mounting bracket. You'll be trying to make sure the connecting rod is parallel with the locking rod. The coupling block will link the connecting rod and the locking rod, so the two rods have to sit side by side and move in the same directions.

You may need to trim the connecting rod if it's too long, as shown in Figure 3-33. You might also need to bend the connecting rod so the end that will be coupled to the locking rod is parallel to it (see Figure 3-34).

When you are checking the connecting rod, make sure you have the door lock set to the unlocked position and the actuator pulled all the way out into the unlocked position. If you measure, trim, and bend the connecting rod while the door lock or actuator is in the wrong position, the door may not unlock, or worse, you may damage the door lock or locking rod when the actuator is activated.

After you have measured, trimmed, and bent the connecting rod, mount the actuator to the bracket as shown in Figure 3-35.

Now couple the connecting rod to the locking rod using the coupling block. You should have something similar to Figure 3-36.

FIGURE 3-33: Trimming the connecting rod

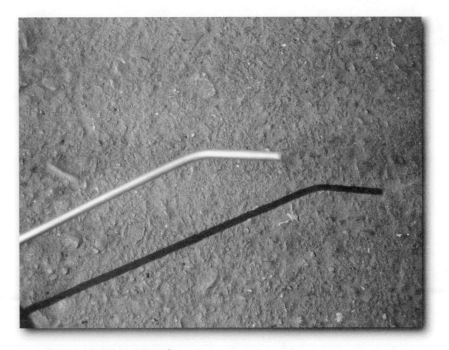

FIGURE 3-34: Bent connecting rod

FIGURE 3-35: Mounting the actuator to the bracket

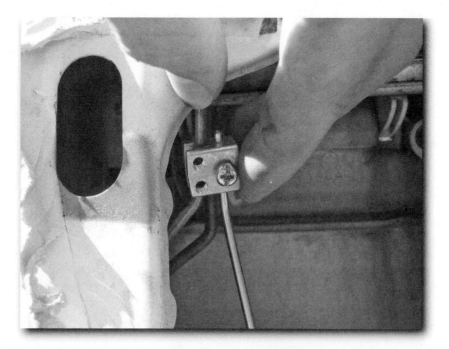

FIGURE 3-36: Coupling the connecting rod to the locking rod

Wire Up the Actuator

Now you need to test the polarity of the actuator to make sure you know which direction the current needs to flow to make the actuator unlock the door. Usually that means the actuator needs to be in the OUT position for the door to be unlocked. Run test wires from the actuator leads to the battery. There are blue and green wires on most two-wire actuators and in this case, the green wire is ground and the blue wire is +12v. Wiring it like that will make the actuator move to the OUT position when power is applied.

The actuator wires come with bullet connectors on the ends already. Cut the connector off the green wire and crimp on a ring connector. Take one of the mount screws holding the actuator to the mounting bracket out and put the ring connector on it as shown in Figure 3-37. Screw it back down and test the actuator using a test wire from the blue actuator wire to +12v. The actuator should activate. If it doesn't, find a new grounding spot for the green actuator wire.

FIGURE 3-37: Actuator connected to RFID control box

Now it's time to connect the RFID control box to the actuator. You'll need to connect a wire to C on the relay connection block. Run that wire through the hole you drilled in the project box for it, and then fish it through the car interior and out to the door. Getting this wire from the inside of the car, through the car body, and into the doorframe is difficult no matter what kind of car you have. Chances are, there's already wiring that leads from under your dash to inside the car doorframe for things like stereo speakers and such. Try to follow those wires and use cable-ties to hold your actuator wire to the bundle.

Once you get the wire into the doorframe, put a shielded female bullet connector on the end and connect the actuator wire.

Put It All Together

The last thing you have to do is test everything before you put the RFID control box together and mount it. Lock your car door and power up the box. Run your access card over the antenna. The box should beep, the relay should close, and the actuator should unlock the door. If it all works, close up the box and put the screws in because you're done!

Troubleshooting

If the box beeps but the actuator does nothing, check your actuator's power connections to both the RFID control box and ground. Sometimes a car's doorframe or certain parts of the door-frame are not grounded, or poorly grounded at best. You may need to run a ground wire into the vehicle's cab as you did with the other actuator power wire.

Another possibility is that you may need to program the KL042 again. You'll have to take apart the project box to see the Leeds and set the DIP switches. Try your card again and watch the LEDs. If the red LED is lighting up, your card is not authorized and needs to be programmed. If the LED is lighting green, then you've got a problem between the RFID relay connector block and your power door lock actuator or vehicle remote.

If you're not getting a read or any beeps, turn the key in your vehicle to ensure you didn't acci-dentally connect to an ACC or accessory power supply. If you still don't get any action, check your power and antenna connections.

You might also try removing the antenna from where you mounted it and try to get the access card to read. Surrounding metal may be causing too much interference to get a good read where the antenna was mounted.

Logging into Windows XP Using RFID

Many companies sell alternative authentication devices and software packages for personal and corporate computers, but most dig too deep into the pocketbook. Biometric fingerprint scanners sometimes take several attempts to work, and the sensor is prone to scratches or other types of damage. Smart cards work fine, but are complicated to implement, and the electronic contacts in the readers and on the cards wear out — remember the old cartridge based game consoles like the Atari 2600 or the original 8-bit Nintendo console? For those of you too young to remember those days, the contacts on the game cartridges and consoles would wear out. You'd either spend all your leisure time frantically jamming cartridges in and out of the machine, trying to get them to work, or maybe you'd get a few minutes of game play in before being shut down by an entire screen of gibberish and fuzz because the cartridge contacts failed.

With RFID being impervious to dust and dirt, and being contactless, it's a perfect candidate for desktop authentication. In this chapter, you're going to build a covert RFID-enabled USB keyboard (shown in Figure 4-1) that keeps its enhanced functionality a secret from the general public. You'll be using open source software to enable the login process on your Windows-based computer.

Caution

This project involves making changes to your Windows PC operating system and registry settings, which could render your PC inoperable. Proceed at your own risk. You should know how to make changes to the Windows registry and be comfortable with the possible risks before attempting this project.

---

in this chapter

☑ Building an RFID-enabled keyboard

☑ Modifying your PC operating system

☑ Editing registry settings

☑ Considering security

FIGURE 4-1: RFID-enabled Microsoft Natural Elite USB keyboard

Parts and Tools

You need the following parts for this project:

- Phidgets USB 125KHz RFID reader from www.phidgetsusa.com
- Passive EM4102 type 125 KHz RFID tag
- Microsoft Natural Elite USB/PS2 keyboard
- Targus 4-port travel USB hub, model PA055
- Phidgets software downloaded from www.rfidtoys.net or www.phidgetsusa.com
- RFIDGina software package downloaded from www.rfidtoys.net

And here are the tools you need:

- Soldering iron and solder
- Desoldering wick or solder vacuum tool
- Philips screwdrivers (large and small)
- Exacto knife, Dremel tool, or side cutters
- Hot glue gun and glue

Build the Hardware

If you don't like the idea of using the Microsoft Natural Elite keyboard and want to build this project using another make and model, make sure the keyboard is USB. Also try to find one that seems to have plenty of empty space inside the casing. The Microsoft Natural Elite has a built-in wrist rest that is part of the casing and not a cheesy add-on like some keyboards. That extra space is a perfect place to put the RFID reader and accompanying circuitry.

Step 1: Prepare the Keyboard

Flip the keyboard over so the keys are on the desk and you're staring at the screws in the back. Take them all out, being careful not to press down too hard while removing them. You need to keep the keyboard together after the screws are out, and pressing down pushes the keys into the desktop, separating the keyboard housing. Once the screws have all been removed, carefully flip the keyboard back over so it's resting on its little rubber feet again.

Carefully lift the top cover off the keyboard, leaving the keys resting on the bottom half of the keyboard casing as shown in Figure 4-2. As you lift the top cover off, there is a keyboard controller circuit board situated just under the space bar that will lift up with the top cover. Notice how the keyboard membrane that stays with the bottom half is pressed up against the keyboard controller, making contact through carbon leads. Be sure to keep in mind how these parts fit together because you'll need to put this back together eventually. Also be aware that the keyboard's USB cable will come up with the top cover as you lift. Once you've separated the top cover, carefully set the bottom half aside. Disconnect the keyboard cable from the keyboard controller and remove the cable, setting it aside as well.

FIGURE 4-2: Bottom half of a USB keyboard

Now you should have the plastic top cover sitting in front of you, face down, so you're looking at the inside of it. The RFID reader and USB hub will be situated in the wrist rest portion of the keyboard, so you'll need to make room for these additional components by cutting off and trimming down some plastic support stanchions. Start by removing the two cable-guide support posts to the left of the keyboard controller as shown in Figure 4-3. Cut these off using your favorite cutting tool, making sure nothing but smooth plastic remains.

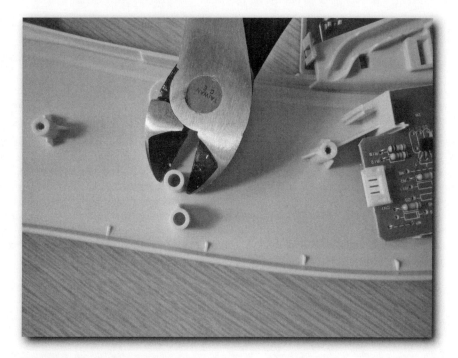

FIGURE 4-3: Trimming cable support posts

The other plastic piece you need to trim is an actual screw mount and support, just to the right of the keyboard controller. Figure 4-4 shows the mount post you need to trim. You might want to remove the keyboard controller and set it aside before cutting this post off. You need to remove completely and smooth down both the screw mount post itself and the bridging support as shown in Figure 4-5. Be sure not to cut or damage the other nearby support stanchion.

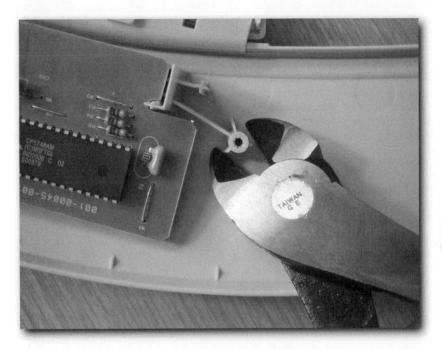

FIGURE 4-4: Cut-off screw mount post and support stanchion

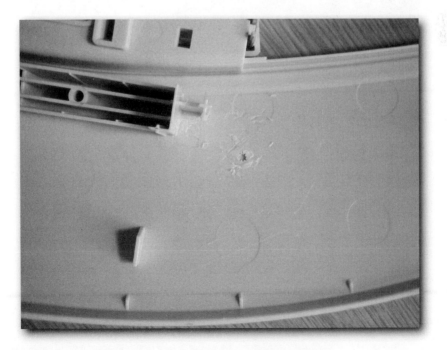

FIGURE 4-5: Completely flat screw mount post and support stanchion

Step 2: Prepare the RFID Reader

Desoldering components is really quite easy if you have the correct tools. You need a soldering iron and a solder wick, which looks just like a thick candlewick, only made of copper. The basic idea is, you heat up the solder points on the board holding the component in place and the wick will soak up the solder, leaving the solder point on the board devoid of solder. The component should lift right out. To do it, you just place the wick over the solder point you wish to desolder, and then press it down into the solder point with the soldering iron. The heat transfers through the wick and heats the solder until it flows to the wick. Because solder only flows to unused portions of the wick, keep trimming off the solder-soaked end of the wick as you move from point to point.

If you have a solder vacuum, it's basically the same idea, except you just heat up the solder with the iron until it's liquid, then without moving the iron, place the vacuum tip as close to the solder point as possible and press the button. The solder is sucked right into the vacuum.

Figure 4-6 shows a standard Phidgets RFID reader board just out of the box. Let the hacking begin.

FIGURE 4-6: Phidgets USB RFID reader

Desolder and Remove Components from the Board

The Phidgets RFID reader board is a little too bulky and square to fit into the keyboard wrist rest comfortably, so you have to remove some components and trim the board down. Start by removing some bulky components from the board.

Flip the reader over so you're looking at the flat side with no components on it. The Phidgets RFID reader has a large square USB type B port on it, and that's the first component you'll remove. Start by using your solder wick or solder vacuum to remove the solder from the two large mount points holding the connector in place. Once those are loose, you can desolder the four actual USB data and power pins and lift the connector off the board. The other component you'll remove is the output connector block. Desolder this connector and lift it off the board. Thanks to surface mount technology, this should leave you with a relatively flat circuit board.

Trim the Board Down to Size

To make the board fit properly, you have to trim some of the excess circuit board material from the corners, rounding the edges. With the board sitting component-side up, with the antenna section facing up and away from you, use an Exacto knife or Dremel tool to trim off the upper left-hand and upper right corners of the board. Make them as rounded as possible, following the curve of the antenna pathways. Trim off as much material as you can, but be very careful not to cut or scratch the pathways on the circuit board or you will severely reduce or completely destroy the effective read range. Once that's done, you can move on to trim off the lower right corner of the board. Watch out for components and pathways. Check both sides of the board before cutting.

With the three corners trimmed, you can move on to the lower left corner. This corner takes some special attention. You're going to want to completely notch out this corner of the board, following the output pathways as closely as possible without damaging them. When you're finished, you should have something that looks like Figure 4-7.

Step 3: Prepare the USB Hub

The USB hub will be crammed inside the keyboard with the RFID reader so the finished product only requires a single USB cable connected to your PC. Otherwise two cables would be needed, one for the RFID reader and one for the keyboard itself.

To get the hub to fit inside the tight confines of the keyboard casing, you remove the USB hub circuit board from its casing, and then remove any bulbous and cumbersome components from the board.

Desolder and Remove Components from the Board

Flip the USB hub over and remove the small Philips head screws from the back. There's a screw under the label as well, so be sure to remove that one before trying to pry apart the case and end up with shattered plastic all over your carpet. Separate the casing and remove the circuit board. Remove the clear plastic covers over each of the USB type A ports as well. The type A ports are the short flat rectangle shaped ports that line the bottom, as shown in Figure 4-8.

FIGURE 4-7: Phidgets USB RFID reader with trimmed edges and components removed

FIGURE 4-8: Targus USB hub board

As you did with the Phidgets reader, you have to make this board as flat as possible by removing components. Start with the large square USB type B connector. Desolder the mount points first, and then the data and power pins. Move on to the four USB type A ports, again desoldering the mount points first, and then the data and power pins. Once you have removed all the USB ports from the board, remove the external power connector from the board.

Trim the Board Down to Size

Now that the board is basically flat, to make it fit nicely you have to trim off the top corners as shown in Figure 4-9. With the board sitting the same way it was for soldering the jumper wire across the power connector solder points, the side of the board that had the USB type A ports should be facing you. Use your cutting tool to trim the top left corner off the board. Cut straight through the mounting hole, like you're cutting a doughnut in half. It might appear that you are cutting a pathway while doing this, but it's only a ground path, and you can cut through it safely. Now trim the top right corner the same way.

Jumper Power Connections

Once you've removed the power connector, you have to jumper two solder points that the connector was bridging internally, otherwise the USB hub won't power up when connected to your PC. With the board sitting component-side up and the corner where the power connector used to be now situated in the upper left corner, the three holes left by the power connector form a triangle of sorts. Solder a jumper wire from the top hole to the one sticking out to the left.

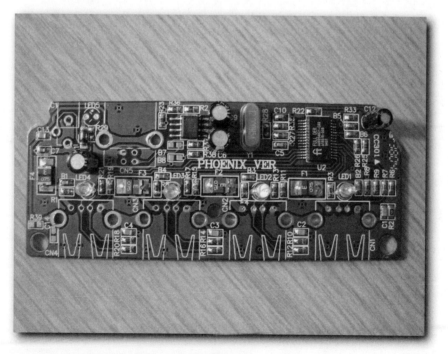

FIGURE 4-9: Trimmed and prepped USB hub board

Step 4: Connect Components

Now it's time to start connecting components. You'll be using some wire from the keyboard's USB cable. Don't worry; the cable is long enough to spare a few inches.

Connect the Keyboard Controller to the Hub

Grab the keyboard USB cable and measure out about 6" from the end with the keyboard controller connector on it and cut it, as shown in Figure 4-10. The keyboard controller connector connects the cable to the keyboard controller circuit board. Don't cut from the other end with the USB connector on it or you'll be very unhappy when it comes time to plug the keyboard back into your PC.

Take this 6" pigtail and strip off all the white wire housing, exposing the red (+5V), black (gnd), green (data -), and white (date +) wires, and you should have something like Figure 4-11. If there is a ferrite choke ring used near the keyboard controller connector, remove it and save it for later. There may also be an extra bare metal wire with about an inch of black plastic housing on it, shown as the top wire in Figure 4-12. This wire is only a conductor for the shielding you just stripped off, so you can completely remove it from the controller connector and toss it, leaving you with something like Figure 4-13.

FIGURE 4-10: Cutting from the controller connector end

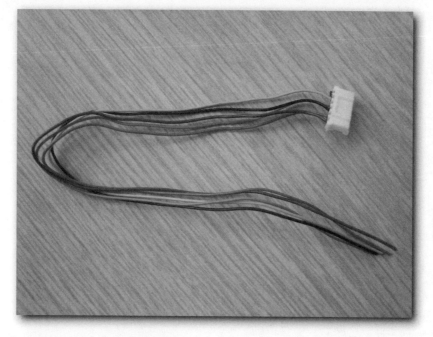

FIGURE 4-11: Six-inch long pigtail wires

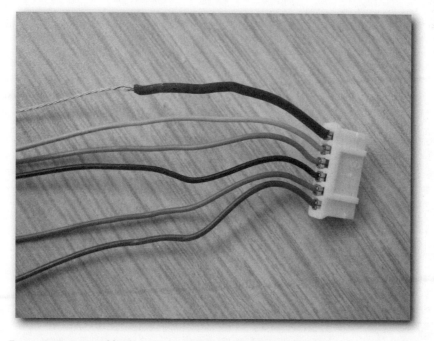

FIGURE 4-12: Stripped keyboard wire with bare shielding conductor

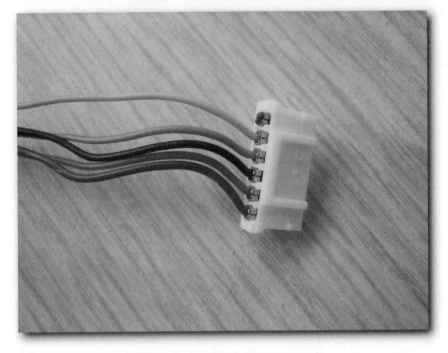

FIGURE 4-13: Keyboard connector with shield conductor removed

Pick one of the USB type A ports on the USB hub board, preferably one toward the left side. Make sure the wires are long enough to go from the port you've chosen to the keyboard controller board. With the USB type A port side of the board facing you, the power and data solder points are ordered left to right: red, green, white, and black. Solder the wires to the USB type A port's power and data pins in that order. Take a look at the bottom left of Figure 4-14, which shows these solder connections for the left-most USB type A port. After you've soldered everything, plug the keyboard controller connector back into the keyboard controller board.

Connect the Keyboard Cable to the Hub

Now you can solder the remaining keyboard USB cable to the USB hub's type B port. Strip off a few inches of housing from the end of the cable. If you removed a ferrite choke ring from the keyboard controller connector pigtail, you'll want to use it now on the keyboard USB cable. For this end of the cable, don't cut the bare metal shield conductor wire off. Solder it to the USB hub board along with the power and data wires to reduce noise and interference. If you have a ferrite choke ring, don't run it through the choke with the other wires — let it go straight to the hub board.

FIGURE 4-14: Hub board connected to USB keyboard cable and keyboard controller pigtail

Take the USB hub board, component side up, and turn it so the type B port is facing you and the type A ports are facing up and away. With the type B port on the USB hub board facing you, the power and data pins form a square. Moving clockwise, solder the red wire to the upper right pin joint, the black to the lower right, the white to the lower left, and the green to the upper left. Now solder the keyboard cable's shield conductor to one of the type B port's case mount solder joints. You should wrap this bare metal conductor in electrical tape, use liquid electrical tape to insulate it, or even use the hot glue gun to pin it down and stop it from moving around and possibly shorting connections on the USB hub board.

Connect the Phidgets RFID Reader to the Hub

Gather some red, green, white, and black connecting wire to connect the Phidgets reader to the USB hub. You'll need four wires, each about 8" long. With the Phidgets USB reader sitting component side up, the antenna side should be facing up and away from you (as previously shown in Figure 4-7). You're going to connect the Phidgets USB type B port to one of the USB hub's type A ports. Solder the connecting wire to the type B port in the same order as you connected the keyboard connector pigtail wire to the USB hub: red to the upper right corner, black to the lower right, white to the lower left, and green to the upper left. Now connect the Phidgets reader to the USB hub, soldering the wires to one of the USB hub's type A ports in the same order as before: red on the far left pin, green next, white, then black.

Now lay the Phidgets reader down into the keyboard casing in the wrist rest area as shown in Figure 4-15 to see how it fits.

FIGURE 4-15: Phidgets RFID reader wired and set in keyboard casing

Step 5: Test Connections

It's always best to test everything out before you start mounting things in place and reassembling parts. The first thing you'll have to do is install the Phidgets device driver MSI package on your PC. You can download this file from www.rfidtoys.net, or www.phidgets usa.com. I won't bother going through the install process screen by screen — it's straightforward. You just double-click the install file, click next a few times, and you're done.

Next, open the Device Manager on your PC by going to the Control Panel and double-clicking System. When the System dialog box appears, click the Hardware tab, and then click the Device Manager button. The Device Manager window opens. In the Device Manager window, click the plus sign next to Human Interface Devices to expand it as shown in Figure 4-16.

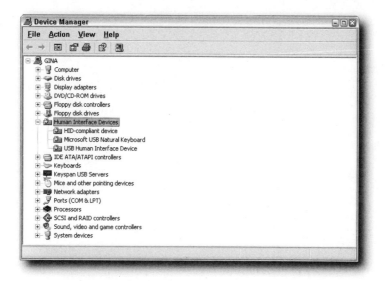

FIGURE 4-16: Windows Device Manager

You won't need the actual keys of the keyboard for this test; simply seeing the keyboard in the device list will be sufficient. Connect the keyboard USB cable to your PC. The LEDs on the USB hub board should light up. Now take a look at the Device Manager window. You should see a couple of new devices. You should see a new Microsoft USB Natural Keyboard and generic USB Human Interface Device listing, which represents the Phidgets USB RFID Reader. Perhaps later on, Phidgets will update their driver to call the RFID reader by name in the device list, but for now it just shows up as a generic device.

Download the Phidgets RFID testing software called RFIDTest from www.rfidtoys.net and run it. Figure 4-17 shows the software listening for tags. You should see the green LED on the Phidgets RFID reader light up, and if you pass a tag over the reader, you should see the ID come up in the software as shown in Figure 4-18.

FIGURE 4-17: RFIDTest software listening for tags

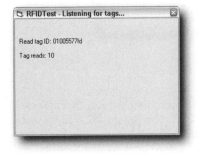

FIGURE 4-18: RFIDTest software showing the tag ID and read count

Step 6: Add More Ports (Optional)

You may have noticed you have two ports on the USB hub left unused. You can use these ports for just about anything you want. One possibility is to add a USB port or two to the keyboard casing, allowing other USB devices to be plugged into the keyboard.

There is plenty of extra room in the upper left corner of the keyboard casing (under the Microsoft name on the face of the top cover) that you could used for an extra USB port, if you wanted to cut the hole and wire up the connector. Figure 4-19 shows where you could install an additional USB connector. Just be sure to secure the connector with quite a bit of hard epoxy type glue. Hot glue will not stand up at all to devices or cables inserted and removed from the port. Be sure to rough up the casing plastic before gluing and don't let any glue seep through the holes in the connector or you won't be able to insert anything.

FIGURE 4-19: Possible location for an external USB port

Step 7: Mount Components Inside the Casing

Now that you have tested the components, it's time to mount them into the keyboard casing. Figure 4-20 shows the basic locations where these components will reside inside the keyboard casing.

Mount the Hub Board

Make sure the casing is laying face down, with the wrist rest section toward you. Set the hub board in place between the two screw mount posts on the left side of the keyboard controller. Make sure you run any connecting wires above the board, and don't let them get near the edge of the casing where the keyboard covers come together or you could damage them when you reassemble the keyboard. When you set the board, the top two corners you trimmed off should be facing away from you and almost line right up with the screw mount posts. The bottom edge of the hub board should sit right on the bottom edge of the keyboard casing, forcing the upper right corner of the hub board up off the casing a little bit. As long as the bottom edge of the board is resting along the bottom edge of the keyboard casing, you're in good shape.

Go back and check Figure 4-20 to make sure you have the board set in the casing the correct way. Then lift the bottom edge of the hub board and use your hot glue gun to put a couple dabs of hot glue along the edge, and then press it back down to secure it to the keyboard casing. Make sure your wires are above the board.

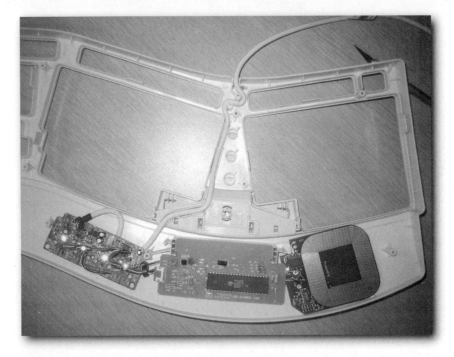

FIGURE 4-20: Components mounted in the keyboard casing

Mount the RFID Reader

Set the Phidgets RFID reader in place on the right hand side of the keyboard controller as previously shown in Figure 4-15, and even better in Figure 4-20. Make sure you run the wires from the hub to the reader under the keyboard controller. It might be a good idea to use some hot glue to secure those wires to the keyboard casing so they don't move around and become pinched during assembly. Dab some hot glue on the corners of the RFID reader board and press it down into the keyboard casing.

Step 8: Reassemble the Keyboard and Test

Putting the keyboard back together may be slightly annoying, mostly due to the way the keyboard membrane connects to the keyboard controller circuit. Remember how the membrane was situated when you took the keyboard apart, making a connection by simply being pressed against the keyboard controller? The hard part about putting it back together is the fact the membrane needs to be on top of the keyboard controller, not under it. So, when you go to put the top cover back on the keyboard, you will have to let the controller drop out of it, position the membrane, and then make sure you position the two in exactly the right place so the support posts and resting socket in the top casing line up with the keyboard controller correctly.

Assemble the Keyboard

Take the top casing and flip it over so the top face is upward and the new modifications you just added are facing down. You may have to use your finger to hold the keyboard controller in place so it doesn't fall out and yank the USB hub out with it. Lift the interface end of the keyboard membrane up so you can place the interface edge of the keyboard controller board under it, as it was when you took it apart. With the membrane in place and the keyboard controller set, lower the top housing down on the rest of the keyboard assembly. Make sure everything fits and there are no wires sticking out.

Hold the keyboard together with your fingers and flip it over so you can put the screws back in. Be sure to keep the keyboard held together with your fingers while putting in the first couple of screws. Don't press down too hard on the back of the keyboard as this will push the keys down into the desk and force the keyboard casing apart. You will have one screw left over, which used to go into the screw mount you removed in order to put in the RFID reader. Once all screws (except the extra one) are in, flip the keyboard right side up.

Test the Keyboard

Plug the keyboard back in to your PC. You should see the devices show up in the Device Manager as before, but you now need to make sure you can type on the keyboard. Open Notepad or something you can type in and hit some keys on both sides of the keyboard, and the number pad. If you're not seeing any characters on-screen, but you still see the devices in Device Manager, chances are you have the keyboard membrane on the wrong side of the keyboard controller circuit board. Take the keyboard apart and switch it up.

Configure Your Computer for RFID Authentication

You'll be using a simple middle-man approach to get your RFID-enabled keyboard working as an authentication device. By inserting some middle-man software between the login screen and the actual authentication process, you will be able to use RFID tags to log into your computer. When you present the tag to the reader, it will be checked against a database. If found, the user name and password associated with that tag will be pulled from that database and passed to the authentication process as if you had typed in the account information yourself!

Step 9: Replace Your Windows GINA

What does GINA mean? Well, it's sort of an acronym for Graphical Identification and Authentication. I say "sort of" because of the N in GINA, a true acronym would be GIAA. Okay, semantics aside, the GINA is basically what you see when you go to log on to Windows. The screen sitting there asking you for your username and password is what the GINA essentially is. It asks you, in a graphical manor (a window) what your account credentials (username, password, and the like) are, and then authenticates those credentials against whatever authentication methods are available to it. For instance, if your PC is part of a Windows domain or active directory structure, it may check your account information against a domain controller.

A setting in the registry tells Windows what DLL file to use for its GINA functions. You are going to replace the standard GINA with a new DLL called PollGina that allows all the standard Windows GINA functions to pass through to the original Windows DLL, but adds the ability for external applications to specify account credentials. Figure 4-21 shows the original Windows GINA authentication process as well as the new authentication process, which leverages RFID technology.

As shown in Figure 4-21, normally Windows processes logon events from WinLogon to the MSGINA module. From there, MSGINA gets your account information and passes it off to various authentication mechanisms, the nature of which depends on your operating system version and whether or not your PC is part of a network domain. Once these mechanisms authenticate you, they pass data back to MSGINA and then back to WinLogon, and you are allowed to log in.

By telling Windows to use pGina as the official GINA DLL, WinLogon invokes PollGina and waits for successful authentication. PollGina itself does not do the work of MSGINA, but instead acts as a middleman. Because of PollGina's position as middleman, it can link account information, such as username and password, to RFID tags. If an RFID tag is presented to the reader and account data has been attributed to that tag, PollGina passes that account information to the real MSGINA for processing as if you had typed it in yourself. Once MSGINA has done its work, PollGina passes back control to WinLogon and you are allowed to log in.

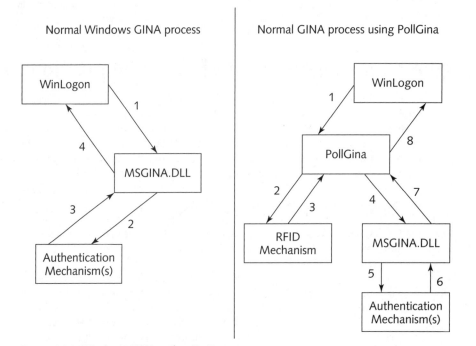

FIGURE 4-21: Windows GINA authentication processes

Please be aware that replacing the GINA in your Windows computer and making registry changes could render it completely inaccessible if an error is made or there is a compatibility problem with your system. Be sure to have a *full* backup of any PC you intend to install this software on, as it may render your PC useless. You are assuming all risk involved by proceeding. If you do run into trouble, I will cover possible recovery options later in this chapter.

The PollGina software used in this project changes the way your PC processes authentication. It disables fast user switching, and if your system normally requires pressing Ctrl+Alt+Del before you log on, PollGina disables that requirement as well.

Download and Extract RFIDGina Software

Download the RFIDGina software package from www.rfidtoys.net. RFIDGina is a collection of software files that enable the RFID reader in your new keyboard to act as an authentication device. They all come wrapped up in an easy downloadable ZIP file:

- **PollGina.dll:** The GINA replacement file

- **RFIDAuth.exe:** Used to associate RFID tags with accounts

- **RFIDGina.reg:** Registry file with RFIDGina settings

- **rfidPoll.dll:** The RFID library for PollGina

- **RFIDTest.exe:** Used to test the Phidgets RFID reader

The ZIP file contains PollGina and rfidPoll. PollGina is used to interact with the standard Windows GINA authentication system, and rfidPoll is basically a plug-in that links the Phidgets RFID reader to PollGina.

PollGina is an open source solution that acts as a wedge between the user (you) and the normal Windows GINA. The purpose is to let alternative authentication methods, like your fancy new RFID-enabled keyboard, work with standard Windows authentication systems. PollGina is open source software, written by Nathan Yocom of XPA Systems (www.xpasystems.com.).

There is no installer for PollGina. Instead, you have to copy files to their proper locations yourself. After downloading the ZIP file, extract all the files to a temporary location like C:\TEMP. To install PollGina, move the PollGina.dll and rfidPoll.dll files from the temporary location to your default Windows operating system folder, which is usually C:\WINDOWS.

You'll also find a registry settings file and some other pieces of software in there called RFIDAuth and RFIDTest. You will use those later, so keep them handy.

Update the Windows Registry

You'll need to modify some registry entries and add some others to get RFIDGina working. If your Windows installation is typical, the operating system is installed in the standard C:\WINDOWS folder. If you've copied the PollGina.dll and rfidPoll.dll files to that folder, you can simply use the RFIDGina.reg file to update your registry settings. Just double-click the RFIDGina.reg file to import the correct settings into your local registry. You are asked to confirm the registry file import, as shown in Figure 4-22. Click Yes and a screen like Figure 4-23 tells you the import was successful. You need to make sure you are logged in as an administrator on the machine, or the import will fail.

Manually Update the Registry

If you've got a non-standard Windows installation, you'll need to make these changes manually. Otherwise, you can skip this portion.

Open your registry editor (Start → Run → regedit). The first thing you have to do is change the standard GINA that Windows uses to the customized PollGina replacement. To do that, you have to add or modify the GinaDLL string value (REG_SZ). Start by navigating to the registry key:

HKEY_LOCAL_MACHINE\SOFTWARE\Microsoft\Windows NT\CurrentVersion\WinLogon

Look for a string value named GinaDLL. If there is a string entry already named that, you need to modify its value. If there isn't one, you need to add a new string value by clicking Edit → New → String Value as shown in Figure 4-24. Name the new string value **GinaDLL**, keeping in mind that the name is case-sensitive. The value of GinaDLL should be the full path to the rfidPoll.dll file you copied to your default Windows operating system folder. Since you don't have a standard Windows installation, you'll have to update the value with the appropriate path to PollGina.dll. Figure 4-25 gives an example path to PollGina.dll.

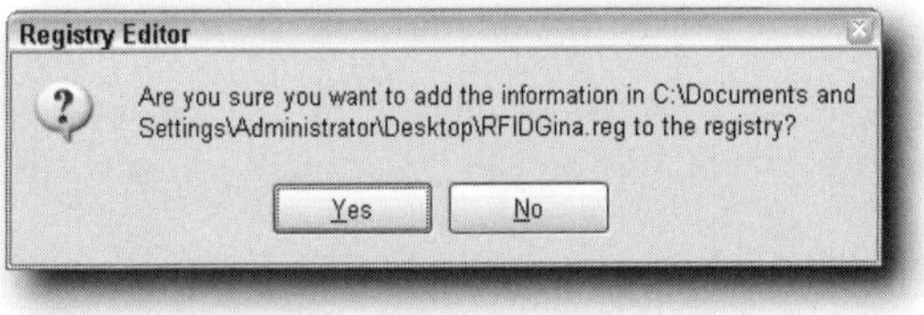

FIGURE 4-22: Importing RFIDGina.reg into the Windows registry

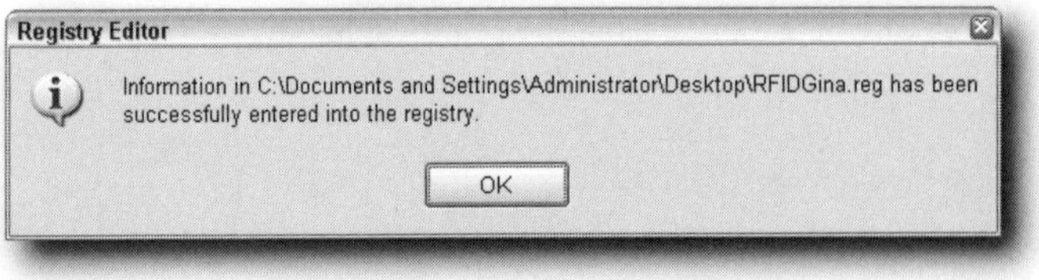

FIGURE 4-23: Successful import of the RFIDGina.reg file

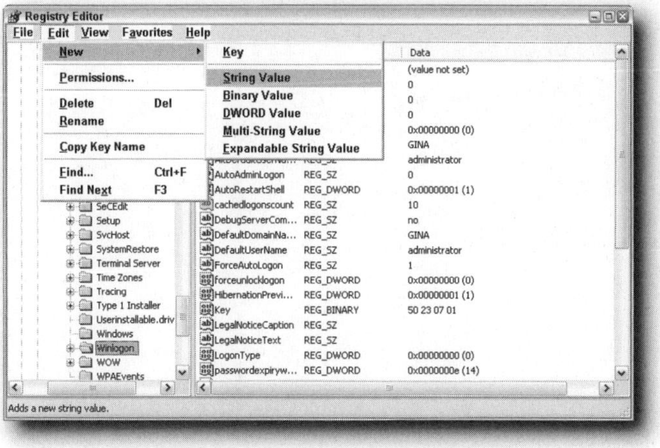

FIGURE 4-24: Adding a new string value to the registry

Now add some registry keys that hold additional RFIDGina settings. Navigate to the following:

```
HKEY_LOCAL_MACHINE\SOFTWARE
```

Add a new key called **PollGina**. Then add a new string value to the PollGina key called **pollLib**. The value should be the correct path to the rfidPoll.dll file, similar to what you just did with the GinaDLL string value above.

This time you'll be adding a DWORD value, not a string value. Name this new value **pollTime**. When you go to set pollTime's value, you have the option of supplying values in Hexadecimal or Decimal. Click Decimal and type **500** as shown in Figure 4-26.

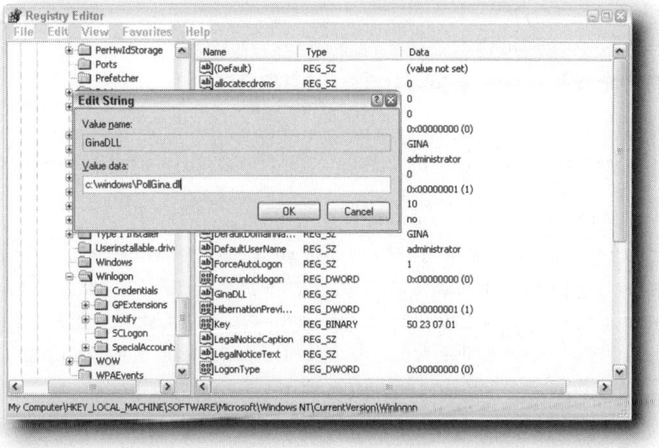

FIGURE 4-25: Modifying the registry string value

FIGURE 4-26: Setting the pollTime DWORD value

Congratulations. You've replaced your standard Windows GINA and set up the RFID polling library. Reboot your computer for your changes to go into effect. After rebooting, log in as usual so you can begin matching your RFID tags to user names and passwords.

Recovery Methods

After you've made the registry changes above, if you find yourself with a system that will not boot you can attempt a recovery. You will need to purchase an offline registry editor like the one sold at www.registrytool.com. You can also use free utilities such as the NT Password & Registry Editor at http://home.eunet.no/~pnordahl/ntpasswd/. You can boot the troubled machine with a boot disk or remove the hard drive and place it in a working machine. Reverse the registry changes you made to their original settings using the registry editing utilities listed above and reboot the system. It should boot just fine. If not, a full recovery from backup may be necessary.

Step 10: Set Up RFID Tags for Authentication

The registry holds the RFID tag IDs and associated account credentials. To make creating and updating this information easier, you can download the RFIDAuth software from www.rfid toys.net.

Note   Just in case you're a hardcore registry hack or want to write your own software, you can make the changes yourself. The settings are stored in HKLM\SOFTWARE\rfidPoll. Tags are stored as subkeys, and account credentials are stored as REG_SZ values named Username, Password, and Domain. If your account is a local machine account, leave Domain blank. It's only used if the machine is a member of a Windows domain and the account is a domain account.

After downloading the RFIDAuth.zip file and extracting files, you can just run RFIDAuth .exe — there is no installation process. You should see something like Figure 4-27.

FIGURE 4-27: RFIDAuth software for matching tags to account information

You simply click the Add New Tag button, and a dialog box asks you for the RFID tag ID, user name, password, and domain information (see Figure 4-28). If your computer is not part of a Windows domain, leave the domain section blank. If your computer is a domain member, and your account is a domain account, enter your Windows domain name in the Domain field. If you're unsure, leave it blank or ask a network administrator for help.

Click OK and you'll see the tag added to the list. If you want to edit your account information associated with a tag, just double-click the tag in the list and enter your changes. Figure 4-29 shows the RFIDAuth software with an RFID tag stored in the registry.

FIGURE 4-28: Filling in the tag ID and account information

FIGURE 4-29: RFID tag added to the list

To remove a tag, just click its ID in the list to highlight it, and then click the Remove Tag button. A screen appears asking you to confirm the removal, as shown in Figure 4-30. Click Yes and the tag and associated account information are removed from the list as well as completely removed from the registry.

Okay, you're ready to test. Assuming you associated your account information with an RFID tag you have ready to test, reboot your machine and attempt to log in with it. Wait until you can see the login screen asking for account information, and then pass the RFID tag over the reader area of the keyboard. You should be logged right in.

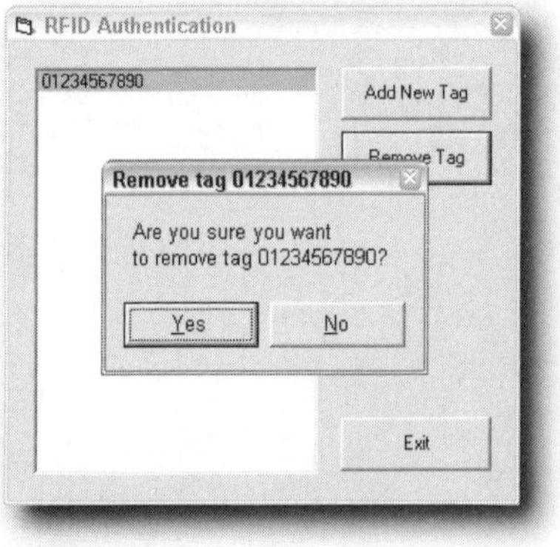

FIGURE 4-30: Removing tags and account
information from the registry

A Word on Security

The point and purpose of this project was to show the concepts involved in enabling authentication using RFID. There are a couple of security concerns that would need to be addressed before something like this could be used wide scale on any computer systems important enough to secure, like company workstations, for instance.

RFID Security

RFID tag IDs can be duplicated. If someone were able to gain knowledge of your RFID tag ID, they could duplicate it and easily log in to your PC with their forged RFID tag. Keep your tag ID secret from others.

Also, the passive 125 KHz EM4102 type tags used for this project are not secure. Any 125 KHz RFID reader that supports EM4102 can read these types of tags, possibly allowing someone to sneak up on you and get your tag ID without your knowledge. However, due to the short read range of these tags and the fact your new RFID keyboard is designed as a covert authentication device, the chances of anyone actually doing this is slim. If you would like to employ more secure RFID technology in your authentication solution, you can certainly do so. However, with greater security comes greater cost. You will also have to write your own DLL solution for interfacing with PollGina to pass RFID tag information, because rfidPoll.dll is written specifically for the Phidgets RFID reader. Look for information about how to do this at http://pgina.xpasystems.com, or use the link provided at www.rfidtoys.net.

Registry Security

The rfidPoll.dll file checks tag IDs read from the Phidgets RFID reader against account data, which is all stored in the registry. Tag IDs and account information are stored in plain text, readable by anyone with access to the registry. However, there are a couple possible solutions.

Securing Registry Keys

One possible solution would be to have an administrator secure these registry keys using the registry editor so no basic user accounts can access them. The PollGina software that authenticates user accounts can still access them because it runs as SYSTEM, which has full access to everything. After securing these keys, only the administrator would be able to add, update, and remove tags and account information from the registry.

Encrypting Registry Data

Since all of the software involved here is open source, downloadable and modifiable by anyone, it's possible to add encryption options to rfidPoll.dll and RFIDAuth.exe so the tag and account data stored in the registry is encrypted. That would render account information and tag values completely unreadable by anyone who wanted to directly access the registry to get at account information or tag IDs.

Building an RFID-Enabled Safe

Continuing with the access-control theme, you're going to take an electronic fire safe and modify it, adding RFID functionality.

Today, electronic fire safes are cheap and easy to find. Most are based on a digital keypad and a dial like the one shown in Figure 5-1. You punch in the correct combination on the number pad, and then turn the dial to open the safe. Inside the safe door, there is a locking mechanism, usually built around a solenoid, which will not let you turn the dial until the solenoid is activated. The idea is to build an add-on that activates the solenoid when the RFID reader is presented with an authorized tag, completely bypassing the digital keypad circuitry.

You can do this project two ways. The first approach involves interfacing with the keypad circuitry to activate the RFID reader and control circuit when the keypad is activated. This approach can be a little more difficult to implement, but it takes advantage of the safe's existing circuitry and keypad. However, even though most electronic safes are built around the same simple concept, the keypad circuitry used is different for each safe. It might not even be possible to interface with the circuitry in your safe, or worse, it might damage the keypad control circuitry rendering the keypad inoperable. If in doubt, use the second method.

The second approach is to build a timer circuit that activates the RFID control circuitry and reader board for about 10 seconds once you press a push-button on the front panel. During this time, you can present your tag and turn the dial if the tag is authorized.

in this chapter

☑ Modifying an electronic fire safe

☑ Building a transistor-controlled keypad interface

☑ Programming a BASIC Stamp 2 microcontroller

☑ Building an RFID-enabled lock control circuit

The reason you can't just let the RFID reader continuously scan for tags all comes down to battery life. A 9V battery has approximately 500 mAh of power to give, however a BASIC Stamp and RFID reader require about 250 mA. If you divide 500 mAh by 250mA, you get two hours. A two-hour operating life means this is not a practical battery-powered application when continuously scanning for tags.

The plan of attack for this project is to mount an RFID reader, shown in Figure 5-2, inside the keypad panel and put the RFID control circuitry in the safe door with the safe's lock control circuitry. The trick here is to mount the RFID reader as far away from the metal safe door as possible, because the metal in the safe's door totally mutes the radio signal needed to read the tags if the reader board is too close. You'll be using a very cheap but very powerful 125 KHz RFID reader board from Parallax and Grand Idea Studio that is well suited to the task.

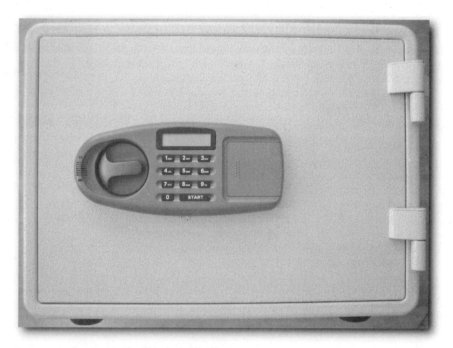

FIGURE 5-1: Electronic safe with digital keypad

FIGURE 5-2: Parallax 125 KHz RFID reader by Grand Idea Studio

Parts and Tools

You need the following parts for this project:

- Electronic safe with digital keypad and solenoid-actuated locking mechanism
- Parallax RFID reader module by Grand Idea Studio from www.parallax.com
- Parallax BASIC Stamp 2 (BS2) from www.parallax.com
- 9V battery and battery clip with leads
- Two general-purpose circuit boards, Radio Shack part number 276-148a
- A 24-pin IC socket, Radio Shack part number 276-1996
- Two +5V reed relays, Radio Shack part number 275-232
- An NPN switching transistor, Radio Shack part number 276-1617
- A 7805 +5V voltage regulator, Radio Shack part number 276-1770
- A 560-ohm resistor (green/blue/brown color code)

- A computer (PS/2 port) keyboard/mouse extension cable with male and female ends
- Two 1N4005 type general-purpose diodes, Radio Shack part number 276-1104
- Connecting wire

And you need these tools:

- Soldering iron and solder
- Hot glue gun with plenty of hot glue
- Large set of pliers
- Small flat-blade screwdriver
- Medium Philips head screwdriver
- Digital multimeter

Get To It

The first thing you need to do is open and take apart the safe. Then you'll program your micro-controller and build the circuitry. So let's get started.

Step 1: Take Apart the Electronic Safe

Usually, the electronics are split into two parts, the external access circuitry and the internal lock control circuitry. You're going to disassemble the safe door so you can remove the front control panel and internal lock control circuitry.

Open the Safe

Use the keypad to open the safe. Once the safe is open, look around on the backside of the door for screws holding a protective metal plate over the lock control circuitry and locking mechanism.

Remove the Protective Plate

After you remove the screws from the protective plate, it should look something like Figure 5-3, revealing the lock control circuitry and locking mechanism. Inside this cubbyhole, you should find plenty of extra room for housing your RFID control circuitry and 9V battery.

FIGURE 5-3: Lock control circuitry and locking mechanism

Disassemble the Locking Mechanism

Start by removing the center screw and washer holding the armature to the front panel actuator dial, as shown in Figure 5-4. The armature assembly should come off and you should be able to pull the dial face and actuator post out of the front of the control panel.

After you have removed the actuator assembly, you can focus on removing the actual locking mechanism. It's held on by an e-ring and washer. Use a flat-blade screwdriver to pry the e-ring off its post by pulling it straight back. Don't try to pry it upwards off the post — that might bend or break the e-ring and you wouldn't be able to put the safe back together. Once the e-ring is off, you can remove the locking mechanism (see Figure 5-5).

FIGURE 5-4: Removing the actuator dial armature

FIGURE 5-5: Removing the e-ring with a flat blade screwdriver

Now that the entire locking assembly is out of the way, you'll see a large nut holding part of the front control panel in place. Use a large set of pliers or the correct size socket or wrench (if you have one) to remove this nut (see Figure 5-6). Once the nut is off, pull out the metal through-shaft that used to house the dial actuator. Now you're half way to removing the front control panel.

Disconnect the front control panel from the lock control circuitry by pulling the wiring harness out as shown in Figure 5-7. Pull apart the quick connect between the locking solenoid and lock control circuitry (see Figure 5-8) and then carefully pull the circuit board off the plastic support posts. Make sure you press in the little plastic locking flaps on the support posts so you don't rip the posts out of the safe door.

FIGURE 5-6: Removing the nut holding the actuator through-shaft

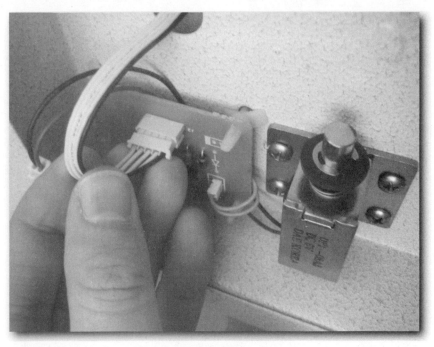

FIGURE 5-7: Disconnecting the lock control circuitry

FIGURE 5-8: Separating the solenoid from lock control circuit

Remove the Front Control Panel

Once you've disconnected the lock control circuit board from the front control panel and removed it from the safe door, you can remove the front control panel. Open the battery cover and remove the batteries. Behind the batteries are two screws securing the front control panel to the safe door, as shown in Figure 5-9. Remove those screws and carefully remove the front control panel, slowly pulling the wiring harness through the wiring hole in the safe door (see Figure 5-10).

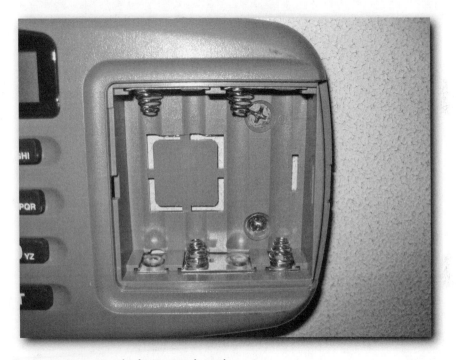

FIGURE 5-9: Removing the front control panel

FIGURE 5-10: Removing the front access panel from the safe door

Step 2: Program the BASIC Stamp 2

If you've never worked with Parallax microcontrollers before, you should purchase one of the BASIC Stamp 2 starter kits direct from Parallax (www.parallax.com). Kits include a Stamp microcontroller and an easy-to-use starter board, which makes programming and testing the Stamp microcontroller a snap. The BASIC Stamp 2 Discovery Kit is a good one to get because the kit board has an IC socket for your Stamp, which makes it easy to program your Stamp and then place it in your final product. It also has a breadboard built in and comes with lots of components to use for building and testing your own circuit designs.

The two basic things your Stamp microcontroller will be doing is listening for authorized tag IDs from the RFID reader board, and activating the locking solenoid when a reader is presented with an authorized tag. The following code constantly checks for RFID tags until the power is cut to the Stamp and RFID reader. Remember, you can download the source code file from www.rfidtoys.net.

Note   Before you connect the BASIC Stamp 2 to your PC and run the code, be sure to update it with the IDs of the RFID tags you want to have access to the safe.

BASIC Stamp 2 Microprocessor Code

```
' ============================================================================
'
'   File....... RFID.BS2
'   Purpose.... RFID Tag Reader / Simple Security System
'   Author..... Jon Williams -- Parallax, Inc.
'   E-mail..... jwilliams@parallax.com
'   Started....
'   Updated.... 07 FEB 2005
'
' ============================================================================
'   Updated.... 02 JULY 2005
'   Purpose.... Update code to suit RFID Safe project
'   Author..... Amal Graafstra -- RFID Toys
' ============================================================================
'
'   {$Stamp BS2}
'   {$PBASIC 2.5}
'
' ============================================================================


' -----[ Program Description ]----------------------------------------------
'
' Reads tags from a Parallax RFID reader and compares to known tags (stored
' in EEPROM table).  If tag is found, the program will disable a lock.


' -----[ Revision History ]-------------------------------------------------
'
'   Updated.... 02 JULY 2005
'   Purpose.... Update code to suit RFID Safe project
'   Author..... Amal Graafstra -- RFID Toys

' -----[ I/O Definitions ]--------------------------------------------------

Latch          PIN    0                    ' Solenoid control
RX             PIN    15                   ' Serial from RFID reader
LED            PIN    14                   ' LED indicator


' -----[ Constants ]--------------------------------------------------------
```

Continued

BASIC Stamp 2 Microprocessor Code *(continued)*

```
#SELECT $Stamp
  #CASE BS2, BS2E, BS2PE
    T1200       CON     813
    T2400       CON     396
    T4800       CON     188
    T9600       CON     84
    T19K2       CON     32
    TMidi       CON     12
    T38K4       CON     6
  #CASE BS2SX, BS2P
    T1200       CON     2063
    T2400       CON     1021
    T4800       CON     500
    T9600       CON     240
    T19K2       CON     110
    TMidi       CON     60
    T38K4       CON     45
#ENDSELECT

SevenBit      CON     $2000
Inverted      CON     $4000
Open          CON     $8000
Baud          CON     T2400


#SELECT $Stamp
  #CASE BS2, BS2E
    TmAdj       CON     $100                ' x 1.0 (time adjust)
    FrAdj       CON     $100                ' x 1.0 (freq adjust)
  #CASE BS2SX
    TmAdj       CON     $280                ' x 2.5
    FrAdj       CON     $066                ' x 0.4
  #CASE BS2P
    TmAdj       CON     $3C5                ' x 3.77
    FrAdj       CON     $044                ' x 0.265
  #CASE BS2PE
    TmAdj       CON     $100                ' x 1.0
    FrAdj       CON     $0AA                ' x 0.665
#ENDSELECT


LastTag       CON     3


#DEFINE __No_SPRAM = ($Stamp < BS2P)        ' does module have SPRAM?


' -----[ Variables ]----------------------------------------------------
```

```
#IF __No_SPRAM #THEN
  buf            VAR     Byte(10)              ' RFID bytes buffer
#ELSE
  chkChar        VAR     Byte                  ' character to test
#ENDIF

tagNum           VAR     Nib                   ' from EEPROM table
idx              VAR     Byte                  ' tag byte index
char             VAR     Byte                  ' character from table


' -----[ EEPROM Data ]--------------------------------------------------

Tag1             DATA    "010249F390"          ' valid tags
Tag2             DATA    "0123456789"
Tag3             DATA    "0987654321"

' -----[ Initialization ]-----------------------------------------------

Reset:
  LOW Latch                                    ' make sure solenoid is locked
  LOW LED                                      ' make sure LED is off

' -----[ Program Code ]-------------------------------------------------

Main:
  #IF __No_SPRAM #THEN
    SERIN RX, T2400, [WAIT($0A), STR buf\10]   ' wait for hdr + ID
  #ELSE
    SERIN RX, T2400, [WAIT($0A), SPSTR 10]
  #ENDIF

Check_List:
  FOR tagNum = 1 TO LastTag                    ' scan through known tags
    FOR idx = 0 TO 9                           ' scan bytes in tag
      READ (tagNum - 1 * 10 + idx), char       ' get tag data from table
      #IF __No_SPRAM #THEN
        IF (char <> buf(idx)) THEN Bad_Char     ' compare tag to table
      #ELSE
        GET idx, chkChar                       ' read char from SPRAM
        IF (char <> chkChar) THEN Bad_Char     ' compare to table
      #ENDIF
    NEXT
    GOTO Tag_Found                             ' all bytes match!

Bad_Char:                                      ' try next tag
  NEXT
```

Continued

BASIC Stamp 2 Microprocessor Code *(continued)*

```
Bad_Tag:
  tagNum = 0
  HIGH LED                              ' light red LED
  PAUSE 10000                           ' wait for power loss
  GOTO Main

Tag_Found:
  HIGH Latch                            ' activate solenoid
  PAUSE 5000                            ' keep latch open
  LOW Latch                             ' lock solenoid
  GOTO Main

  END
```

Step 3: Build the Interface Circuitry

The Parallax RFID reader doesn't require much power to operate. It only needs about 230 mA of current when scanning for tags. However, because this is a battery-powered application, you can't let the RFID reader continuously scan for tags. A 9V battery has approximately 500 mAh of power to give to your project, but a BASIC Stamp and RFID reader together require about 250 mA. If you divide 500 mAh by 250 mA, you get only two hours. A two-hour operating life is not practical for a continuous scan for tags, so a method must be created that only powers the Stamp and RFID reader when they are needed and cuts power to them when finished.

You can do this project two ways. First, you can interface with the keypad circuitry to activate the RFID reader and control circuit when the keypad is activated. This approach is more difficult to implement, but takes advantage of the safe's existing circuitry and keypad. However, even though most electronic safes are built around the same simple concept, the keypad circuitry used is different for each safe. It might not even be possible to interface with the circuitry in your safe, or worse, it might damage the keypad control circuitry rendering the keypad inoperable. If you don't have exactly the safe used in this project, or don't know how to test for and locate a suitable interface pin on your safe's keypad controller, use the second method.

In the second approach, you simply use a push-button or a switch to power the RFID control circuitry and reader board only while it is needed.

Keypad Interface

If you don't want to interface with your safe's keypad circuitry, you can skip this section and move on to "The Push Button Method." The keypad interface is a simple transistor controlled relay. When you press the START button on the keypad, the relay activates and allows current to flow from the 9V battery and powers up the BASIC Stamp 2 and RFID reader. An unused output on the keypad control IC switches the transistor on. See Figure 5-11 for a circuit diagram.

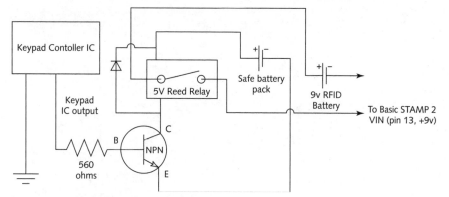

FIGURE 5-11: Keypad interface circuit diagram

Build Keypad Interface Circuit

First, be sure there are no batteries in the safe's battery pack. Break out a general-purpose circuit board and place a 5V reed relay somewhere in the center, making sure there is extra room on all sides. Solder the relay posts to the contact pads on the backside of the board. Trim them down if they stick out too much.

Drop an NPN switching transistor on the board so the collector pin sits adjacent to one of the relay's coil pins (refer back to Figure 5-11 for an example). Not all NPN transistors have the same pin-out though, so check yours before soldering it in place. Connect the transistor's collector pin to the relay's coil pin using a solder bridge across the two contact pads.

Add a 560-ohm resistor so that one lead is next to the transistor's base pin. Connect the resistor to the transistor's base pin using a solder bridge. Since the general circuit board is just a collection of through-hole contact pads with no pathways, you can just bridge component leads with a generous amount of solder.

Place the resistor's other lead near the other end of the relay, keeping it close. The point is to keep the finished circuit a very tight package so it will fit properly in the safe's front control panel with the RFID reader board. Now solder a long jumper wire to the free resistor lead. This jumper wire will connect to the safe's electronic keypad IC.

Solder a red wire from the safe's +6V battery pack post to the relay's other coil pin (the one not connected to the transistor). Solder a black wire from the safe's ground battery-pack post to the transistor's emitter pin.

Now unravel the PS/2 keyboard extension cable. Measure out about 6" from the male connector and cut the cable. Strip all but an inch of housing off the cable, exposing six multicolored wires, a bare metal shield conductor wire, and a cable stress-reduction string. Trim off the bare metal shield conductor wire and the stress-reduction string, leaving only the six multicolored wires. Solder the brown wire from the PS/2 cable to one side of the relay's switched contacts. Then solder the green wire to the other switched contact. You should now have something like Figure 5-12 in front of you.

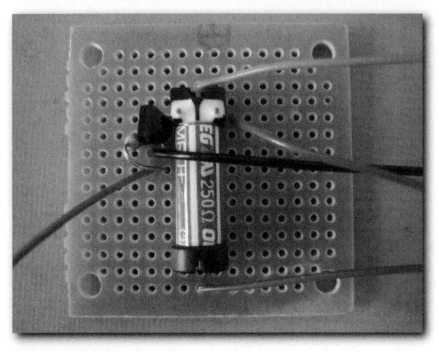

FIGURE 5-12: Keypad interface circuit

 Note When working with relays, you add diodes across the relay's coil pins to sink the high voltage currents generated when the relay is switched off. When a relay is switched off, the electromagnetic field collapses through the relay's coil windings and generates a high voltage spike. This voltage usually has no place to go except through the rest of the circuit and can end up damaging sensitive components like transistors and ICs.

Get yourself a diode and solder its cathode lead (the side with the colored band) to the relay coil pin that is not connected to the transistor. Solder the diode's anode lead to the other relay coil pin, the one connected to the transistor. This lets the inducted voltage generated by the collapse of the relay coil's electromagnetic field flow from one side of the coil to the other, through the diode, without damaging the transistor the relay is connected to. If you connect the diode in the wrong direction, the current meant to switch on the relay flows through the diode instead, possibly burning out your transistor.

Connect the Keypad Interface Circuit

Locate a suitable output from the safe's keypad circuitry. One method is to use a multimeter. Connect your multimeter to ground and place the positive probe on one of the unused pins on the keypad IC. Your meter should read 0 (zero). Now press the START button on the safe keypad and see if you get a reading. If not, move to the next pin and keep testing.

If you decide to test your safe keypad IC for an unused output, be aware of two things. First, make sure you do not accidentally short two or more pins with the tip of your multimeter probe. That could damage the keypad controller IC. Also, unless you have actual documentation about the IC you are testing, there's no certain way to know what might happen if you use any output pin you may find. It may damage the IC or cause the keypad to behave in an unforeseen manor. This is a hack in the messiest sense of the word, so proceed at your own risk.

On this particular safe, there are only two unused outputs on the control IC (see Figure 5-13), either one of which can be used. Solder the jumper wire coming from the 560-ohm resistor to the keypad IC output pin. Once you've soldered the jumper wire to the IC output, secure it to the keypad control circuit board with some hot glue. This will significantly reduce stress on the solder joint and fragile IC lead.

Figure 5-13: Jumper wire connected to the keypad controller IC

Test the Keypad Interface Circuit

At this point, you may want to test your transistor with a multimeter to make sure it switches on when the START button is pressed. Put batteries in the safe's battery pack and set your meter to test for DC voltage. Set your positive (+) meter test lead on the battery pack's positive post. Place the negative (-) test lead on the transistor's collector pin. Press the START button on the keypad and you should get a voltage reading until the keypad LCD powers off. Put the meter into continuity mode, place a test lead on each of the relay's switched contact pins, and try again. You should get a continuity reading when the transistor is switched on. If you don't, you might try replacing the 560-ohm resistor with a 530-ohm resistor and trying again. If still nothing, try reducing the resistance between the transistor's base pin and the keypad's IC output until the transistor switches on.

Once you've tested the circuit, trim off as much excess circuit board as you can. Trim along unused through-holes. There isn't a lot of extra space inside the front control panel, so we want to make this board as small as possible.

With the circuit board trimmed, heat up your trusty hot glue gun and secure the interface circuit toward the top of the keypad casing, near the battery posts (see Figure 5-14). Hot glue works both as an adhesive and as an insulator, so be sure to use enough to create a large pad for your interface circuit to rest on, keeping it secure and insulated from the keypad controller circuitry under it. If you feel you need more insulation, you can cut a piece of rigid construction grade paper between the keypad controller board and your keypad interface board.

FIGURE 5-14: Finished keypad interface circuit

The Push-Button Method

If interfacing with your safe's keypad circuitry isn't possible or makes you uncomfortable, you can simply use a switch or push button to activate the RFID circuitry.

I chose to use a momentary push button (see Figure 5-15) instead of a switch because I'm the type of person that would forget and leave the circuit turned on, draining the battery and rendering it useless.

Installing a switch is straightforward. The only trick is to figure out a place to put the switch that will not interfere with mounting the RFID reader board later, so set your RFID reader board in place while hunting around for a spot. Also check to ensure you won't be drilling through any important parts or pieces on the front of the access panel.

Once you find a place, put the threaded nut that came with the switch down as shown in Figure 5-16. Make sure it rests flat against the plastic of the access panel. There are several curved edges inside the access panel, and by putting the nut in a flat position you can be assured it will fasten tightly down on the switch, holding it in place.

Use a permanent marker to put a dot on the access panel plastic directly in the center of where the nut is laying (see Figure 5-17).

Figure 5-15: Standard push-button switch

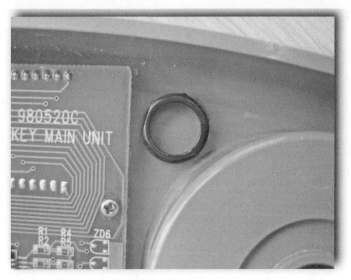

Figure 5-16: Place the threaded nut to ensure a proper fit

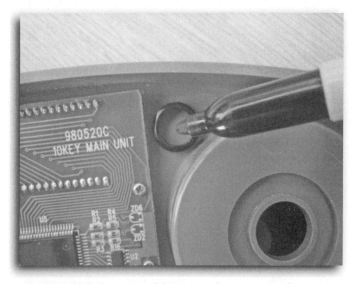

FIGURE 5-17: Mark the center of the nut on the access panel

Drill a hole big enough for the switch, but don't make it so big that the switch will sit loose in the hole. Sometimes it's best to drill the same size hole as the switch shaft diameter, making it somewhat difficult to insert the switch through the hole. This will help keep the switch from moving around or coming loose. Often, using the nut alone won't hold the switch in place over a lifetime of use and it will come loose.

Insert the switch. Then thread the nut on the back down tightly. You should have something that looks like Figure 5-18.

Now unravel the PS/2 keyboard extension cable. Measure out about 6" from the male connector and cut the cable. Strip all but an inch of housing off, exposing six multicolored wires, a bare metal shield conductor wire, and a cable stress-reduction string. Trim off the bare metal shield conductor wire and the stress-reduction string, leaving only the six multicolored wires. Solder the brown wire from the PS/2 cable to one of the switch leads. Then solder the green wire to the other switch lead. Now fold down the switch leads so the switch assembly is as short as possible and you should have something like Figure 5-19.

FIGURE 5-18: Switch installed in front access panel

FIGURE 5-19: Lead wires soldered to switch

Step 4: Mount the RFID Reader Board

You will be soldering the remaining PS/2 connector wires to the RFID reader board and securing the board into the safe's front control panel.

Take out the RFID reader board. Solder a jumper wire from the ENABLE pin to the GND pin on the RFID board. This immediately puts the board into an enabled state when it powers up.

Solder the red wire from the PS/2 connector to the VCC pin on the RFID board. Then solder the black wire to the GND pin and the orange wire to the SOUT pin.

Use the hot glue gun to put a generous amount of glue onto the keypad control circuit board, creating an insulating adhesive layer for your RFID reader. With the component side up, press the RFID board down into the hot glue, keeping in mind you still want a thin layer of glue insulating the two boards from each other. The risk of a short is very small as the RFID reader board has no exposed solder points on the side glued in place, but if you feel you need more protection, you can glue an insulating piece of construction grade paper between the RFID board and keypad controller board.

If you went the keypad interface route, you should now have something like Figure 5-20 sitting in front of you. Otherwise, the green and brown wires from the PS/2 connector lead to your switch instead of the keypad interface circuit.

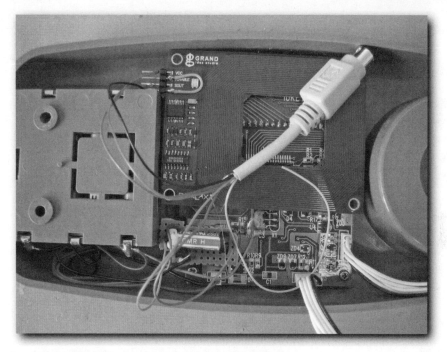

FIGURE 5-20: Finished control panel with keypad interface

Step 5: Build the RFID Control Circuitry

Now that you've finished the keypad interface circuit and mounted the RFID reader board in place, you can focus on building the RFID control circuit, which you'll mount inside the safe's door with the lock control circuitry. Figure 5-21 shows a circuit diagram of the BASIC Stamp based RFID control circuit.

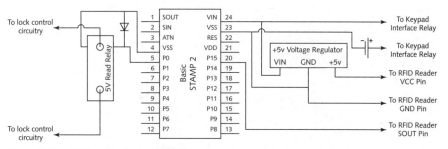

FIGURE 5-21: RFID control circuit diagram

Using another general-purpose circuit board, place a 24-pin IC socket on the board. Keep the socket off to one side so there is plenty of room for extra components on the board. Also, make sure you keep plenty of extra room around the end of the IC socket with the dip in it. The dip signifies where pin 1 of the IC should go. Check Figure 5-22 to see what kind of placement requirements the IC socket has.

Note You count pins on ICs by placing the IC in front of you with the marked end at the top. Most ICs have a dibit or marking at the end to signify where pin 1 is. With the marked end at the top, pin 1 is on the top left. Count down the left side of the IC, and then move across to the bottom right and count up the right side of the IC, making a big U shape as you count.

You don't have to use an IC socket, but I highly recommend doing so. It lets you handle the circuit board and solder components without having to worry about damaging your BASIC Stamp 2 microcontroller. It also makes reprogramming the Stamp much easier, since you can easily remove it from the board.

Place a 5V reed relay on the board, leaving enough room around it for additional connecting wires and components.

Solder jumper wires from the relay's coil pins to pins 4 and 5 on the IC socket. You count pins starting from the top left, which is pin 1. Pin 4 is the Stamp's VSS (ground) pin, and pin 5 is the Stamp's P0 I/O pin (pin 0 in the code).

Now you should be working with something like what was shown in Figure 5-22.

FIGURE 5-22: Placement of the IC socket and 5V reed relay

Take out the 9V battery clip and solder the black lead to pin 23 on the IC socket. BASIC Stamp microcontrollers have two VSS (ground) pins, and pin 23 is that second pin.

Solder a 7805 +5V voltage regulator to the board and fold it down to keep the circuit as thin as possible. You don't want components sticking too far out as there isn't much room in the safe's door to house this additional board. Solder a black jumper wire from the center ground pin on the voltage regulator to pin 14 or pin 4 of the IC socket.

Take the female end of the PS/2 extension cable and measure out about 6" from the end. Cut the cable and strip off all but about 1" of the housing, exposing the multicolored wires inside. Trim the bare metal-shield conductor wire and the stress-reduction string like you did earlier on the male end. Solder the black wire from the PS/2 connector to a ground pin, either pin 14 or pin 4 on the IC socket.

Use a butt connector to connect the red lead from the 9V battery clip to the PS/2 connector's green wire. Solder the red wire from the PS/2 connector to the 5V output pin on the +5V voltage regulator.

Solder the brown wire from the PS/2 connector to pin 24 on the IC socket. Pin 24 is the first pin on the top right, and correlates to the Stamp's unregulated voltage input pin (VIN).

Solder a jumper wire from pin 23 on the IC socket to the input pin on the +5V voltage regulator. If you've placed the +5V regulator close enough to the IC socket, you may just be able to use a solder bridge instead of a jumper wire.

Solder the orange wire from the PS/2 connector to pin 20 on the IC socket. Pin 20 is the Stamp's P15 I/O pin. Solder the yellow wire from the PS/2 connector to pin 19 on the IC socket. Pin 19 is the Stamp's P14 I/O pin.

Figure 5-23 shows the voltage regulator connected and the PS/2 wires soldered to the IC socket.

The safe's lock-control circuitry basically does what the relay you placed on the RFID control circuit board will do — it allows current from the safe's battery pack to activate the locking solenoid. The safe's lock-control circuitry will have contacts on the board, which connect directly to the safe's battery pack (and maybe a couple signal lines as well) to let the control circuit know when to activate the solenoid. Locate the point on the lock-control circuit board where the current to the locking solenoid is switched on and off by the lock-control circuitry. Solder two 6" jumper wires from those points to the relay's switched contacts on your RFID control circuit board. This is like having two switches installed for one light bulb. Both switches have to be off for the light to be off, but either switch can turn the light on.

Figure 5-24 shows the two possible points you can solder your switched relay contacts to on this particular safe's lock-control circuitry.

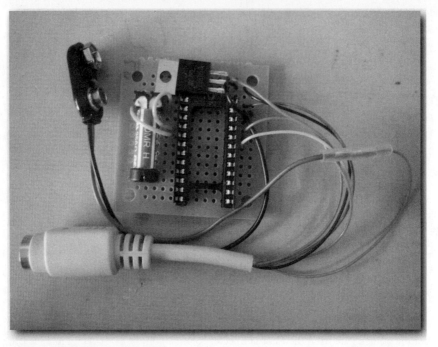

FIGURE 5-23: RFID control circuit

FIGURE 5-24: Connect relay to lock control circuitry

Step 6: Test and Reassemble the Safe

You'll want to run a test before reassembling everything. The first thing you'll want to do is insert the BASIC Stamp microprocessor into the IC socket, making sure pin 1 is in the correct position.

Test the Safe and RFID Functionality

Push the PS/2 connector from the front control panel through the hole in the door, followed by the lock control wiring harness. Secure the front control panel using the two screws located behind the batteries, but don't bother putting the locking mechanism dial and through-shaft back in place yet.

Letting the lock control circuitry and RFID control boards just hang (see Figure 5-25), make sure the boards aren't shorting out and connect the lock control circuit to the solenoid. Connect the lock control circuit to the front control panel wiring harness. Before connecting the 9V battery, make sure the safe's batteries are in place and test the safe using the keypad. After testing the safe's normal operation, connect the 9V battery to the 9V battery clip and test the RFID functionality.

Keep in mind that the RFID reader will have a reduced read range due to the close proximity of the safe's metal door behind it, so you have to hold up tags directly in front of the LCD screen and keypad area, probably even touching the control panel. Press the START button on the front control panel and hold the RFID tag up quickly; it should authenticate and the safe should unlock.

If you build the push button version, you must hold the button in while presenting your tag. Once the safe is unlocked, you can turn the dial and open the door, and then release the push button.

FIGURE 5-25: Testing the RFID control circuit

Reassemble the Safe

Remove the safe's batteries from the front control panel and disconnect the 9V battery from the RFID circuit. Reassemble the rest of the safe, starting with the front control-panel dial. Put the through-shaft back in place and secure it with the large nut. Put the locking mechanism back in place and replace the washer and e-ring. Push the dial-post through the through-shaft and assemble the locking armature.

Push the lock-control circuitry back onto its support posts. Make sure the solenoid control wires and lock-control wiring harness are all out of the way of the locking mechanism. Find a place for the 9V battery and RFID circuit board. Your RFID board doesn't have the luxury of resting on plastic insulating posts, so cut a piece of thick construction paper or other insulating material down to size and secure it with hot glue to the back of the RFID control board. Once that's secure, find a place to mount the board and glue it in place as shown in Figure 5-26. Connect the 9V battery to the battery clip and glue it in place using a small dab of glue. The wonderful thing about using hot glue is that it's relatively easy to fix mistakes. You just pull the glued pieces apart, strip the glue off, and start again. So, the day you need to replace the 9V battery it should be easy to remove the battery and re-glue a new one in. Of course, you could always just get a battery-holding clip and glue that in place using a stronger glue or epoxy.

Replace the protective cover over the locking mechanism and control circuitry, and screw it down.

Congratulations. You are now the proud owner of an RFID-enabled safe!

FIGURE 5-26: RFID control circuit and battery glued in place

Taking Inventory with an RFID-Enabled Smart Shelf

S mart shelves are one of the many things businesses dream about when they think RFID. You can apply the concept of a smart shelf to not just shelves, but to filing cabinets or just about any item or document-storage container. In fact, many places that deal with mountains of paper, including medical clinics and blueprint drafting houses, use smart shelves. After tagging medical charts, clinics have implemented smart shelving in order to track where a chart has gone. Dealing with and storing paper medical charts are the most daunting tasks for medical clinic office staff because even inactive records must be kept for several years. Being able to locate a chart quickly by querying the smart-shelf system saves time for everyone involved, from office staff to doctor to patient.

In 2003, Wal-Mart announced its plans to implement RFID and has been pressing their suppliers to tag product pallets and cases with RFID labels ever since. Not only do they want to be able to track products through the supply chain, but also they eventually plan on deploying the smart shelf concept in stores for inventory control and auditing. That would allow Wal-Mart to inventory not just product type counts like 25 "apples" and 37 "oranges," but it would let them inventory each apple and orange. With each item in the store being uniquely identifiable, similar items such as a particular make and model of a hammer could be grouped together under "XYZ hammers," and all the different makes and models could be grouped under just "hammers." Yet another group could be created rounding up all the hammers and other hardware tools under "hardware and tools." The smart-shelf technology itself doesn't necessarily care what the items are; it just reads and reports. You can design the backend information-processing software to give any desired level of detail wanted on both the per-item level as well as the enterprise level.

in this chapter

☑ Working with high-frequency 13.56 MHz RFID technology

☑ Leveraging the anti-collision feature

☑ Learning about passive RFID resonant loop antennas and magnetic coupling

While a smart shelf has obvious business uses, you can also use it at home to inventory a DVD collection, CDs, books, or just about any thing you'd keep on a shelf. In this chapter, you're going to build a shelf that can take inventory of the tagged items resting on it. To do this, the reader and tags have to support anti-collision so each tag can respond with its ID and not talk over the other tags. When two tags try to respond to a reader request at the same time, it's called a *collision*. The end-result is that the reader doesn't hear either tag. Typically, low-frequency tags and readers don't support anti-collision. You can find some types that do, but they still aren't able to achieve the kind of range that high-frequency tags and readers can with the same low-power consumption.

For this project, you're going to step up the frequency a bit and move away from the 125 KHz – 134 KHz low-frequency technology used in previous chapters. This project uses high-frequency 13.56 MHz technology, which still uses passive near-field magnetic coupling to communicate between tags and reader, yet offers anti-collision features and a bit more range than low frequency technology.

Unfortunately stepping up the frequency usually means stepping up the costs, too. Luckily, there are some cheap OEM readers out there, which you can use for your 13.56 MHz projects. One such reader is the SkyeTek M1 module shown in Figure 6-1. This little reader is both cheap and amazing.

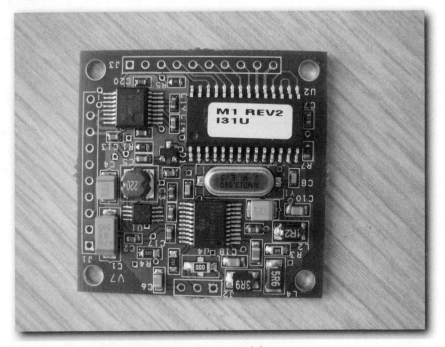

Figure 6-1: SkyeTek M1 13.56 MHz read/write module

This little (and I do mean little) module has it all. It can communicate with hosts using several different methods, including RS-232, TTL, SPI, and I2C. The communications protocol used between host and M1 module allows up to 255 individually addressable modules to reside on a single communications line and work independently. You can even update the firmware on this module to support future tag protocols. Even though this project barely scratches the surface of what the M1 can do, I hope you will be able come up with your own projects that utilize many of the features this module has built in.

Parts and Tools

You need the following parts for this project:

- SkyeTek M1 13.56 MHz RFID read/write module from www.skyetek.com
- Feig 13.56 MHz pad antenna, part number RR-IDISC-ANT34-24 from www.digikey.com
- Four short wood screws for mounting Feig antenna
- DB-9 female to male RS-232 cable, Radio Shack part number 26-269
- ClosetMaid 24" horizontal shelving unit, part number M26 (08565)
- Optional female SMA connector, DigiKey part number 4959-ND
- SmartShelf software downloaded from www.rfidtoys.net
- Connecting wire

And you need these tools:

- Philips screwdriver
- Soldering iron and solder

Build It

The first you'll need to do is put together the shelving unit itself. You can use the ClosetMaid 24" unit given in the parts list, or use another shelf. The only requirement is that it's not made of metal and has minimal metal parts holding it together. Metal will interfere with the 13.56MHz radio spectrum this RFID project uses and will significantly decrease read range and tag reliability.

Step 1: Build the Shelf

This project uses a 24-inch shelving unit to store tagged inventory items. The size of this shelf is the absolute maximum that the Feig antenna and SkyeTek M1 module can handle. The M1 module is a low power reader, but it still creates a large enough magnetic field through the Feig antenna to read the shelving area.

If you want to read more shelves or inventory a larger area, you can do so a few different ways. In the first method, you simply add more readers and antennas. Space out the antennas so you get good coverage without much overlap. Overlap causes interference and reduces effective read range and accuracy. The second method is to get a high-power reader and a high-power antenna to read the entire shelf with one setup, but this can be very expensive. The third and more complicated method is to connect multiple antennas to a single reader. Some readers allow for up to four different antennas to be connected to them, but these too are expensive.

If you don't have a reader with multiple antenna connections, there is a way to connect multiple antennas to a single reader, but you need to use only one antenna at a time. Building that kind of setup is outside the scope of this project, so at the end of this chapter I will give you some information on building your own antenna for this shelf project and include some resources that give in-depth detail about building multiple shelf antenna arrays.

Mount the Antenna

There are two shelves in this shelving unit: a top and a bottom shelf. You're going to mount the external antenna shown in Figure 6-2 to the underside of the top shelf. When the antenna is mounted to the top shelf, the system can inventory tagged items on both the top and bottom shelf.

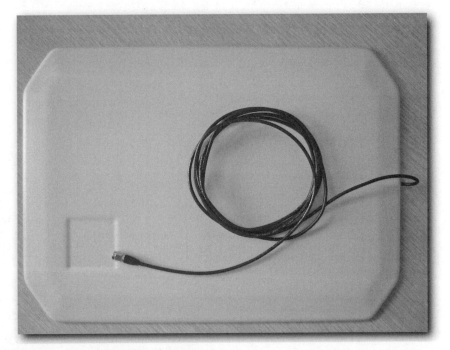

FIGURE 6-2: Feig 13.56 MHz pad antenna

Flip the pad antenna over and you will see screw mount holes like the ones in Figure 6-3. There are eight holes, two per corner, to allow mounting in different directions. There is only one set of four holes that are all notched the same way; the other holes allow for hanging configurations where only two mount screws are used. You want to use all four mount points, so locate the mount holes that are all notched in the same direction.

Place a piece of plain letter paper over the back of the antenna so all the holes are covered and tape it into place so it won't move on you. Figure 6-4 shows the whole backside of the antenna covered with a single 8.5" × 11" piece of letter paper.

Press the paper into the mount holes with your fingers, indenting the paper. This marks the paper so you can see where the holes are. Then, without moving the paper, use an ink pen and make little dots to mark the mount holes as shown in Figure 6-5. Make the dots small and in exactly the same place for each hole. The mount-hole slide notches are short and there is very little tolerance for screw position, so mark the paper with as much precision you can muster.

FIGURE 6-3: Mount holes on the back of the pad antenna

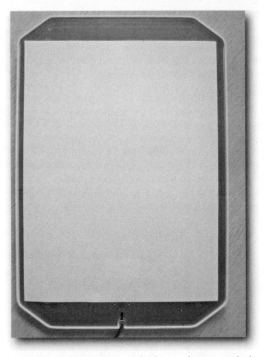

FIGURE 6-4: Letter-size paper laid over the mount holes

FIGURE 6-5: Marking screw holes on the indented paper

Now carefully take the paper off the antenna and tape it on to the underside of the board you will be using as the top shelf. Once you've securely taped the stencil, use a small drill bit or some other marking method to transfer the screw-mount-hole positions to the shelving board. Screw the mount screws into the board and test your antenna mounts. After you have successfully mounted your antenna, dismount it and leave the mounting screws in place.

Build the Shelf

I'm not going to tell you how to build a shelf. If you need instructions, follow the ones included with the shelving unit. Just make sure you use the board with the antenna mount screws in it as the top shelf.

Step 2: Wire the Reader

The way the M1 read/write module is set up allows for easy wiring and soldering. There are clearly marked through-holes on the board for power, antenna connections, communications lines, and so on. The first thing you're going to do is connect the antenna.

Connect the Antenna

Of all the features the M1 module has, the internal antenna is an unexpected one. This module has already crammed all its components into a 1.5" × 1.5" square, but SkyeTek engineers found enough room to place an internal antenna capable of reading tags up to 3.5" away. While this is impressive, the field isn't nearly large enough to cover the shelf, so you need to use the Feig pad antenna. Luckily, the design of the M1 board allows for a very easy switch between internal and external antennas.

On the underside of the module, there are three through-holes marked GND, ANT, and INT. Figure 6-6 shows these antenna connections along the top of the M1 module. The ANT point is the antenna "hot" lead. To use the internal antenna, you simply jumper ANT to INT and you're in business. To use an external antenna, you just connect GND and ANT to the external antenna's leads.

The Feig pad antenna already has a male SMA connector on it, as shown in Figure 6-7. You can find a female SMA connector to solder to the M1 module, or you can cut the SMA connector off the pad antenna cable and just solder the cable directly to the M1 module. I didn't have a female SMA connector, but I did have an SMA barrel connector designed to join two male connectors together. Some quick work with a Dremel tool and I was able to separate the barrel connector into two pieces, making sure not to cut all the way through and trim off the center post.

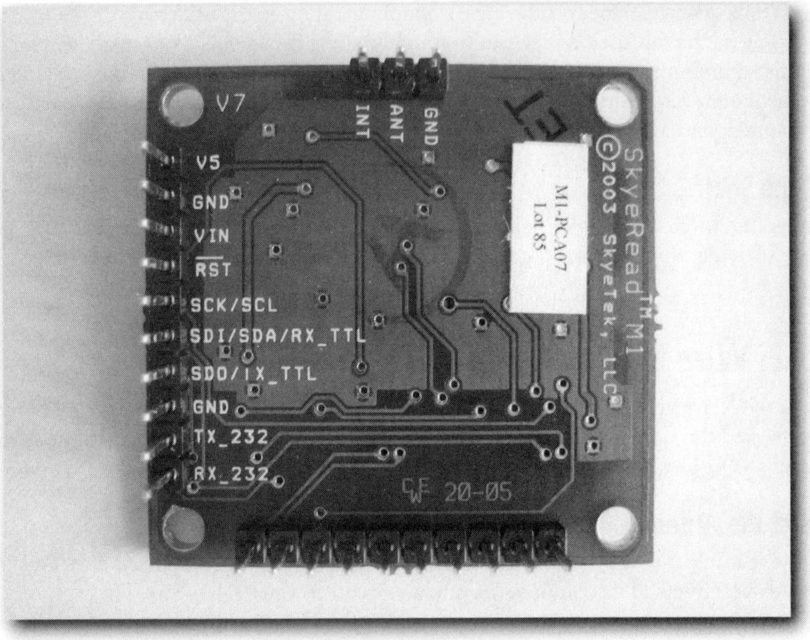

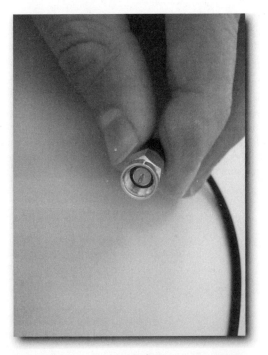

FIGURE 6-6: Underside of the SkyeTek M1 module

FIGURE 6-7: Feig antenna's male SMA connector

If you already have an SMA connector you want to use, either solder it directly to the board as close as possible to the connectors, or use a short chunk of RG58 or any other 50-ohm coaxial cable. If you've decided to cut the SMA connector off the antenna cable and solder the cable directly to the M1 module, cut as close to the SMA connector as possible. Figure 6-8 shows my cut up barrel connector soldered to the M1 module.

Caution   If you soldered the connector directly to the board, remember it is very fragile. When you connect the antenna cable, make sure you hold the female SMA connector while you screw on the cable connector. If you twist the cable connector on without holding the female end, it may rip off the board and damage the circuit pathways. You could also encase the connector in a generous amount of epoxy to help secure it to the board.

Figure 6-9 shows the pad antenna cable threaded on to the M1 board's new SMA connector.

FIGURE 6-8: Half an SMA barrel connector soldered to the M1 board

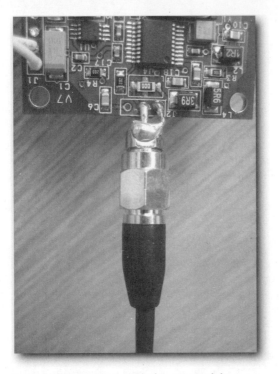

FIGURE 6-9: Antenna connected to M1 module

Wire the M1 Module for RS-232

Even though there are several communications options for the M1, you'll be using RS-232 because it's the easiest to interface with a PC. You can use the TTL interface if you want to connect to a microcontroller without much fuss.

| Note | If you want to use the IC2 or SPI interface, you'll need to load different firmware onto the reader. Contact SkyeTek for instructions on how to download the firmware and update the module. |

Take the RS-232 serial cable and cut the male end off, leaving the female end and about 6' of cable. Strip some of the housing off the cut end of the cable so you can get at the conductors inside. Use a continuity meter to test the conductors to find the correct wires for pins 2, 3, and 5 on the female connector. You should be able to see the pin numbers clearly stamped into the plastic on the female connector.

Once you've identified the conductors, solder them to the M1 board as shown in Figure 6-10.

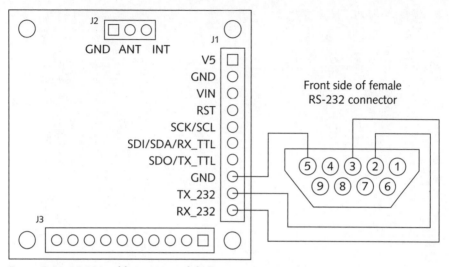

FIGURE 6-10: RS-232 cable to M1 module (top view) wiring diagram

Wire the M1 for Power

The M1 module has two options for power: a regulated 5V supply and an unregulated 1.8V to 5V supply for power sources such as batteries. I've chosen to use the regulated 5V supply as shown in the figures, but you can use the VIN pin if you wish. Just don't exceed the 5V limit. If you are unsure, use a Radio Shack +5V regulator, part number 276-1770 in-line with your power supply. Check Figure 6-10 for the correct power pins to use on the M1 module. Ground is pin 2 on jumper block J1, which runs down the right side of the M1 board shown in Figure 6-10. Pin 1 at the top is the regulated 5V input, and pin 3 is the 1.8V to 5V input.

Place your reader inside a plastic project box to keep it safe from shorts, dirt, and accidental smashing.

Step 3: Tag Your Inventory

You can choose from a variety of different kinds of 13.56 MHz tags to tag your items for inventory. The general rule is, the larger the tag, the more reliable the read will be. The M1 reader can read several different types of 13.56 MHz tags including ISO-15693, ISO-14443, Tag-It HF, and I-Code 1.

Types of Tags

Because of the high frequency used (13.56 MHz), these types of tags can use antennas, which are made from thin circuit pathways, rather than thick copper windings. You can embed these antennas into just about anything, including printable labels with adhesive backs. Figure 6-11 shows a book tagged with a large print label.

Typically, 13.56 MHz is known for its lack of tolerance for metal and liquid, but the keychain tag shown in Figure 6-12 is readable by the smart shelf when surrounded by keys on a key ring.

FIGURE 6-11: A book tagged with a large format print label

FIGURE 6-12: A 13.56 MHz keychain tag

You can embed high-frequency tags into just about anything, including wristbands, adhesive stickers, printable labels, etc.

Choose a Location

When you're tagging an item, be sure to pick a spot on the item that is not near any metal if possible. Proximity to metal will impede the performance of the tag, reducing its effective range. Try to orient the tag so that it's horizontal to the shelf. Tags that are perpendicular to the shelf have far less read range than parallel tags. This is because the tags have to be magnetically coupled to the reader antenna and it's rather difficult to keep the entire loop antenna of a perpendicular tag in the reader's magnetic field.

Step 4: Connect and Take Inventory

Now that you have the reader module wired up for an external antenna, 5V power, and communications, you can connect it to your PC and run the software.

Connect the Module

Mount the pad antenna to the underside of the top shelf of your shelving unit. If you used SMA connectors, connect the antenna to the M1 module. Plug the serial cable into your PC's first serial port, COM1, and power up the reader.

Install the SmartShelf Software

Download and install the SmartShelf inventory software from www.rfidtoys.net. The installation is straightforward. The software is nothing more than a simple example of how an inventory system might work using the M1 module. It does not contain any item logging capabilities, but with some tinkering, I'm sure you could come up with a nice inventory software package.

Taking Inventory Using RFID

The SmartShelf software uses a Microsoft JET database called Inventory.MDB, which is installed along with the software. It is unpopulated, but you can use Microsoft Access to populate the database with tagged items. Because RFID tags identify each individual item, unlike UPC barcodes, the database contains two tables, which you use to identify the item.

The first table is the Items table, which contains the unique tag ID, the name of the item, a short note about the item, and a Category ID, which places the item into a category. For example, a UPC barcode can identify an item as "Fuji apple" or "Children's cough syrup," while an RFID tag identifies the individual apple or individual bottle of cough syrup. Pricing and counting inventory should link these individual items together, much like the UPC barcodes do. The Category table in the database file serves this purpose, allowing you to group individual items together.

In Figure 6-13, I've populated the tables with my own personal items, so I'm not leveraging the Category functionality as a retail store might be.

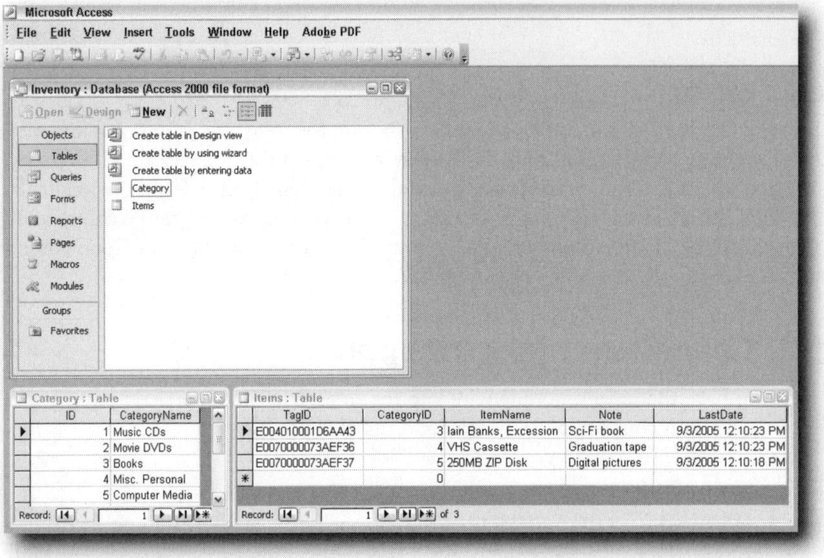

FIGURE 6-13: Tables in Inventory.MDB

Run the Software

Start up the SmartShelf software on your PC. Set your communications port, port speed, and inventory check rate before you click the Active checkbox. The M1 reader's default port speed is 9600 baud, so leave it set to 9600 unless you need to change it. You can change the inventory check rate from 5 seconds to 60 seconds, and you can make this change while the system is active.

You can see the tagged items in Figure 6-14 and the inventory taken by the software in Figure 6-15. There is one item detected by the shelf that is not in my inventory database, nor does Figure 6-14 show it. That's because I stuck a label to the underside of the bottom shelf. That tag serves as sort of a performance check. If I can't read that tag ID it means the field isn't able to penetrate the entire shelving area, and the reader may not be catching other tags.

The software takes an inventory of what's on the shelf and crosschecks the tag IDs found against the Inventory.MDB database. Any items with tag IDs not found in the database are still shown, but they do not have any item data associated with it. The software also updates the LastDate field in the Items table for each item found, keeping track of the last date and time it found the item on the shelf.

FIGURE 6-14: Inventory items on the smart shelf

FIGURE 6-15: SmartShelf software taking inventory

A Simple Example

The SmartShelf software is a very simple example of how you can create a real-time inventory system. To turn this into a viable retail inventory-management tool, you would most likely build in a category counting system, taking a count of the total items per category, such as 6 Fuji apples. You could also identify when each apple was placed on the shelf, and estimate when each apple would go bad and need to be removed. You would probably also cross reference the LastDate fields of each item with stock and sales records to see how long each item has been on the shelf and when each item is sold. This could also serve for a loss-measurement tool by checking for items that are no longer detected in inventory but have no sales record.

The source code for the SmartShelf software is available for download from www.rfidtoys .net. If you want to make your own interface software for the M1 module, make sure you download the SkyeTek protocol documentation from www.skyetek.com/downloads .php. It's a very easy protocol, which supports communication in both binary and ASCII modes.

Step 5: Build Your Own Antenna (Optional)

Building your own RFID antenna is not a trivial task. Passive tags and readers use near-field magnetic coupling to communicate, and this requires a resonant antenna. To get the antenna to resonate and have the correct impedance, you need to use a few special tools and a little black magic. Tools you need include an inductance meter, a capacitance meter, and a multi-meter. An impedance meter and oscilloscope or network analyzer wouldn't hurt either.

I'm going to go over the basics of building and tuning an antenna first, and then I'll cover, step-by-step, how you can actually build a rectangle antenna.

Near-Field Magnetic Coupling

Normal antennas used on devices like your cell phone or FRS radio radiate energy into the air. Passive RFID technologies use magnetic coupling to communicate, so the antenna does not radiate energy. The antenna serves as a sort of electromagnet, creating a field that surrounds and saturates the tag's antenna. The magnetic relationship between tag and reader could be compared to two coils inside a transformer. Energy is transferred from reader to tag, powering the tag. Both tag and reader can modulate the field to communicate with each other.

Resonance and Impedance

The magnetic field generated by the antenna is proportional to the current flowing through it. To get a high amount of current, the antenna needs to resonate at the intended frequency. You achieve resonance with parallel capacitance. You use series capacitance to adjust the antenna to the correct impedance, which is 50 ohms. Figure 6-16 shows a simple example.

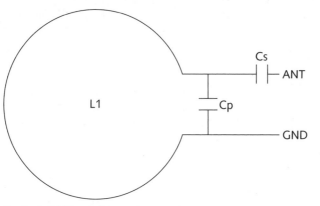

FIGURE 6-16: Simple loop antenna

The maximum size loop antenna the SkyeTek M1 module can drive is about 9" in diameter, or 9" × 9" for a square loop antenna. Larger, more high-powered readers can drive larger antennas and even whole antenna arrays. More power means more cost though, a lot more.

Parallel Capacitance

The easiest way to get the value for Cp is to calculate it based on an inductance reading from L1. You'll need an inductance meter, which can display very small Henry (the unit of measure for inductance) readings. These meters typically read the inductance of coils that have many loops, which usually gives them a higher inductance. If your meter can't read the inductance of your loop antenna, or only displays a very inaccurate insignificant digit (like 0.007), then consider looping your antenna once or twice to increase its inductance. Spiral the loops outward so the wires do not overlap each other.

Once you have your inductance measurement, use the calculation in Figure 6-17 to get an approximate value for Cp. You can also use the web-based calculator at www.rfidtoys.net.

```
Cp = (10^9) / (L * pi * 13.56) ^2)
L = inductance of your coil antenna in nH
Cp = the resonant capacitance in pF


Break it down:
Cp = 1000000000 / (L * 7258.61)


For an L of 1050nH (1.05 uM),
Cp - 131.2 pF
```

FIGURE 6-17: Calculate resonant capacitance

The value calculated for Cp is just an approximation to get you close to the value needed. You need to use a combination of fixed value capacitors and an adjustable capacitor to dial-in the exact capacitance. I'll go into detail on that later.

Impedance

Finding the series capacitance needed to come up with the correct impedance is much more tricky. Start with a capacitor value and mix-and-match until you get the correct impedance. If you don't have an impedance meter, you can measure the impedance using a high-quality multi-meter.

To measure impedance, you have to connect the antenna to the reader and power it up. Use the SmartShelf software to set the reader to actively scan every 5 seconds. Measure voltage RMS and amperage. Take your measurements between the M1 module and the antenna/capacitor network. The diagram in Figure 6-18 shows where to take these measurements.

As shown in Figure 6-18, you can calculate the impedance using voltage and amperage measurements. You can also convert the equation to give you the estimated amperage at the proper 50-ohms impedance. This enables you to connect your meter and play with an adjustable capacitor to dial-in the correct amperage reading. Once you have the correct amperage, double-check your voltage reading and recalculate to make sure you're stable at 50-ohms impedance.

Build the Antenna

The antenna described and shown in the figures is a larger rectangle antenna I built for a more powerful reader, but the concept is the same for loop antennas. If you plan to build your own antenna, start with a loop antenna, as they are easy to build. If you want to go ahead and build a rectangle antenna, this section shows you how.

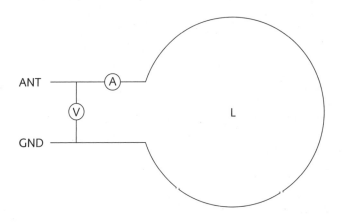

V / A = Ohms impedance

Example: 20mV / 10uA = 2K Ohms
Break it down: 0.02V / 0.00001A = 2000
Convert it: 0.02V / 50 Ohms = 0.0004A

FIGURE 6-18: Measure impedance

Start with the same 24" shelving unit, and turn over of the shelf boards so you're looking at the unfinished bottom side of it. This board is going to be the substrate for your antenna. Since you're dealing with high frequency, you can afford not to use standard copper wire to create the antenna. You can use copper tape, which is much easier to work with since it already has an adhesive backing.

I searched high and low for copper tape like I've seen used before, but I couldn't find any short of going to specialty electronics stores and paying a bundle. However, while searching through the local hardware store for some random parts, I came across something ridiculously cheap and perfect for the antenna project: Corry's Slug & Snail barrier (see Figure 6-19).

The slug tape works great for an antenna project like this. Take your shelf board and draw some straight lines on it to run your copper tape along. Leave a space between the edge of the tape and the edge of the board that is at least double the width of the tape itself. Once you have the lines drawn, lay your tape down and cut the ends of it at 45 degrees as shown in Figure 6-20. You don't want the tape to overlap when it's all laid down.

Note If you are using the SkyeTek M1 module, make sure the length of the rectangle antenna isn't over 9" on any side.

When you're done, you should have a loop that looks something like Figure 6-21.

FIGURE 6-19: Corry's Slug & Snail copper tape barrier

Figure 6-20: Laying down copper tape

Figure 6-21: Rectangle loop antenna

Once you have your loop, solder the individual pieces of copper together as shown in Figure 6-22.

Now that you have your loop completed, you might consider adding a ground ring around it to help stabilize the antenna. These antennas tend to detune when metal is introduced to the field, even RFID tag antennas. A ground ring looks like Figure 6-23. Notice that it's not a loop.

Once your ground ring is in place, it's time to start experimenting with capacitors. Measure your antenna's inductance with an inductance meter. Then perform the calculations previously shown in Figure 6-17 to find the approximate value for Cp, the parallel capacitance needed to achieve resonance.

You might consider soldering some headers to the antenna so you can easily add and remove capacitors to adjust the value. Solder an adjustable capacitor along with your fixed value capacitors to allow for some fine-tuning, as shown in Figure 6-24. If you have an o-scope, you can fine tune for resonance by taking a reading off the loop inductor and adjusting the capacitor until you see peak wave resonance at 13.56 MHz.

FIGURE 6-22: Solder the copper tape pieces together

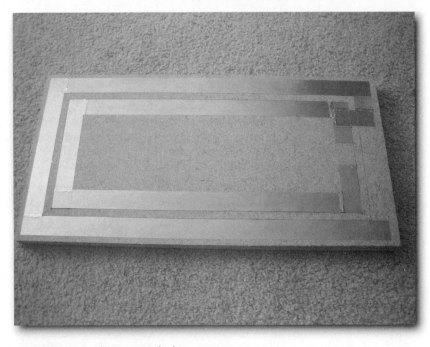

FIGURE 6-23: Ground ring around a loop antenna

FIGURE 6-24: Loop antenna and capacitor network

Measure for impedance and adjust using voltage and current measurements as previously shown in Figure 6-18. Use an adjustable capacitor here as well to fine tune impedance. The M1 module should put out about 10 Vpp, so the RMS voltage should be around 3.535 volts.

Other Resources

Unless you have some very expensive lab-grade equipment, building a working RFID antenna seems to be a process of trial and error. I built six different antennas before I actually got one working. If you're having difficulty, start with a two-loop wire antenna about 4" in diameter and see if you can't get an ISO credit-card style tag or a thicker clamshell tag to work with it. ISO card tags have very good range and usually work even with slightly de-tuned reader antennas.

There are also links to other resources available at www.rfidtoys.net. One great resource for building large multi-array shelf antennas comes from www.rfidusa.com, under their Education & Training section. Check the Articles & White Papers area for an article called "RFID Shelf Antennas."

Letting Fido in with an RFID Pet Door

One problem people run into when implementing passive RFID solutions is they assume tags will always work reliably as long as they are within range of the reader. With passive systems, range is highly dependant on antenna orientation because readers and tags must be magnetically coupled in order to communicate.

The point and purpose of this project is not to show you how to build a secure pet door, but to detail some additional features of the SkyeTek reader module and show the importance of tag and antenna orientation as it relates to read range.

You'll be using the same SkyeTek M1 module and Feig antenna unit used in Chapter 6. This time, however, you'll connect the module to a Basic STAMP 2 microprocessor, untethering it from a PC and allowing it to function autonomously.

Parts and Tools

You need the following parts for this project:

- SkyeTek M1 13.56 MHz RFID read/write module from www.skyetek.com

- Feig 13.56 MHz pad antenna, part number RR-IDISC-ANT34-24 from www.digikey.com

- Parallax BASIC Stamp 2 (BS2) from www.parallax.com

- Two general purpose circuit boards, Radio Shack part number 276-148a

- A 24-pin IC socket, Radio Shack part number 276-1996

- +5V reed relay, Radio Shack part number 275-232

- A 7805 +5V voltage regulator, Radio Shack part number 276-1770

- Plastic project box from www.web-tronics.com, part number PB-2P

- A 9V AC to DC wall-jack power adaptor, Radio Shack part number 273-1767

- BASIC Stamp code downloaded from www.rfidtoys.net

And you need the following tools:

- Philips screwdriver
- Soldering iron and solder

Build It

I like using the BASIC Stamp microprocessor because it's easy to use and lots of people are familiar with it. There are other cheaper microprocessors that consume less power, but they just aren't as flexible, easy, and accessible as the BASIC Stamp line from Parallax.

Step 1: Program the BASIC Stamp 2

I've said it before, but the SkyeTek M1 module is a nifty little OEM reader. One of the M1's features that will greatly reduce your Stamp programming, processing, and memory overhead is the query function. Instead of asking for all tags, storing that data, and parsing through each tag ID, you can query the reader for a particular tag. If the tag is present, you'll get a simple two-digit positive confirmation. If not, you'll get a simple two-digit negative confirmation. Easy!

The following is the BS2 code for this project, which you can download from www.rfid toys.net. The code allows only one tagged pet to enter; however, you can easily modify the code to expand functionality for more than one pet.

Pet Door BS2 Code

```
' ================================================================
'
'   File....... RFID_PetDoor.BS2
'   Purpose.... RFID Tag Reader / Simple Security System
'   Author..... Jon Williams -- Parallax, Inc.
'   E-mail..... jwilliams@parallax.com
'   Started....
'   Updated.... 07 FEB 2005
'
' ================================================================
'   Updated.... 02 JULY 2005
'   Purpose.... Update code to suit Fido project
'   Author..... Amal Graafstra -- RFID Toys
' ================================================================
'
'   {$STAMP BS2}
'   {$PBASIC 2.5}
'
' ================================================================
```

```
' -----[ Program Description ]-----------------------------------------
'
'   This code issues a SELECT command to the SkyeTek M1 reader module
'   along with a tag ID. The M1 reader will return with code 14 if the
'   tag ID is present, or a code 94 if not. This saves the work of having
'   to query for all tags and parse through them to find the authorized
'   pet tag.
'
'   Upon confirmation the authorized tag is present, the Latch pin will go
'   high unlocking the pet door so Fido can go through. If you need to find
'   more than one tag, extra steps will have to be taken to submit multiple
'   tags to the reader. Only one tag ID can be submitted per request.
'
' -----[ Revision History ]--------------------------------------------
'
'   Updated.... 02 JULY 2005
'   Purpose.... Update code to suit Fido project
'   Author..... Amal Graafstra -- RFID Toys
'
' -----[ I/O Definitions ]---------------------------------------------

TX              PIN    0                ' Serial TX to reader
RX              PIN    1                ' Serial RS from reader
Latch           PIN    10               ' Lock control pin

' -----[ Constants ]---------------------------------------------------

#SELECT $STAMP
  #CASE BS2, BS2E, BS2PE
    T1200       CON    813
    T2400       CON    396
    T4800       CON    188
    T9600       CON    84
    T19K2       CON    32
    TMidi       CON    12
    T38K4       CON    6
  #CASE BS2SX, BS2P
    T1200       CON    2063
    T2400       CON    1021
    T4800       CON    500
    T9600       CON    240
    T19K2       CON    110
    TMidi       CON    60
    T38K4       CON    45
#ENDSELECT

SevenBit        CON    $2000
Inverted        CON    $4000
Open            CON    $8000
Baud            CON    T2400
```

Continued

Pet Door BS2 Code *(continued)*

```
#SELECT $STAMP
  #CASE BS2, BS2E
    TmAdj       CON      $100                   ' x 1.0 (time adjust)
    FrAdj       CON      $100                   ' x 1.0 (freq adjust)
  #CASE BS2SX
    TmAdj       CON      $280                   ' x 2.5
    FrAdj       CON      $066                   ' x 0.4
  #CASE BS2P
    TmAdj       CON      $3C5                   ' x 3.77
    FrAdj       CON      $044                   ' x 0.265
  #CASE BS2PE
    TmAdj       CON      $100                   ' x 1.0
    FrAdj       CON      $0AA                   ' x 0.665
#ENDSELECT


' -----[ Variables ]----------------------------------------------

ReaderBuf VAR   Byte(5)                         ' response buffer from reader
TagLen    CON   18                              ' length in bytes of TagID
TagChar   VAR   Byte                            ' holds single byte of tag ID
TagIdx    VAR   Byte                            ' index counter

' -----[ EEPROM Data ]----------------------------------------------

'A note about tag IDs and tag types. The first two characters of
'the TagID need to specify the tag type from the table.
'For example, if the tag is an ISO15693 tag with an ID of
'A089138945D482EE, then TagID must = 01A089138945D482EE. You could
'use two CON values and combine them later when sending commands
'to the reader, but doing it this was reduces complexity.

'Tag Types
  '01 = ISO15693
  '02 = I-Code1
  '03 = Tag-It HF
  '04 = ISO14443A
  '05 = ISO14443B
  '06 = PicoTag
  '07 = RFU
  '08 = GemWave C210

DATA   @10, "01E007000006D501A3"               ' tag data

' -----[ Initialization ]----------------------------------------------

Reset:
  HIGH Latch                                    ' unlock door
```

```
' -----[ Program Code ]-------------------------------------------------

Rest:
  PAUSE 250                                     ' pause for a quarter second.

Main:
  'The SkyeTek reader allows us to check for specific
  'tag IDs, so instead of polling for all tags and
  'having to parse out a possibly large number of
  'tags, we can ask the reader to process tag IDs
  'for us and just return a simple "yes" or "no".

  'sent start of request character
  SEROUT TX, T9600, [13]

  'start request string
  SEROUT TX, T9600, [DEC 4014]

  'read tag data from EEPROM and output to reader
  FOR TagIdx = 0 TO TagLen - 1                   'tag length is 18 bytes
    READ TagIdx + 10, TagChar                    'get tag ID byte from EEPROM
    SEROUT TX, T9600, [TagChar]
  NEXT

  'send end of request character
  SEROUT TX, T9600, [13]

  'wait for response from reader
  SERIN RX, T9600, 2000, Tag_Not_Found, [STR ReaderBuf\5]

  'response from reader should be either
  'YES = "<LF>14<CR><LF>"
  'NO = "<LF>94<CR><LF>"
  'Syntax Error = "<LF>84<CR><LF>"

  'check response from reader
  IF (ReaderBuf(1)="1") AND (ReaderBuf(2)="4") THEN Tag_Found
  IF (ReaderBuf(1)="9") AND (ReaderBuf(2)="4") THEN Tag_Not_Found

  GOTO Tag_Not_Found                             ' unexpected response,
                                                 ' play it safe and keep
                                                 ' door locked


Tag_Found:
  HIGH Latch                                     ' unlock door
  PAUSE 10000                                    ' keep latch open and
                                                 ' don't bother to lock
                                                 ' it again. Let a negative
                                                 ' response from the reader
                                                 ' lock the door... Fido
                                                 ' might be taking his time.

  GOTO Main
```

Continued

Pet Door BS2 Code *(continued)*

```
Tag_Not_Found:
   LOW Latch                           ' deactivate solenoid
   GOTO Rest                           ' rest and try again

   END
```

I want to point out a couple things in the code listing. The first has to do with the SkyeTek communications protocol. To initiate a command, you must send a line feed character, which is ASCII code 10, represented as <LF> in the code comments. A carriage return, <CR>, followed by a line feed, <LF>, character ends the command. The command itself is based on the SkyeTek protocol specifications, which you can download from their website at www.skyetek.com.

In short, you'll be sending <LF>4014TTYYYYYYYY<CR><LF> to the reader, where TT is the tag type and YYYYYYYY is the tag ID you're looking for. Some tag types have more or less than eight characters, like the ISO15693 type tags the code is geared to look for. If you have a different kind of tag that the M1 can read, you'll have to change the tag type and tag ID used in code before programming your BASIC Stamp.

What you get back from the M1 depends on whether or not the tag you're looking for is present. If the tag is present, the M1 returns <LF>14<CR><LF>. If not, the M1 returns <LF>94<CR><LF>. Processing these two possible return codes is a snap compared to trying to store and parse a large number of possible tag IDs returned from a "request all tags" command.

If something is wrong or the reader does not respond for some reason within 2 seconds, the code assumes the tag was not found and processing jumps to the Tag_Not_Found code.

Step 2: Prepare the Stamp Board

The BASIC Stamp will be controlling a locking solenoid, much like the safe project in Chapter 5. The Stamp needs a carrier board that sports a Stamp controlled relay and +5V regulator for the SkyeTek M1 reader. The M1 comes in a few different flavors. Some come with an internal regulator (as the Stamp does), and some require regulated 5V power.

Grab Your Soldering Iron

Slap an IC socket down on the general-purpose circuit board. This should be second nature for you by now because, according to Murphy's Law, soldering a programmable microprocessor directly to the board means the code you loaded will have a flaw or you'll need to remove it later on for some other reason. Having an IC socket saves you from the pain and regret associated with having to desolder an entire 24-pin IC from the board.

Once you have your IC socket secured, solder a trusty 5V reed relay in place, as shown in Figure 7-1.

Note You could easily use a switching transistor instead of a reed relay. I just happened to have a ton of these reed relays lying around and they work fine for this type of application.

FIGURE 7-1: IC Socket and reed relay soldered to the board

Solder one of the relay's coil pins to ground. Solder the other coil pin-to-pin 15 on the Stamp, which is I/O pin 10 in the code (I know, it can get confusing sometimes). Check out Figure 7-2 to see a wiring diagram of the circuit. Figure 7-3 shows the same circuit using a transistor instead of a reed relay.

 Caution If you choose to use a transistor, you *must* include the protection diode shown in Figure 7-3; otherwise, the high voltage generated from the solenoid coil will damage your transistor, and it may also damage your BASIC Stamp.

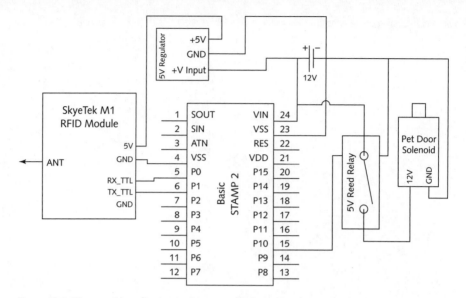

FIGURE 7-2: Stamp wiring diagram using a reed relay

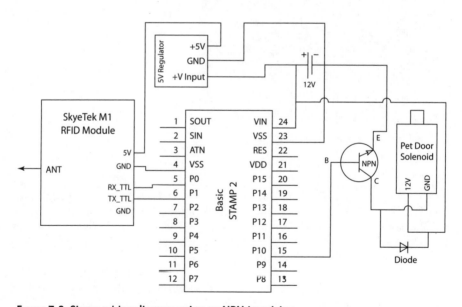

FIGURE 7-3: Stamp wiring diagram using an NPN transistor

Now you need to add a 5V regulator for your M1 reader. Solder it to the carrier board and connect the center ground lead to one of the Stamp's two ground pins using a jumper wire or solder bridge. Make sure you also connect pin 24 (VSS) on the Stamp with the voltage input pin on the regulator.

Bridge one of the switched leads from the reed relay to the unregulated voltage input pin on the voltage regulator, or to pin 24 (VSS) on the Stamp. Solder a wire to the other switched lead on the relay. This wire will lead to one of the solenoid leads. Now you should have something like Figure 7-4 in front of you.

FIGURE 7-4: Stamp carrier board with a reed relay and 5V regulator

Solder the other solenoid lead to an available ground to complete the circuit.

Power

The only thing left to wire up is power. The BASIC Stamp and RFID reader consume far too much energy to power this project using batteries. You'll need to use an AC to DC wall jack adaptor to power your pet door circuit. You can use any kind of DC power adaptor ranging from 6 volts to 12 volts, as long as it supplies at least 300 mA of current. You can cut off the tip of the DC adaptor power leads and directly solder them to the board, or you can solder up a power jack (see Figure 7-5). Make sure the jack is the correct type and size and matches the tip of the AC-DC adaptor you plan to use.

FIGURE 7-5: Two power jacks of different size and mount styles

Solenoid Voltage

No matter what type of power supply you go with, you'll want to make sure your locking solenoid requires the same voltage or less to operate. It wouldn't do much good to try and power a 12V solenoid with a 9V power source. However, if your solenoid operates on significantly less voltage than your power supply, you'll have to add a resistor in series so you don't overpower and damage your solenoid.

You can calculate the resistor value needed using an equation based on Ohm's Law (I = V / R). Well, more accurately, there is a typical voltage divider equation for two series resistors, which you can tweak. The equation is D = (R1 / (R1 + R2)) * V.

This equation lets you calculate voltage drop (D) across one of two series resistors when you know both resistor values. You already know the voltage drop you want, which is the operating voltage of the solenoid. You also have one resistor value (the solenoid coil resistance). So instead of calculating for voltage drop, you need to calculate the value of the additional resistor you'll need by rearranging the equation to look like this: R2 = ((R1 * V) / D) - R1.

This new equation lets you calculate the value of the resistor you'll need to put in series with the solenoid so it won't burn out. First, you need to measure the resistance of the solenoid coil to get a value for R1. For the sake of this example, let's assume your power supply is 9 volts and your solenoid uses a 6V coil that measures 300 ohms. That means you want 6 volts out of the total 9 volts from the power supply to drop across your solenoid coil. See Figure 7-6 to find out how this calculates.

```
D = solenoid operating voltage
V = power supply voltage
R1 = resistance of solenoid coil
R2 = series resistance needed

Equation:
R2 = ((R1 * V) / D) - R1

Break it down:
R2 = ((300 * 9) / 6) - 300
R2 = (2700 / 6) - 300
R2 = 150
```

FIGURE 7-6: Calculating your voltage divider resistor value

According to the equation, you'll need a 150-ohm resistor in series with the solenoid to drop the voltage from 9 volts down to 6 volts so the coil in the solenoid won't burn out when powered on.

The only thing left to consider is the resistor wattage rating. If the solenoid coil pulls significant current, you'll need a heavy-duty resistor. You can calculate current using Ohm's Law by dividing the voltage by resistance. Using the example, a 6V solenoid coil with 300 ohms resistance will draw 0.02 A or 20 mA. Because resistors are rated in watts, you need to calculate wattage by multiplying voltage by current. Again, by taking 6 volts and multiplying it by 0.02 amps you get 0.12 watts. Most resistors you buy in stores such as Radio Shack are quarter-watt resistors, and 0.12 is well under 0.25, so using a typical $1/4$-watt 150-ohm resistor in this example would be perfectly fine.

Step 3: Wire the SkyeTek M1 Module

You'll need to use the TTL lines built into the M1 reader to communicate with the Stamp rather than the RS-232 lines. Typical RS-232 lines use much higher voltages to communicate than TTL serial lines, and you could damage your Stamp module if you connect it to the RS-232 lines on the M1.

Communication Lines

The M1 reader TTL receive and transmit lines are located on pins 6 and 7 of the J1 block, as shown in Figure 7-7. You won't need to use the communications ground (pin 8) because the power supply ground (pin 2) is a common ground between the M1 and BASIC Stamp. Connect the RX_TTL line on the M1 to pin 5 (IO pin 0 in code) on the Stamp, and the M1 TX_TTL line to Stamp pin 6 (IO pin 1 in code).

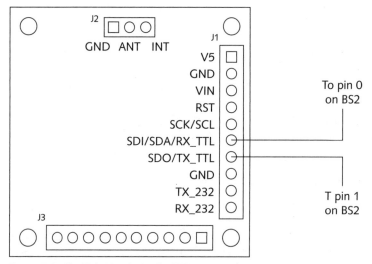

FIGURE 7-7: SkyeTek M1 pinout for TTL communication

Power

To get power to the M1 reader, wire the +5V power pin (pin 1 on the J1 block) to the 5V output of the voltage regulator on the Stamp carrier board. Connect the ground pin (pin 2) to the ground on the carrier board. You should have something like Figure 7-8.

FIGURE 7-8: M1 reader connected to carrier board

Connect the Antenna

Just like in Chapter 6, you'll need to connect an external antenna to the M1 module. The internal antenna built into the board doesn't have sufficient range to be of any use for this project.

On the underside of the module, there are three through-holes marked GND, ANT, and INT. The ANT point is the antenna "hot" lead. To use the internal antenna, you simply jumper ANT to INT and you're in business. To use an external antenna, you just connect GND and ANT to the external antenna's leads.

You can either solder a female SMA connector to the M1 module board as shown in Figure 7-9 and then connect the Feig antenna via the SMA connector (shown in Figure 7-10), or you can chop the SMA connector off the Feig antenna cable and solder it directly to the M1 module. I suggest you go the SMA connector route since the M1 module and accompanying circuitry will most likely be inside your house, which means you'll have to fish the antenna wire from outside the door to the inside where the reader is.

FIGURE 7-9: Female SMA connector soldered to the M1 board

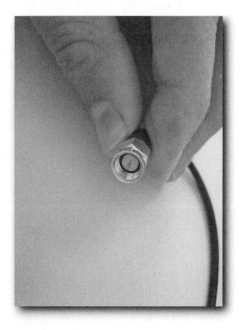

FIGURE 7-10: Feig antenna's male SMA connector

Step 4: Put It All in a Project Box

This part is fairly simple. You just get a PB-2P project box from www.web-tronics.com and drill a hole in it for the SMA connector to fit through (see Figure 7-11). If you didn't go the SMA-connector route, you'll have to notch the project box for the antenna wire, or just drill a hole for the antenna wire if you've not soldered it to the board yet.

FIGURE 7-11: Hole for SMA connector

Drill another hole for the positive and negative power wires that will connect to the locking solenoid and you can close it up. Figure 7-12 shows the finished project box along with the AC adaptor used to power it.

Step 5: Prepare the Pet Door

The only thing that needs to happen with the pet door is to figure out how to lock it so outside animals can't get in unless they are "authorized." There are many types of pet doors that have manual locking mechanisms, which is great because it means the door material itself is rigid. Most standard pet doors use a flexible rubbery material for the doorway, which just won't work for this project. I'm holding a typical locking pet door in Figure 7-13 that uses rigid plastic for the swinging entry door.

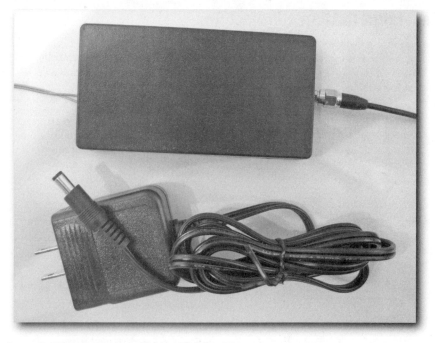

FIGURE 7-12: Project powered by an AC-DC adaptor

FIGURE 7-13: Typical pet door with a rigid plastic doorway and built-in lock

The Solenoid

The method I've chosen is a simple solenoid, which you can use in conjunction with the built-in locking mechanism. You can still manually set the built-in lock to keep all animals out, only let them out and not back in, or let them in but not out. If you set the manual lock to let pets in but not out, then the end-result would be that only your pets could get in, but nothing would be getting back out again.

There are many solenoids to choose from, but there are a few important things you'll have to keep in mind as you select yours. You'll need to make sure you buy one that pulls in the plunger. Many are the "push out" kind. You'll also need to make sure the pull solenoid has enough draw, or distance the plunger pulls in when activated, as well as a tension spring that keeps the plunger extended while the solenoid is not active. Finally, make sure you get a solenoid that operates on a voltage you can supply to it. If you're powering your access control circuit via a 9V power source, you can't very well power a 12V solenoid with it, so keep that in mind when picking out your solenoid. You can get plenty of great solenoids at any hobby shop or at various online websites. I chose to recycle some of my parts, so I pulled the rather large and ugly looking 6V solenoid from the electronic safe used in Chapter 5 for this project.

Installation is quite simple in most cases — just find a mount point you're comfortable with and make sure the door cannot get past the plunger when it's up, but can open freely when the solenoid is activated. Screw the solenoid into place and you're set. Check out Figure 7-14 to see my electronic safe solenoid mounted in place.

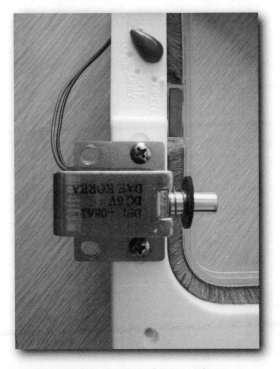

FIGURE 7-14: Solenoid mounted to a pet door

Admittedly, there is one problem with this approach. The solenoid could deactivate while the pet door is still open (as your pet is making their lazy way through), locking it in the open position as shown in Figure 7-15. However, there are a couple ways around this.

FIGURE 7-15: Door locked open by the solenoid

One thing you could do is shave down the solenoid at a 45-degree angle, shown in Figure 7-16. It should look something like your door latches are shaped. It would work just like a door latch too — the pet door would swing back and press the solenoid plunger inward until the door passes and the plunger springs back up, locking the door in the closed position. You'd have to make sure the solenoid spring is weak enough to let the door press down the plunger.

A more complicated but technically cooler way to deal with this problem would be to put some kind of sensor on the pet door that keeps the solenoid activated until the pet door closes again. You could use a NO (normally open) roller switch that closes only when the door is open, allowing an alternate path for current to flow through the solenoid until the door closes.

Connect It

Once you have your solenoid mounted to the pet door, connect it to the solenoid leads coming from the RFID control box.

FIGURE 7-16: Solenoid plunger shave angle

Step 6: Place the Antenna

This step encompasses the entire point of putting this project in the book: to communicate the importance of antenna positioning in a passive RFID system, both reader antenna and tag antenna. As you should already know, passive RFID systems use magnetic coupling between the reader and tag to communicate. This works somewhat like a loosely coupled air-core transformer, where the coils are next to each other and transfer energy via inductance. What's important here is the shape of the magnetic field and how both inductors (tag and reader antennas) are aligned within it.

Remember when you were a kid in school and they brought out the white paper, magnets, and iron filings? You poured out the filings on the paper, ran the magnet under the paper, and dragged them around for a while. Then they had you keep the magnet in one place and gently tap the desk or shake the paper until the iron filings all lined up along the magnetic field lines, showing you what one particular plane of the magnetic field actually looked like. A typical bar magnet has a 3D magnetic field that looks something like Figure 7-17. It's almost like a rugby ball shape that forms around the bar magnet.

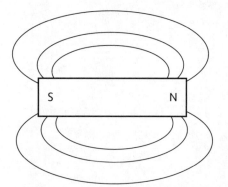

FIGURE 7-17: Magnetic field around a bar magnet

To get the most range out of your tags, the magnetic field generated by the reader antenna must encompass the tag antenna completely. Tag antennas should be parallel with the reader antenna so there is sufficient energy inducted to power the tag. Figure 7-18 shows the difference between parallel and perpendicular alignments.

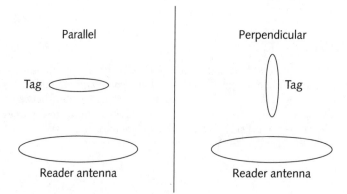

FIGURE 7-18: Parallel and perpendicular antenna alignment

When placing the reader antenna, you have to think about how the tag will be aligned with the antenna. I've included Figure 7-19 to help give you a proper mental image to work with. There are two basic ways you can mount the reader antenna. You can place the antenna on the door itself, or you can place it on the ground in front of the door.

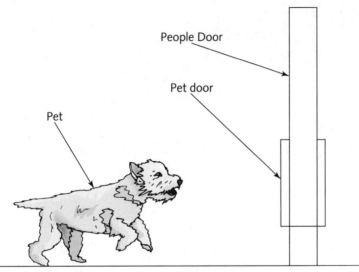

People Door

Pet door

Pet

FIGURE 7-19: Typical door, pet door, and pet scenario

On the Door

Most people's first impulse is to place the reader antenna on the door, but this presents an interesting problem when you consider tag alignment. Most people figure they can use a key-fob style RFID tag on the pet collar, but unless you're using a very expensive active RFID setup for your pet door, it won't be reliable. The reason is that the keyfob-type tag will hang down from the collar (see Figure 7-20) and in most cases, the tag will twist around on your pet's collar. The antenna inside the keyfob will be presented at various degrees between parallel and perpendicular to the reader antenna, making range unpredictable. Figure 7-21 details this by giving a bird's eye perspective on the problem.

FIGURE 7-20: Keyfob tag hanging from a pet collar

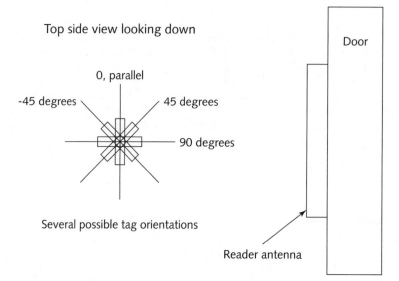

FIGURE 7-21: Bird's eye view of the tag-twist problem

So, unless you can keep your pet's tag from twisting around, or you have a reader with enough transmit power to get sufficient range, you might consider placing the reader antenna on the ground in front of the pet door.

On the Ground

There is a way to make sure the tag on your pet's collar doesn't twist around. You can cut up a wristband style tag (see Figure 7-22) used for hospital patients and such, and then sew it to the fabric of the pet collar.

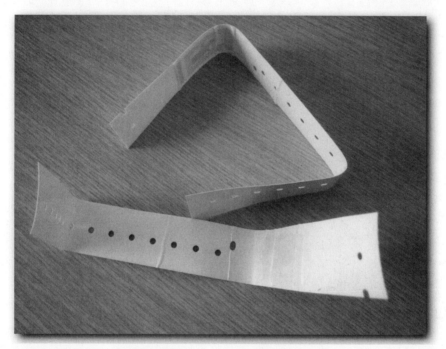

FIGURE 7-22: Wristband-style RFID tags

These wristbands have a tag embedded in the rubbery band material. You can cut the band with scissors, leaving enough rubber on either side of the tag as shown in Figure 7-23 so you can sew it to the pet collar without damaging the antenna.

Now just sew it on to the collar at the bottom near where nametags and other such items hang and you're set. If you're not big on sewing, use some epoxy or some other non-sewing type glue any non-sewer would use. Figure 7-24 shows the tag glued on to a pet collar. Once on your pet, the collar might shift around a little, but the weight of the nametag should keep the RFID tag facing downward toward the reader antenna.

FIGURE 7-23: RFID tag embedded inside a rubber wristband

FIGURE 7-24: RFID tag glued to a pet collar

At an Angle

You could even lean the antenna up against a wall, giving it an angle. Just make sure you position the tag on the pet collar so it's as close to parallel with the reader antenna as possible.

Connect It

Once you have the antenna placed, run the wire through your door or wall and connect it to the control box. Power up your control box and you should be in business. The idea behind presenting this type of project is to get you to start thinking about how passive, magnetically coupled tags and readers work to transfer energy and data. The reliability of RFID tags depends greatly on their alignment with the reader antenna. Anyone designing, developing, or deploying a passive RFID solution needs to consider this issue carefully before rolling it out.

I hope this chapter has also given you some insight as to how you can use microprocessors to interface with many different types of RFID reader devices. It's important to point out that the more advanced readers such as the SkyeTek M1 let you offload a lot of processing work to the reader itself. The fact that you can query the M1 for a specific tag greatly reduces the work involved compared to reading and storing all present tags and then sorting through them. Due to the very small amount of available memory, trying to store and process multiple tag IDs with a BASIC Stamp would be very difficult if not impossible.

Tracking Employees and Time with Active RFID

With this project, you're going to be using higher frequency 433 MHz technology, as well as active RFID transponders. With active tags, you get far more range out of your RFID system because the tags and reader do not need to be magnetically coupled in order to communicate. The tags contain a small battery that powers the transmission and reception of data, just like a cordless phone or FRS radio.

Another limitation of active tags is that they have a finite lifespan. When the battery goes out, the tag is junk. You could crack the case open and replace the battery, but good luck getting the casing back together again. On the other hand, most tags have a 5-year lifespan from the date of manufacture. With the growth rate of this technology, by the time your tags start dying off it might be time to upgrade your entire RFID system anyway.

Active RFID tags work differently from passive tags in that they transmit their identification information constantly. The reader device does not have to query them as it does passive tags. There are RFID systems that use semi-active tags, which are tags that lay dormant until queried by a reader. At that point, the tag powers up and uses its battery to power the response transmission.

Since both readers and active RFID tags emit RF energy, their antennas are much more typical and do require resonant loops like those used in passive RFID systems. This leaves a lot of room for flexibility when dealing with antennas, transmission paths, and effective range.

For the most part, active RFID serves one single purpose: long-range functionality. Passive systems just cannot communicate over the long distances attainable by active RFID. The increased range of active RFID allows you to leverage it in solutions where passive RFID would not work. One of those purposes is object tracking.

In this chapter, you will be building a system for tracking tag-carrying employees and tagged objects. There are two basic concepts you'll be dealing with: location and time. You will be leveraging active RFID tags to track the location of assets and employees within a massive complex, as well as derive arrival times, break times, and when people leave for the day from the tracking log. For this project, you'll be using the Wavetrend L-RX201 reader unit, shown in Figure 8-1. There are a lot of pros and cons related to this unit, but this reader and the active tags that work with it are perfectly suited for tracking assets and personnel. There are other active RFID options out there, but they are generally high powered and high priced.

FIGURE 8-1: Wavetrend L-RX201 reader

Parts and Tools

You need the following parts for this project:

- Female DB-9 connector, Radio Shack part number 276-1538
- CAT5 cable and RJ45 modular ends
- Wavetrend L-RX201 reader
- Wavetrend L-TG501 personnel tag
- Wavetrend L-TG800 metallic asset tag
- Ferrite snap-on chokes

And you need the following tools:

- RJ45 modular end crimper
- Soldering iron and solder

Hardware

Before you get into building the project itself, take a look at the hardware you'll be using.

Wavetrend L-RX201 Reader

Wavetrend makes two types of readers and tags. The W series devices are meant for high-density, shorter-range applications where a high number of tags will be present within a smaller area. This is perfect for solutions such as supply-chain automation where large numbers of tagged items will be located within a small controlled area, and you can be assured that they will stay within that controlled space. The L series readers and tags are designed for long-range applications where the number of tags within a given coverage area will be relatively low and their location within the coverage area cannot be assured. This project will feature L series devices due to the fact not many people are running supply chains through their homes.

The reader itself is an RS-232 serial device meant to interface with a PC or other serial RS-232 host. It also supports the RS-485 communication between readers, allowing you to form a network of linked readers that all communicate with the serial host or PC through a single interface.

 Note If you want to see how you can cover more area without additional readers, check out Chapter 9.

L-RX201 Ports and Power

The reader uses standard RJ45 ports for power and communications, as shown in Figure 8-2. The left port supports RS-232 and serial TTL communications with a serial host or PC. You can use the right port to connect to the left port of another reader to share power and communicate via RS-485.

You can chain up to 255 readers in this way; however, you must consider power distribution and signal interference. Only a few readers can share power. If you want to link more readers, you have to connect another power source further down the chain. Signal interference is also an issue, so make sure you use ferrite chokes around all link cabling.

FIGURE 8-2: Wavetrend RJ45 ports

L-RX201 Features

One thing about this reader is that it's cheap when compared to other active RFID solutions I've been able to find. Be sure to check the forum at www.rfidtoys.net for more hardware suggestions and sources.

RS-485 Network

The fact you can network this reader with other readers on an RS-485 network is a big plus. Multiple readers can communicate with the controlling serial host or PC through a single serial interface, which greatly reduces hardware costs and software complexity. By chaining a number of readers, you can monitor a huge complex with only a single PC running some simple software.

Adjustable Gain

This is an active RFID system, so there are a few features you won't find in most passive readers. Programmable gain control is one of them. You can actually program the reader to reduce its signal gain, which might seem like a dumb thing until you consider the fact you can fine tune coverage areas with this feature. When you are working with multiple readers, you can customize each reader to blanket a certain area, and not overlap coverage with a nearby reader. Overlap would result in two readers reporting a tag's presence, which could really compromise your software and reporting system.

Tip

Reducing gain may actually increase range if you're dealing with a noisy environment. Too much signal gain amplifies noise and could drown out tag signals.

RSSI

Another feature is RSSI, or Return Signal Strength Indicator. When the reader receives a tag transmission, you can get the signal strength of that tag along with the tag data. That means you can create a software-based "squelch" feature, allowing you to dynamically fine-tune coverage zones using software, rather than adjusting the hardware gain control. If you have more than one reader installed and two or more readers pick up a tag, you can figure out which reader the tag is closest to based on signal strength.

If you put your imagination to it, you can do many things with RSSI. You could create a crude distance measurement tool between the reader and tagged item, such as a car entering a garage. As the tagged car gets closer to the reader antenna mounted on the back wall, the signal strength will go up. Software can detect when the signal strength peaks over a certain value and light an indicator light or sound a buzzer, notifying the driver they are in position. Think of it as a high-tech "tennis ball hanging by a string".

Site Codes

Site codes allow readers to separate and filter tags at the hardware level by listening for tags only from a specific site code. If you are ordering in quantity, you can ask that your tags be given a unique site code or set of unique site codes if you have multiple sites in your organization that need separate codes. Because the hardware is doing the filtering, the serial host (PC or otherwise) that the reader or RS-485 reader network is connected to won't have to deal with receiving and sorting tags by site code. However, if you end up with a mixed batch of site-coded tags, you can tell the reader to listen for site code 0, and it will report all tags from all site codes.

Proprietary Drawbacks

The software shown in this chapter was created with the Wavetrend SDK. Unlike all the other software in this book, I can't print or make source code available. Wavetrend is so serious about protecting its SDK that I had to sign an NDA (Non-Disclosure Agreement) before I was allowed to use it.

The SDK is available for a fee, however it is not trouble-free — other integrators and I have had our share of issues with it, which I am unable to detail for you, as the NDA prevents me from doing so. Simply keep in mind that it worked for the purposes of this project, but your mileage may vary.

If custom application development isn't required for your situation, you may consider a second option: iAutomate. Because iAutomate (www.iautomate.com) has integrated the Wavetrend reader with HomeSeer, home automation software from www.homeseer.com, you can use HomeSeer as a middleman. Read this chapter and make sure you check out Step 4 for more information on how to use HomeSeer as an alternative to writing your own custom software application.

Wavetrend L Series Tags

Wavetrend makes a few different types of L series tags. All tags support tamper detection, which can alert the reader if the tag is removed from the surface it was affixed to. That's a great feature if you're dealing with an asset-management situation. Even though all tags support tamper detection, when you actually order the more expensive tamper detection version of tags, you get a little magnet and a high-bond glue pad that are basically required to enable utilize the tamper detection features of the tag.

Many of the tags support movement alarms and tag age counters as well. The tag age counter helps you calculate the tag's age and approximate remaining battery life based on the number of transmissions it's made. At one transmission every 1.5 seconds, a tag's approximate lifespan is 5 years. You can also order tags with different transmission rates, which can increase or decrease the lifespan, depending on what rate you choose.

L-TG501 Tag

This tag, shown in Figure 8-3, is like an oversized clamshell ISO tag. It's meant to be used as a personnel tag, or it can be affixed with pre-cut VHB (very high bond) glue strips to nonmetallic items such as the inside of a car windshield. Personally, I cringe at the idea of gluing something with a limited lifespan to my windshield, but you'll probably get enough use out of the tag in 3–5 years to make gluing it worthwhile, should you decide to do so.

FIGURE 8-3: L-TG501 active RFID tag

I've taken the initiative to show what the inside of a tag looks like so curious minds out there won't undertake the somewhat difficult task unless they really feel the need to see for themselves. Opening the tag is not required for the project — it's just something I wanted to show.

After some careful work with a sanding wheel and Dremel tool, I was able to cut around the perimeter of the plastic to reveal the internal components. Figure 8-4 shows the circuit board inside. You can even see the battery used to power the tag. Sadly, my Dremel work wasn't careful enough and scuffed the antenna a few times. I also took out a circuit pathway, rendering the tag an expensive piece of junk.

Figure 8-4: The inside of an L-TG501 tag

As the NDA I signed may also cover Wavetrend hardware, I am unable to show you a picture; however, on the other side of the tag are all the surface mount components. There is also a list of every team member's first name silk-screened on the antenna section of the circuit board.

L-TG100 Tag

With an external antenna, this tag (shown in Figure 8-5) is geared for long-range tracking of nonmetallic assets. You can affix it to wooden shipping pallets or extruded plastic moldings or just about any nonmetallic product or item. While you could use a personnel tag, the domino tag is considerably smaller, which makes finding mounting points easier.

FIGURE 8-5: L-TG100 "domino" tag

L-TG700 Keyfob Tag

I understand that these active tags require a battery power source. Even still, this tag is quite a hunk of plastic hanging off your key ring. I feel it's too large to be considered a "keyfob," but I guess I've seen worse hanging from other people's key rings. My VW key is big enough to annoy me, but as you can see in Figure 8-6, the TG700 tag is bigger than that. It doesn't quite have the range other tags do, but that's probably because of the smaller antenna size and the fact that it's surrounded by metal keys.

These tags do have an interesting characteristic. They have a button on them, which you can press, that will alert the reader. You could create software that detects the button press and takes appropriate action. For example, the reader could detect the presence of the tag and unlock a door. When you press the button, the system could lock the door, even though the tag is still present, and keep it locked until the tag leaves the area and returns again.

L-TG800 Metallic Asset Tag

If you have metallic assets such as computers or even lawnmowers, this asset tag is the one to use (see Figure 8-7). The internal antenna is designed to mitigate the effects of metallic surfaces. It cannot be affixed to the inside metallic assets, like the inside of the computer to be tracked. Enclosing any kind of tag inside a metal box renders it virtually useless.

FIGURE 8-6: L-TG700 "keyfob" tag

FIGURE 8-7: L-TG800 metallic asset tag

Note   Wavetrend makes other kinds of tags as well, but the ones listed here are probably the most relevant. Check their website at www.wavetrend.net for more information about these tags and to take a gander at the other tags they make, including a wristband personnel tag and a screw-mountable industrial tag.

Where to Get This Stuff

Wavetrend doesn't sell their hardware directly. It's actually rather difficult to obtain the hardware at a reasonable cost because they require their distributors and integrators to pay for training. It seems Wavetrend is more interested in making money by selling software and enforcing training fees than manufacturing hardware. Another problem is that Wavetrend's hardware is licensed to vendors and integrators, who have the option of modifying the way it works to suit their own uses. However, you can get unadulterated hardware from a few sources, two of which I'll list here.

One source is www.autoaccessid.com, but the model numbers of tags and readers are customized with their own numbers, and their own labels are affixed over the Wavetrend hardware. They also don't normally sell single units — they are interested in large-scale integration projects.

Another place you can get hardware is www.iautomate.com. They sell R500HA reader hardware for HomeSeer or Crestron home automation systems. I was told in a phone conversation with the man behind iAutomate that the "powered by Wavetrend" home automation hardware (the R500HA reader) was modified and didn't work the same as native Wavetrend hardware. So, if you want to use the SDK, you can get their R500SP reader, which is the L-RX201 reader module sold under a different part number. I ordered an R500SP unit right off their site and was able to use it with the Wavetrend SDK and TrackStuff software.

Get Started

Now that you're familiar with the hardware, you can get down to actually putting everything together.

Step 1: Wiring the Reader

The reader uses standard RJ45 ports, which makes cabling very easy. You can use the standard CAT5 cable and RJ45 modular connectors used to wire Ethernet networks. Due to the internal design of the L-RX201 reader, any CAT5 cabling will need a ferrite choke, shown in Figure 8-8. Otherwise, the cabling itself might act as a potential antenna; picking up signals from nearby active tags and/or introducing so much noise the reader can't hear tags.

FIGURE **8-8: Ferrite chokes for the CAT5 cable**

You can buy a PC cable along with the reader, or you can make your own. Figure 8-9 shows the pin-out and color code for the left port of the reader using standard CAT5 cable.

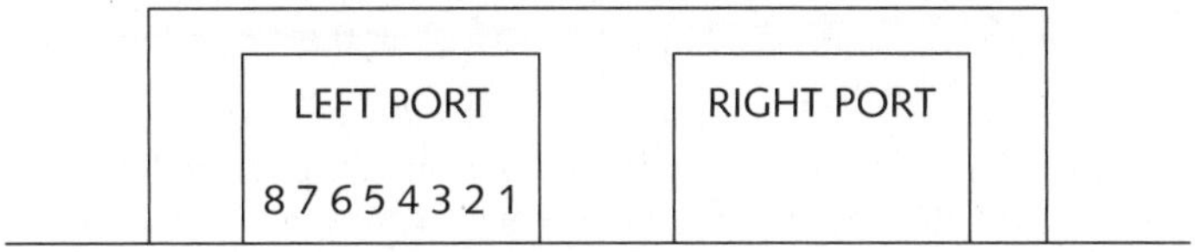

LEFT PORT	RIGHT PORT
8 7 6 5 4 3 2 1	

8 = TTL RX (Brown)
7 = TTL TX (Brown/White)
6 = RS-485 Negative (Green)
5 = RS-485 Positive (Blue/White)
4 = GND (Blue)
3 = +6 - 18VDC (Green/White)
2 = RS-232 TX (Orange)
1 = RS-232 RX (Orange/White)

FIGURE **8-9: Left port pin-out of an L-RX201 reader**

On the other end of the CAT5 cable, you need to solder a DB-9 serial connector to interface with your PC. Grab your female DB-9 connector and solder it to the cable using the color code shown in Figure 8-10. The pin numbers should be clearly stamped into the plastic on the DB-9 connector.

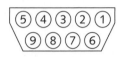

Front side of
DB9 connector

2 = RS-232 RX (Orange)
    Connects to TX pin on reader

3 = RS-232 TX (Orange/White)
    Connects to RX pin or reader

5 = GND (Blue)
    Splice on this end to go to both
    the power supply and DB9 pin 5

FIGURE 8-10: Female DB-9 color-coded solder guide

If you have more than one reader, you need to make a cable to connect them. You want to pass power and RS-485 data down the line. To do that, take some CAT5 cable and modular connectors and check out Figure 8-11 to see how to wire your patch cables. It's a straight-through cable, but only for conductors 3–6. Don't use a standard CAT5 Ethernet cable! The additional conductors in a standard straight-through CAT5 cable will cause communications problems and may damage your readers.

The important thing to realize about the RS-485 patch cables is that the communications lines don't cross over like RS-232 cables. With RS-232, each device has a transmit (TX) and receive (RX) line. For device A and B to communicate, device A's TX line would need to go to device B's RX line so data transmitted by device A would be "heard" by device B. The RS-485 medium is geared for network-type communication, where multiple devices share the same data lines. All the devices on the RS-485 network share the data lines, with each device transmitting and receiving data on the same line used by other devices on the network.

Since pins 3 and 4 are for power and pins 5 and 6 are for the RS-485 network, it would be a good idea to use a twisted pair for each set. Use the blue/white wire for pin 3 and the blue wire for pin 4. Use the orange/white wire for pin 5 and the orange wire for pin 6. Using twisted pairs helps keep line noise and cross talk problems to a minimum.

Note   Remember, you also need to use ferrite chokes on all patch cables. They reduce false reads and RF noise, increasing stability and reliability of all the readers on the network.

Step 2: Time to Tag

Okay, so you've got your reader wired up. It's time to tag people. The easiest way to get people to carry the tag around with them is to integrate it into a security badge. The Wavetrend personnel tags are quite thick, which might make for a clunky badge, but Figure 8-12 and Figure 8-13 should give you a quick idea of how that might work.

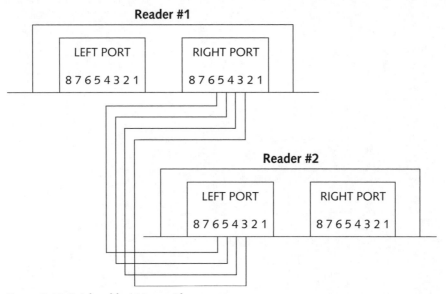

FIGURE 8-11: Patch-cable wiring guide

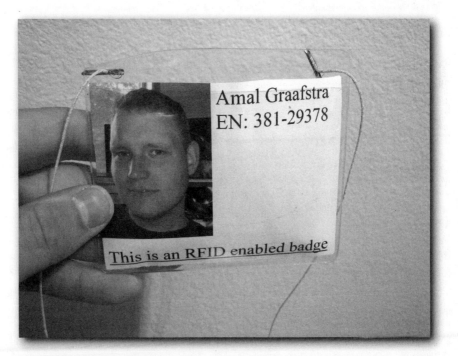

FIGURE 8-12: A homemade RFID-enabled security badge

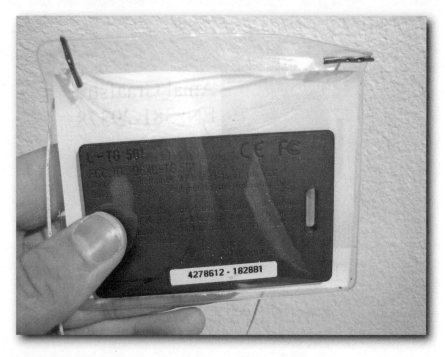

FIGURE 8-13: The L-TG501 tag "integrated" into the security badge

Tag Personnel

The personnel tag is slotted at the top for use with most vertical type card-badges. The flat backside means you could place the front face of your badge over the top of the back of the tag and loop the plastic connector that holds everything to the neck strap or lapel clip through both the badge and the RFID tag. That would actually make for a nicely integrated badge.

Personnel could alternatively wear the L-TG1200 RFID bracelet tag Wavetrend makes. I don't know anyone who'd want to wear this lumpy thing on their wrist all day, but I suppose it has its uses. Patient-monitoring in hospitals would be a likely application for this tag.

Tag Your Assets

While there are more than a few types of tags, the basic types you'd be using to tag assets are the L-TG800 metal asset tag and the L-TG100 domino tag. You can use an L-TG501 personnel tag or even a keychain tag if you want, but the other two are more suited for tagging assets.

The metallic asset tag was shown previously in Figure 8-7. You can affix this tag to the side of any metallic object, like a car, computer case, water cooler, or refrigerator. What you can't do is place the tag inside the metallic asset. You couldn't open the fridge and place the tag inside, for example. Doing that would cut the tag's range down to almost zero, until someone opened the fridge door.

Tag Orientation

The best way to get maximum range from your Wavetrend tags is to mount them vertically. That puts the internal antenna at the top of the tag, rather than aiming it at the ground or off to the side. Figure 8-14 shows various tags in a vertical orientation. Figure 8-15 shows the L-TG800 metal asset tag affixed vertically to a PC case.

FIGURE 8-14: Vertical orientation of various tags

Tamper Detection

As I said earlier, just about all tags support tamper detection. The detection method is an internal reed switch pulled closed by a magnet placed in the correct spot behind the tag. Each tag (even the tiny domino tags) has on the back of it a small circle of smooth plastic. Behind that circle is the reed switch. When you order the tags, you can order the tamper-detection version of most tags. There is no difference between the tamper-detection version and a normal tag; however, when you order the tamper-detection version you get a VHB (very high bond) adhesive pad and a very powerful tiny magnet. Figure 8-16 shows the adhesive strip and magnet you get.

FIGURE 8-15: An L-TG800 metal asset tag affixed vertically to a PC case

FIGURE 8-16: L-TG800 tag with a tamper detection magnet and VHB glue pad

You can see in Figure 8-17 that there is a hole pre-cut in the VHB pad for the magnet. The idea is that you place the VHB pad where you want to mount the tag, and then you place the magnet in the hole and cover the pad with the tag.

FIGURE 8-17: Lining up the tag with the magnet and VHB pad

How Tamper Detection Works

The tamper-detection system used by Wavetrend tags works by sending a special alarm code to the reader when the status of the reed switch changes. That means when you place the tag over the magnet, the tag sends the alarm code on the next couple of transmissions. After that, it goes back to status normal. If someone removes the tag from the asset it's affixed to, the idea is that the magnet will be separated from the tag and the reed switch status will change. The alarm code will then be sent on the next few transmissions, and hopefully the reader and software will pick up on it and take action.

The small window of time for the reader and accompanying software to pick up on a tamper situation would normally be more than enough to detect any tampering, but if there are a large amount of tags in the area, the reader may not catch the transmission and miss the tamper alarm. To help alleviate this issue, place the tagged assets you wish to receive tamper alarms from closer to the reader. That should help ensure you receive those tag transmissions over weaker tag transmissions originating from farther away.

Step 3: Download the Software

Download the TrackStuff software from www.rfidtoy.net. Installation should be very straightforward, so I won't bother covering that here. The software itself is just an example of what you can do using the Wavetrend SDK.

The Database

TrackStuff uses a Microsoft JET database (commonly known as an "Access" database), called TrackStuff.MDB. This empty database comes with the software. You can use Microsoft Access to populate the database with tags and readers. The database has three basic tables: Employees, Readers, and Tracking. Figure 8-18 shows the first two tables populated with my own data.

FIGURE 8-18: Employee and Readers table in TrackStuff.mdb

As you can see in the figure, the Employees table contains names of people (or any tagged object for that matter) and the RFID tag ID associated with that person or object. The Readers table associates a reader ID with a location. If you have more than one reader installed, this enables location data to be tracked as well as time.

The Tracking table stores tag events such as arrivals, absences, and location changes. A tag going undetected for a pre-set amount of time triggers an absence. That time is hard-set in the software to only 10 seconds to make it easy to demonstrate the functionality. Realistically, you'd probably want to set it to 10–15 minutes to allow for quick bathroom visits and such, but record when the employee is out of the building for a 20-minute break.

Time for Action

To get things rolling, connect the reader to an available serial port. Set the correct COM port and baud rate in the software. The reader I have is set for 57600 bps, the default rate from the factory. Once you've set the port and baud rate, click the Open button. The software detects all readers connected to that port and sets them to report any tag data they receive. Figure 8-19 shows the first few seconds of operation on my test bench.

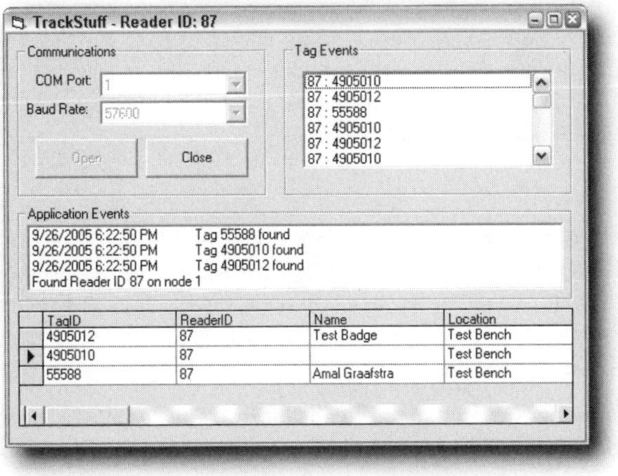

FIGURE 8-19: The first few seconds running TrackStuff

There are two events windows in TrackStuff. The first window is called Tag Events, which shows raw tag events coming in from readers. Basically, whenever a tag transmits its ID, an event is fired that contains relevant data such as the tag ID received and the reader that received it. Before that data is processed, it's posted to the Tag Events window. The other event window is called Application Events. It's the more important event window. Any readers detected, as well as processed tag events, are shown here. By "processed" I mean the TrackStuff software has to actually keep an internal queue of tags it's seen since it's been running, when they were last seen, and so on. You can see in Figure 8-20 that TrackStuff found the three tags were found, even though you can see in the Tag Events window that it received several transmissions per tag ID. This is the kind of filtering and processing required to make an intelligent tracking application.

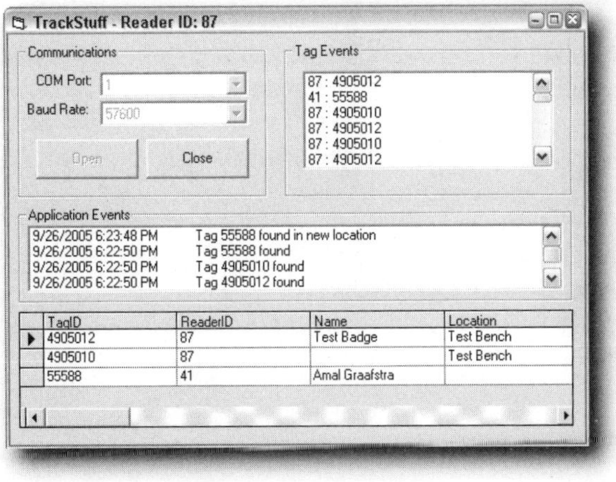

FIGURE 8-20: Tag 55588 changes location

The data grid at the bottom is a peek at the internal queue TrackStuff uses to keep track of tags and such. The database file is not used for this because reading and writing to the database would be too slow to keep up with the stream of tag events coming in from the Wavetrend SDK object. However, the queue also merges data from the database such as names associated with tag IDs and location names associated with reader IDs.

Changing Location

Now you'll see what happens when a tag moves from the area covered by reader ID 87 to another area covered by reader ID 41. Figure 8-20 showed that the software detected the tag in a new location. The best type of multiple-reader deployment keeps overlap to a minimum, but also ensures there are no dead spots without any coverage. That's why you don't see the tag going absent before it's detected in a new location.

This software doesn't even begin to take advantage of the advanced features the Wavetrend readers' support, such as gain control and RSSI indicators. If you like what you see and decide to get the SDK from Wavetrend, you can implement all kinds of advanced features in your own applications.

You can see I've not given reader ID 41 an associated location name. No big deal—you don't need to name your locations. It just helps if you have location names when you're analyzing the tracking log.

Break Time

So now, Figure 8-21 shows tag 55588 going out through a side door for a quick break. After the pre-set time elapses without detecting the tag, it's marked as absent.

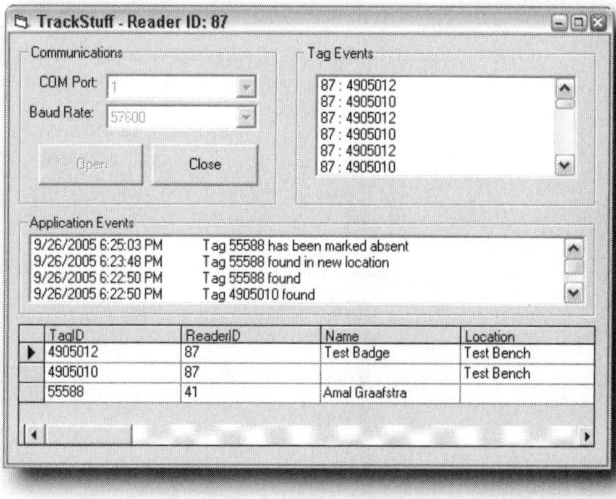

FIGURE 8-21: Tag 55588 goes absent

When the tag goes absent, the tracking log entry recorded does not show the time the software marked the tag—it shows the last time the software *detected* the tag. That relieves the pain of having to calculate the actual time the person left by taking the current time minus the number of minutes it takes for a tag to be marked absent. For instance, if the software is set to mark my tag as absent after going undetected for 10 minutes and I go outside at noon for lunch, then the tracking log should show I left at noon, not 12:10pm.

Figure 8-22 shows the tag coming back in through the front door, which reader 87 covers. Both the tag returning and the location change are registered in the tracking log as simultaneous, yet separate events.

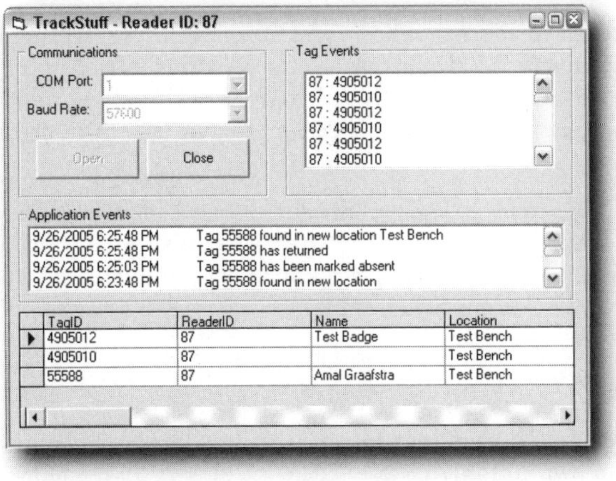

FIGURE 8-22: Tag returns in a new location

The Tracking Log

Now check out Figure 8-23 to see these events unfold in the Tracking table.

Tracking : Table

ID	TagID	ReaderID	ReadDate	Status
94	55588	87	9/26/2005 6:08:03 PM	Tag found
95	4905012	87	9/26/2005 6:08:03 PM	Tag found
96	4905010	87	9/26/2005 6:08:03 PM	Tag found
97	55588	41	9/26/2005 6:08:07 PM	New location
102	55588	87	9/26/2005 6:08:16 PM	New location
103	55588	87	9/26/2005 6:08:27 PM	Tag has gone absent
104	55588	87	9/26/2005 6:08:34 PM	Tag has returned
(AutoNumber)		0		

FIGURE 8-23: Tracking log shows events

You can see that the software initially finds the tags. Then it finds tag 55588 found in a new location. Eventually the tag is marked absent, only to return later in a new location. You could easily write separate analysis software to process log data and derive employee arrival times, hours worked in each location, lunch-breaks, and so on. You could even come up with a web-based method to pull the last known location of a specific employee, providing near real-time location fixes for specific people.

Picture you're a manager holding a meeting and you're missing somebody. You could query the system to find out where they are in the building. Let's say that you're in a huge complex with several long hallways between the offices you're holding the meeting in and the engineering wing. You could trace the last few locations of the missing meeting member and figure out if they are on their way to your meeting or if they got sidetracked in the employee lounge.

Being able to derive hours worked in an area might be helpful for situations where temporary employees are loaned out to departments. You could track which departments were using whom the most. If you expanded your tagging to assets such as overhead projectors or other expensive office supplies, you could easily locate a shared device or figure out which departments were hogging resources.

The range that typical active RFID systems have opens the door for amazing possibilities. Combining long-range active systems for tracking with short-range passive systems for applications such as access control will transform the workplace and other areas of life that, until recently, were something only found in science fiction stories.

Step 4: Use HomeSeer

It may be possible to use Wavetrend RFID hardware for your project without purchasing the Wavetrend SDK and writing your own custom software. There is a plug-in for the home automation software called HomeSeer (www.homeseer.com) made by iAutomate (www.iautomate.com), a Wavetrend hardware vendor. The combination of HomeSeer and the iAutomate RFID plugin allow you to leverage most if not all of the features Wavetrend hardware has to offer. Because you can write your own plug-ins for HomeSeer, you can still customize your RFID application with just about any functionality you can imagine.

The Hardware

The iAutomate website sells both an R500SP reader and a cheaper R500HA reader, which look exactly alike. The R500SP reader is just a Wavetrend L-RX201 reader sold under a different part number. According to iAutomate, the R500HA reader has been modified and will not work with the SDK. I've not been able to test this as I didn't order an R500HA reader.

However, I did test my R500SP reader and the original Wavetrend L-RX201 reader I had sitting around with the HomeSeer iAutomate plug-in and they seemed to work fine. However, if you're going to go the HomeSeer route, I suggest getting the R500HA reader just to be safe. That way if the plug-in code changes in the future, you won't be using unsupported hardware. Besides, the R500HA is cheaper than the R500SP reader.

Setting Up HomeSeer

The HomeSeer software package is a sweet deal for the price. You can download a 30-d ay demo from www.homeseer.com or purchase an RFID package deal from www. iautomate.com that includes the reader hardware, some tags, and the HomeSeer software.

The application itself doesn't really support much on its own. It's like a brain without any nerves connected to it. To get data into the brain, you need to download plug-in software. Some plug-ins you have to buy but many are free, including most of the plug-ins written by HomeSeer. Most third-party plug-ins will cost you extra, but the iAutomate RFID plug-in is free.

Once you have HomeSeer installed, you can use the web-based administration system to download update software. In the update section, you can select plug-ins to download and install. Scroll down to the iAutomate plug-in and check it for download. The download program automatically installs the plug-in and you can get right to configuring it. Figure 8-24 shows the configuration screen. First set the correct COM port, and then you can add your reader and any tags you have. I've added my reader and keychain tag, as shown in Figure 8-24.

Once you have your reader and tags input, click the Update/Save button, then the Reset/Restart button. In the HomeSeer log, you should see something like Figure 8-25 detailing the initialization of the iAutomate plug-in.

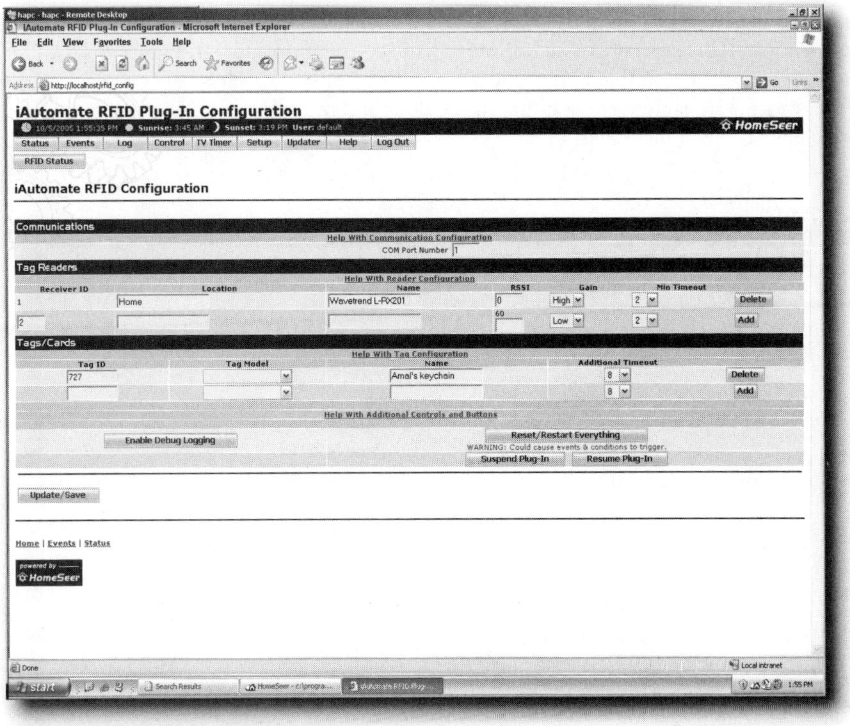

FIGURE 8-24: Configuring the iAutomate plug-in for HomeSeer

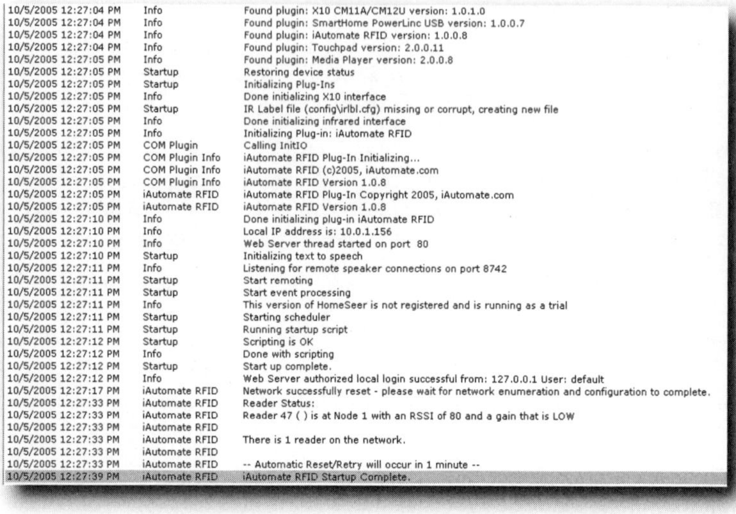
10/5/2005 12:27:04 PM Info Found plugin: X10 CM11A/CM12U version: 1.0.1.0
10/5/2005 12:27:04 PM Info Found plugin: SmartHome PowerLinc USB version: 1.0.0.7
10/5/2005 12:27:04 PM Info Found plugin: iAutomate RFID version: 1.0.0.8
10/5/2005 12:27:04 PM Info Found plugin: Touchpad version: 2.0.0.11
10/5/2005 12:27:05 PM Info Found plugin: Media Player version: 2.0.0.8
10/5/2005 12:27:05 PM Startup Restoring device status
10/5/2005 12:27:05 PM Startup Initializing Plug-Ins
10/5/2005 12:27:05 PM Info Done initializing X10 interface
10/5/2005 12:27:05 PM Startup IR Label file (config\irlbl.cfg) missing or corrupt, creating new file
10/5/2005 12:27:05 PM Info Done initializing infrared interface
10/5/2005 12:27:05 PM Info Initializing Plug-in: iAutomate RFID
10/5/2005 12:27:05 PM COM Plugin Calling InitIO
10/5/2005 12:27:05 PM COM Plugin Info iAutomate RFID Plug-In Initializing...
10/5/2005 12:27:05 PM COM Plugin Info iAutomate RFID (c)2005, iAutomate.com
10/5/2005 12:27:05 PM COM Plugin Info iAutomate RFID Version 1.0.8
10/5/2005 12:27:05 PM iAutomate RFID iAutomate RFID Plug-In Copyright 2005, iAutomate.com
10/5/2005 12:27:05 PM iAutomate RFID iAutomate RFID Version 1.0.8
10/5/2005 12:27:10 PM Info Done initializing plug-in iAutomate RFID
10/5/2005 12:27:10 PM Info Local IP address is: 10.0.1.156
10/5/2005 12:27:10 PM Info Web Server thread started on port 80
10/5/2005 12:27:10 PM Startup Initializing text to speech
10/5/2005 12:27:11 PM Info Listening for remote speaker connections on port 8742
10/5/2005 12:27:11 PM Startup Start remoting
10/5/2005 12:27:11 PM Startup Start event processing
10/5/2005 12:27:11 PM Info This version of HomeSeer is not registered and is running as a trial
10/5/2005 12:27:11 PM Startup Starting scheduler
10/5/2005 12:27:11 PM Startup Running startup script
10/5/2005 12:27:12 PM Startup Scripting is OK
10/5/2005 12:27:12 PM Info Done with scripting
10/5/2005 12:27:12 PM Startup Start up complete.
10/5/2005 12:27:12 PM Info Web Server authorized local login successful from: 127.0.0.1 User: default
10/5/2005 12:27:17 PM iAutomate RFID Network successfully reset - please wait for network enumeration and configuration to complete.
10/5/2005 12:27:33 PM iAutomate RFID Reader Status:
10/5/2005 12:27:33 PM iAutomate RFID Reader 47 ( ) is at Node 1 with an RSSI of 80 and a gain that is LOW
10/5/2005 12:27:33 PM iAutomate RFID
10/5/2005 12:27:33 PM iAutomate RFID There is 1 reader on the network.
10/5/2005 12:27:33 PM iAutomate RFID
10/5/2005 12:27:33 PM iAutomate RFID -- Automatic Reset/Retry will occur in 1 minute --
10/5/2005 12:27:39 PM iAutomate RFID iAutomate RFID Startup Complete.

FIGURE 8-25: HomeSeer log showing the iAutomate plug-in startup

Once you've configured the plug-in, you can go about setting up events. HomeSeer is an event-processing system that handles cause-and-effect type relationships. In Figure 8-26 and Figure 8-27, I've setup a simple event that will trigger when my keychain tag comes within range of my reader. The cause is me walking in the door and the effect is the system greeting me by saying "Welcome home Amal!"

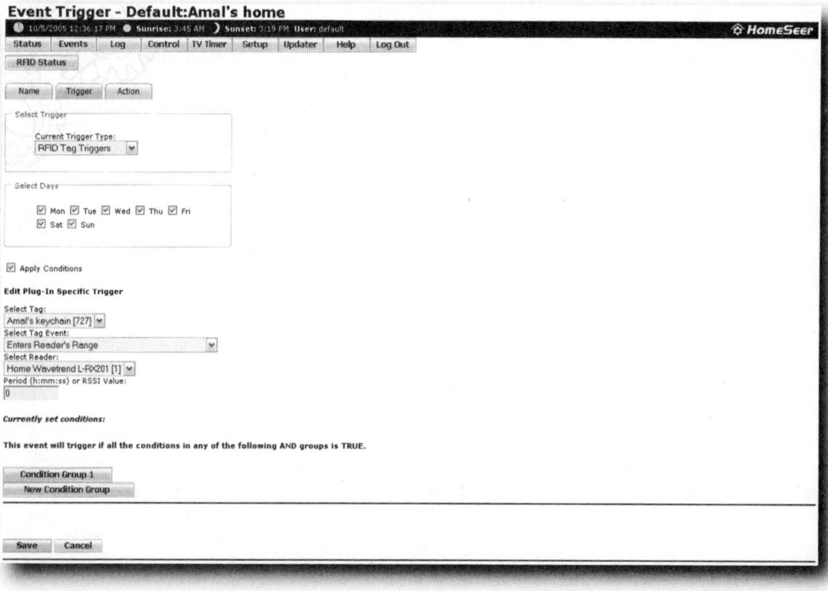
Event Trigger - Default:Amal's home
HomeSeer
Status
Events
Log
Control
TV Timer
Setup
Updater
Help
Log Out
RFID Status
Name
Trigger
Action
Select Trigger
Current Trigger Type:
RFID Tag Triggers
Select Days
Mon Tue Wed Thu Fri
Sat Sun
Apply Conditions
Edit Plug-In Specific Trigger
Select Tag:
Amal's keychain [727]
Select Tag Event:
Enters Reader's Range
Select Reader:
Home Wavetrend L-RX201 [1]
Period (h:mm:ss) or RSSI Value:
0
Currently set conditions:
This event will trigger if all the conditions in any of the following AND groups is TRUE.
Condition Group 1
New Condition Group
Save
Cancel

FIGURE 8-26: Configuring RFID events in HomeSeer

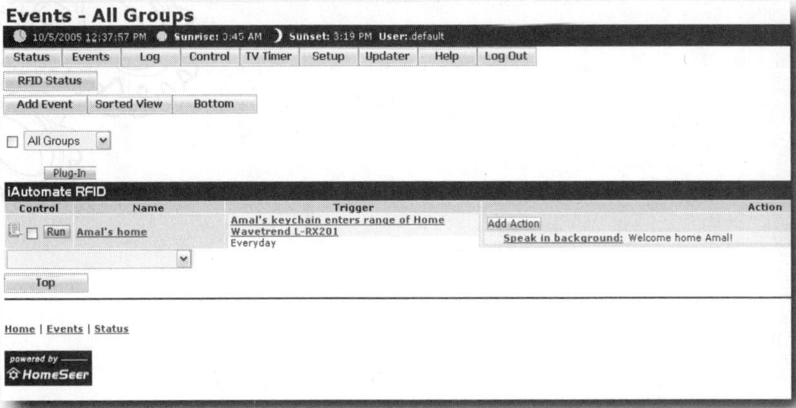

FIGURE 8-27: HomeSeer event list

Interfacing with HomeSeer

Perhaps one of the biggest advantages to HomeSeer is the fact you can create your own ActiveX components to interface directly with HomeSeer. You can download the plug-in SDK for free from the HomeSeer website. The SDK lets you create your own triggers, conditions, and actions taken by HomeSeer. You can even add your own web pages to the HomeSeer administration interface.

The most important thing, though, is the ability to create your own actions. That way you can create your own action logic for tag arrivals, exits, and movement between zones with HomeSeer, and then set up your own software to log those events or do whatever you want. By leveraging HomeSeer and iAutomate's RFID plug-in, you effectively sidestep the Wavetrend SDK.

HomeSeer Configuration Files

If you want to be able to configure HomeSeer programmatically, you're in luck. Inside the HomeSeer/Config folder are several INI files and MDB database files. HomeSeer uses Microsoft JET database files, which you can be open directly in Microsoft Access, or manipulate using ADO within your application code. You can also edit the INI files using Windows API calls, or just open them directly and edit the contents. Once you've made your changes to INI files, however, you may have to restart the plug-in that uses them, depending on the plug-in and how it uses its INI files.

Monitoring Assets and Sending Alerts

Monitoring tagged assets with RFID has been around a long time. Storefronts protect their products using EAS (electronic article surveillance) passive RFID tags, which only have two states: on or off. These tags do not carry any ID information, yet they still protect storefronts from theft by not letting tagged items that have not been turned off to leave the premises.

While the passive EAS type systems work fine for storefronts, many situations call for a more advanced method of monitoring assets. There are usually only one or two entrances customers can enter and exit the store through, and monitoring these passageways using EAS is a rather trivial task. Monitoring employee entrances or backroom doorways is not necessary, nor is it practical. EAS-type systems cannot curb employee theft because employees can just deactivate or even remove the tag from the asset they intend to walk out with.

Active RFID tags transmit their information constantly. Because they are transmitting, reader devices do not need to be stationed at each passageway. They can receive signals from any tagged items within range, enabling the system to actively monitor tags no matter where they are in the store, not just when they pass through special protected areas. Passive tags require energy from the reader to power up and make their presence known. That means they are vulnerable to shielding, which prevents communication between tag and reader. A thief could easily shield a passive EAS tag while passing through any protected passageway, allowing the tag and the item to slip through the storefront's defenses. Because active tags are transmitting all the time, the system detects a tag as missing if it is still within the coverage area but shielded by a would-be thief. The monitoring system will detect the absence of a signal, whether from actual tag absence or maliciously shielding the tag's signal.

in this chapter

- ☑ Asset monitoring and alerting

- ☑ Importance of tag orientation

- ☑ Exploring tamper detection

- ☑ Checking out different antenna types

- ☑ Using multiple antennas to extend the coverage area

In this chapter, you will be building on what you did in Chapter 8. You will use the same Wavetrend reader, shown in Figure 9-1, to monitor tagged assets. Unlike Chapter 8 however, you will be using a single reader to cover a large area that would normally require multiple reader devices. To do that you will build an antenna-switching device that connects multiple antennas to a single reader, allowing you to monitor the presence of tagged assets within the entire extended coverage area.

FIGURE 9-1: Wavetrend L-RX201 reader

Parts and Tools

You need the following parts for this project:

- RG-58 50 ohm BNC cable, Radio Shack part number 278-964
- BNC female-to-female coupler, Radio Shack part number 278-115A
- BNC jack, Radio Shack part number 278-105

- Male BNC plug, Radio Shack part number 278-103

- Female DB-9 connector, Radio Shack part number 276-1538

- Radio Shack circuit board, part number 276-158B

- Wavetrend L-RX201 reader and L series tags

And you need the following tools:

- Philips screwdriver

- Soldering iron and solder

Get Started

Assuming you've read Chapter 8 already, you should be familiar with the Wavetrend L-RX201 reader and tags. I'll give you a quick refresher on wiring the reader and then you can dive into tagging your assets. If you're not familiar with the reader hardware, please go back and read Chapter 8 to get up to speed.

Step 1: Connect the Reader

As you already know, the reader uses standard RJ45 ports and modular connectors like those used in standard CAT5 Ethernet installations.

You can buy a PC programming cable along with the reader, or you can make your own. Figure 9-2 shows the pin-out and color code for the left port of the reader using standard CAT5 cable.

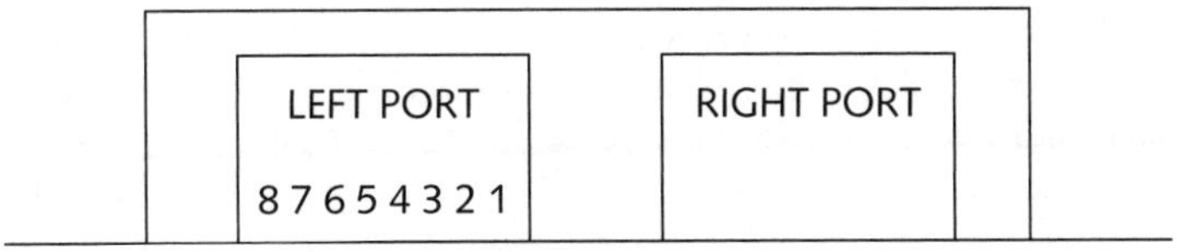

```
 _____
|     _____       _____     |
|    | LEFT PORT |   | RIGHT PORT | |
|    |           |   |            | |
|    | 87654321  |   |            | |
|    |_____|   |_____| |
|_____|
```

```
8 = TTL RX (Brown)
7 = TTL TX (Brown/White)
6 = RS-485 Negative (Green)
5 = RS-485 Positive (Blue/White)
4 = GND (Blue)
3 = +6 - 18VDC (Green/White)
2 = RS-232 TX (Orange)
1 = RS-232 RX (Orange/White)
```

FIGURE 9-2: Left port pin-out of L-RX201 reader

On the other end of the CAT5 cable, you'll need to solder a DB-9 serial connector to interface with your PC. Grab your female DB-9 connector and solder it to the cable using the color code shown in Figure 9-3. The pin numbers should be clearly stamped into the plastic on the DB-9 connector. You can wire the reader for power using the blue (ground) and green/white (+6-18VDC) wires, following the pin-out previously shown in Figure 9-2.

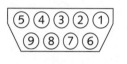

Front side of
DB9 connector

2 = RS-232 RX (Orange)
  Connects to TX pin on reader

3 = RS-232 TX (Orange/White)
  Connects to RX pin or reader

5 = GND (Blue)
  Splice on this end to go to both
  the power supply and DB9 pin 5

FIGURE 9-3: Female DB-9 color-coded solder guide

Step 2: Tag Your Assets

Okay, so you've got your reader connected to your monitoring station. It's time to tag your assets.

Tag Types

While there are more than a few types of tags, the basic types you use to tag assets are the L-TG800 metal asset tag and the L-TG100 domino tag. You can use an L-TG501 personnel tag or even a keychain tag if you want, but the other two are more suited for tagging assets.

Figure 9-4 shows the metallic asset tag. You can affix this tag to the side of any metallic object, like a car, computer case, water cooler, or refrigerator. What you can't do is place the tag inside the metallic asset. You couldn't open the fridge and place the tag inside, for example. Doing that would cut the tag's range down to almost zero, until someone opened the door to the fridge.

The "domino" asset tag shown in Figure 9-5 is useful for tagging nonmetallic assets such as wooden pallets, crates, and plastic bins.

FIGURE 9-4: The L-TG800 metallic asset tag

FIGURE 9-5: L-TG100 domino tag with external antenna

Tag Orientation

The best way to get maximum range from your Wavetrend tags is to mount them vertically. That puts the internal antenna at the top of the tag, rather than aiming it at the ground or off to the side. Figure 9-6 shows various tags in a vertical orientation. Figure 9-7 shows the L-TG800 metal asset tag affixed vertically to a PC case.

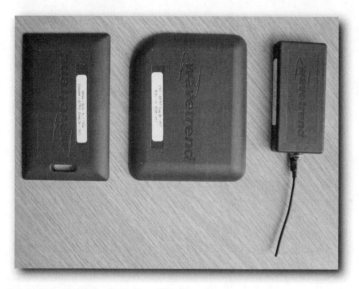

FIGURE 9-6: Vertical orientation of various tags

Step 3: Download the Software

The MonitorStuff application is very similar to the TrackStuff application in Chapter 8, except it checks for tag presence and takes action when a tag goes missing. Because some assets only need to be monitored during certain times, like only at night, for example, each asset record in the MonitorStuff database can specify an optional start and end time to start the monitoring process.

The assets table shown in Figure 9-8 details the fields available to each asset record, including AlertEmail, which, if populated, will be sent an e-mail alert when an asset goes missing.

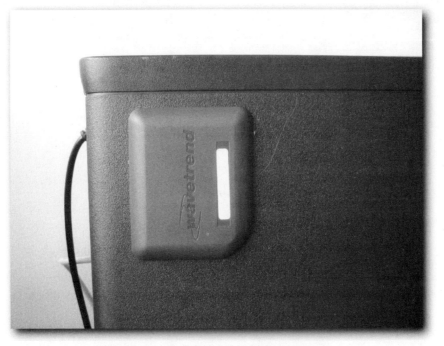

FIGURE 9-7: An L-TG800 metal asset tag affixed vertically to PC case

Assets : Table

	TagID	Asset	AlertEmail	StartTime	EndTime
▶	55588	Car Keys	my@email.com		
	658	Computer			
*					

Record: 1 of 2

FIGURE 9-8: The Assets table from MonitorStuff.mdb

Open the software and choose your serial communications port and baud rate. Click the Open button to open a connection to the reader and start processing tags. As you can see in Figure 9-9, there are far more tags in the area than just the two listed in the Assets table. Unless the table lists the tags, nothing will happen if one of those unmonitored tags leaves the area.

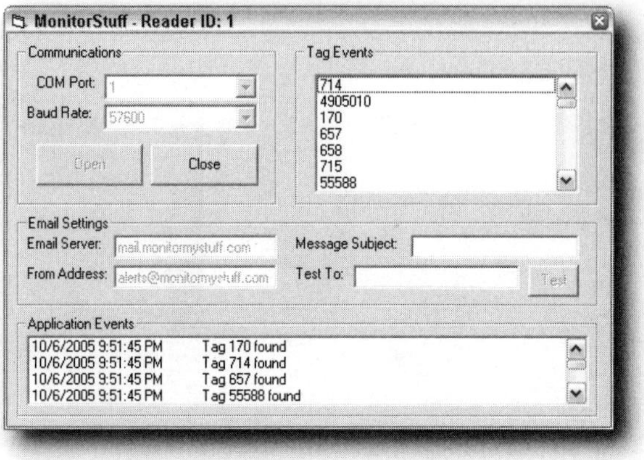

FIGURE 9-9: Monitoring tag transmissions

Now I'll take my car keys outside and put them in my car. The application is hard-set to alert after 10 seconds of it does not hear from a monitored tag. Figure 9-10 shows the tag going missing, and the application alerting on the monitored asset and sending an e-mail alert.

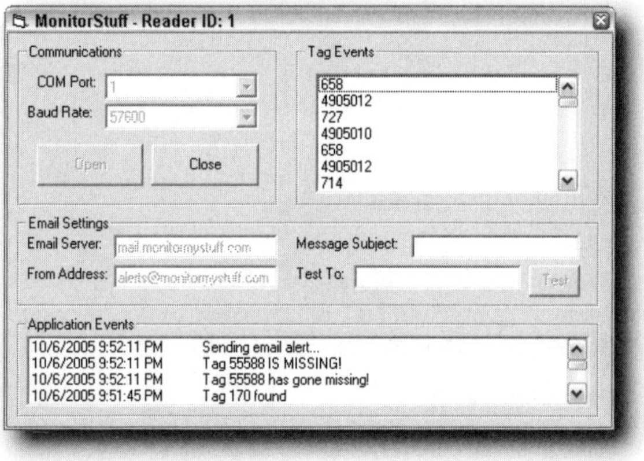

FIGURE 9-10: My car keys go missing

E-mail Alerts

Sure enough, I have an alert message waiting in my e-mail box (Figure 9-11).

Alert from MonitorStuff!

alerts@monitormystuff.com

To: Amal Graafstra

The asset Car Keys with tag 55588 has gone missing!

FIGURE 9-11: Alert e-mail message sent from MonitorStuff

E-mail alerts only work if you have set your e-mail server and e-mail address in the E-mail Settings section. Also, only assets with a valid e-mail address listed in the AlertEmail field in MonitorStuff.mdb database trigger an e-mail.

Specify Times

If you specify StartTime and EndTime values in the MonitorStuff.mdb database for a particular asset, the asset is not counted as missing unless it goes missing within the given time frame. This works great for things like field equipment that is out all day, but should be staying put all night in storage lockers.

Tamper Detection

MonitorStuff does not implement tamper detection, although you could easily implement it in your own software applications using the Wavetrend SDK. The MonitorStuff application is just an example of what you could accomplish with the Wavetrend SDK, but you don't have to use the SDK. The alternative access software approach using HomeSeer and iAutomate's RFID plug-in (mentioned in Chapter 8) supports tamper detection features. You can also use HomeSeer's powerful scripting capabilities to leverage VBS scripts to interact with the reader, allowing you to do just about everything you can do with the SDK, but through the HomeSeer plugin framework instead.

Step 4: Extend the Coverage Area

Now that you have a working asset monitoring and alerting system, I'm going to show you how to extend your coverage area without adding readers.

Reader devices are very expensive, and for this type of asset monitoring application, it won't be necessary to know the location of an asset. It's only important to know that the asset is within the "protected space" of the monitored coverage area. By extending the range of a single reader, you save money by not requiring additional reader hardware.

You can extend the range a few ways. First, you can use a different, more efficient antenna. Second, you can use multiple antennas connected to a single reader. Third, you can use a combination and connect multiple well-designed antennas.

Note There are signal amplification devices out there that can boost transmission power; however, these have several drawbacks. Most are illegal to use because they break transmit power limit laws set forth by the FCC. Probably the most important drawback, however, is the fact you won't get any significant range increase. Signal amplifiers usually only boost transmit power, but do little to help boost received signals. By placing an amplifier on the RFID reader, you're not helping tag signal strengths and you may be introducing enough noise to actually reduce the effective range of your reader.

Radiant Energy and Antennas

Active RFID uses radiant energy to communicate between tags and readers, so the antenna systems don't need to be resonant loops like those used in passive, magnetically coupled RFID setups. That allows for a little more flexibility when it comes to things like cable lengths and antenna types.

There are a many different antenna options out there. A few of them have negative gain characteristics and are meant to attenuate signal. You use these types of antennas to limit the range of readers that don't have built-in range controls. Figure 9-12 shows a couple of attenuator adaptors that you can also use with standard antennas to limit their gain.

Figure 9-12: BNC style 10db and 6db attenuators

Realistically though, you can use virtually any antenna made for the 433 MHz spectrum. Ham radio antennas, panel/patch antennas, dipoles, whips — any of these types of antennas would work fine. It all just comes down to what type of energy pattern and coverage zone you want.

Omnidirectional and Unidirectional

Whip antennas are generally omnidirectional, which means they have a bubble-like coverage area that extends in all 360 degrees around the antenna. Directional antennas, on the other hand, have a shaped coverage area. The advantage is you usually get more range than you would with an omnidirectional antenna, except that extended range is limited to one specific direction.

The shape depends on the design on the antenna. The 433 MHz patch antenna shown in Figure 9-13 is commonly used with active RFID installations. It even has a BNC style connector on the back, as shown in Figure 9-14, which makes it very easy to connect to the Wavetrend reader using a typical BNC 50 ohm coax cable. This type of patch panel antenna has a coverage pattern that extends directly out in front of it, but falls off to the sides and leaves almost no coverage in the back. Figure 9-15 illustrates the horizontal reception plane of this style patch antenna. A perfect application for this antenna would be something like recording vehicle IDs as they passed through parking garage gates.

FIGURE 9-13: Directional 433 MHz patch antenna

FIGURE 9-14: BNC connector on the back of the patch antenna

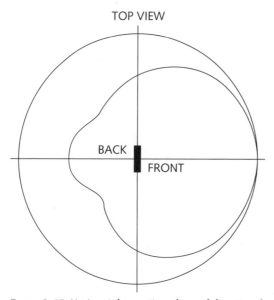

FIGURE 9-15: Horizontal reception plane of directional patch antenna

Note You can purchase this antenna from Wavetrend or one of their distributors, but it's not made specifically by Wavetrend. You can get a 433 MHz patch antenna from many places, usually for hundreds cheaper. I got mine at a bargain from www.netgate.com. Wavetrend and their distributors sell the same antenna for over $200 more than what I paid.

Connecting Multiple Antennas

You can add coverage areas without additional readers by using multiple antennas. Unless you know a lot about antenna design, don't bother with trying to connect multiple antennas to the reader at the same time — you'll most likely end up significantly reducing your range. I'm talking about connecting multiple antennas through antenna switching.

You can theoretically use a large number of antennas, as long as only one of them is connected at a time. There are many types of antenna switches out there, but most are manual devices. Manual switches require that the user flip the switch, which will not be sufficient for this project. The alternative is to build an automatic antenna switch that toggles back and forth between two (or more) antennas. I'm going to show you how to build an automatic switch for two antennas.

Relay-Based Switching

Ham radio operators use many remote type antenna switches. They use relays to do the actual switching at the antenna end, while a control box sits next to the radio operator. Even though it's an electronic switching system, it's still a manual process. You want to build your own relay-based switching system that automatically switches between two different antennas every few seconds.

By default, Wavetrend tags transmit their IDs every 1.5 seconds. If any one antenna is connected for about 5 seconds, it allows ample time for a tag within range of that antenna to transmit at least two or three times. If your reader doesn't hear a tag transmission the first time due to interference or a transmission collision, the tag gets a couple more chances before the antenna is deactivated. You can build a simple timer circuit coupled with a flip-flop to switch back and forth between two antennas.

Most relay-based antenna switches are geared for high-powered radio setups and use heavy-duty relays. This is not a high-powered setup, so you can afford to use my old standby; the 5V Radio Shack reed relay. It switches much faster than a typical relay and it creates a more direct path for RF energy to travel. Figure 9-16 details what a reed relay looks like inside, which is quite different from a typical relay. The switched section sits directly in the center of the coil, allowing a straight path for the RF energy to travel.

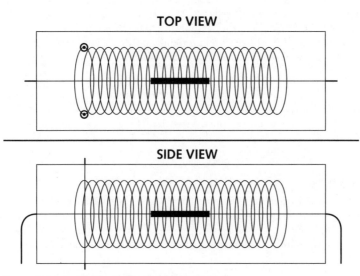

FIGURE 9-16: Inside the Radio Shack 5V reed relay

As you can see in Figure 9-17, a traditional switching relay introduces several twists and turns into the energy path. High-frequency RF energy likes to travel in straight lines both through the air and within conductive wiring. Introducing 90-degree path changes can create loss, reducing the effective range of your RFID antenna system.

Loss

One of your worst enemies when it comes to range will be loss. High frequencies like 433 Mhz want to travel in straight lines, even within antenna cables and circuit pathways. Antenna cables themselves introduce loss, but bending an antenna cable at a sharp 90-degree angle (or more) will create additional loss. Inserting a relay into the RF energy path from transmitter to antenna will also create loss Normally, all these small losses don't matter too much because the radio system being used is dealing with fairly high power levels, but your RFID system is listening for faint tag transmissions and is very sensitive to loss. It's a good idea to avoid it wherever possible.

Traditional Relay

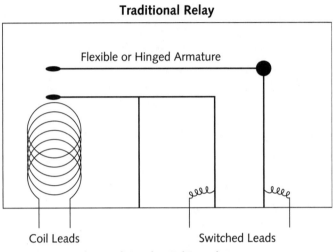

FIGURE **9-17: Inside a traditional switching relay**

A Peek at the Switch Circuit and Board

Figure 9-18 shows a circuit diagram of the automatic antenna switch. It's build around an LM555 timer circuit, a 7473 logic flip-flop IC, and two reed relays. The 555 timer circuit generates a timed pulse, the output of which triggers the flip-flop. Each time the 555 timer IC emits a pulse, the flip-flop switch states. The output that was currently active goes inactive and the inactive output goes active. The outputs switch back and forth with each pulse from the 555 timer circuit.

Figure 9-19 and Figure 9-20 show the board. I mounted components to both sides of the board, but you won't have to do that.

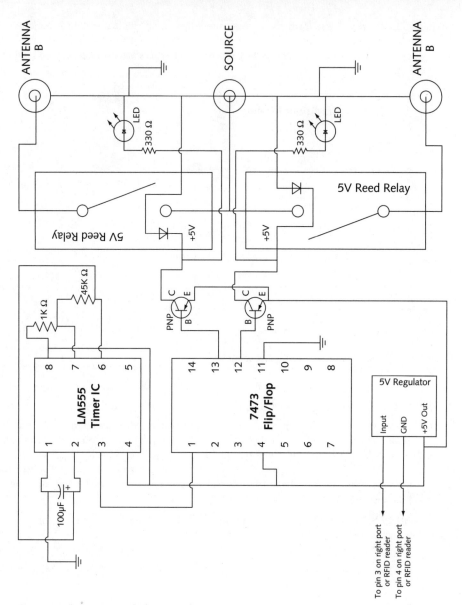

FIGURE 9-18: Antenna switch circuit diagram

FIGURE 9-19: Top side of the finished antenna switchboard

FIGURE 9-20: Bottom side of antenna switchboard

Note The components shown in the diagram in Figure 9-18 have been split up on the board, with some on the top side (Figure 9-19) and some on the bottom side (Figure 9-20). I opted to put some components on the bottom side of the board because I was going to mount it in a small project box and thought I needed to conserve space. Halfway through, I found out the project box I ordered was no longer made and couldn't find a box that size from another manufacturer, so I didn't need to save all that top-side space on the board after all. You don't need to put your components on both sides of the board when building your antenna switch. Keep in mind though, if you want to put your board into a project box, you might need to do things a little differently. For instance, you might not want to solder the indicator LEDs directly to the board—you may want to mount them to the project box along with the BNC connectors and use jumper wire and short lengths of 50 ohm coax cable to connect them to the board.

Build the Switch Circuit

First grab your circuit board and stick two relays into it, as shown in Figure 9-21. You should make sure there's room enough on the edges for the BNC connectors that come next.

FIGURE 9-21: Positioning reed relays

Solder them to the board, and then grab your BNC connectors. Figure 9-22 shows the bottom of these connectors. There is a small flat surface as well as a metal tab with a hole for soldering to the shielding.

FIGURE 9-22: Bottom side of the BNC connector with a flat edge

Get this connector ready to be soldered to the board. Take a small length of wire and strip all the housing off. Loop it through the shielding solder hole and crimp it down like Figure 9-23. Now solder it to the BNC connector.

Now when you place the BNC connector on the circuit board, you'll have a shielding wire to solder to the board. Position the connectors and solder their shielding wires. That should hold the connectors in place while you strip some more wire. Take your wire and solder it to the center posts on the BNC connectors, and then run them down through the holes in the board and solder them. You should have something like Figure 9-24 sitting in front of you now.

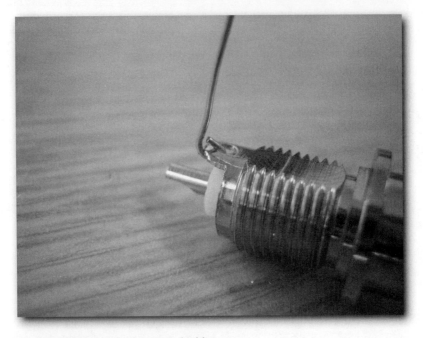

FIGURE 9-23: Wire crimped to BNC shielding

FIGURE 9-24: BNC connectors soldered to the board

Now solder the ends of the two outside BNC connectors to the ends of the relay switched leads as shown in Figure 9-25.

FIGURE 9-25: BNC center post connected to relay lead

Now take the middle BNC connector's center post lead and connect it to the inside switched lead on both relays. Once you have that all done, secure the fragile BNC connectors to the board with some strong epoxy. Make sure not to make too big of a mess with it; you still have more parts to add. Once the epoxy has hardened, you'll have something like Figure 9-26 and Figure 9-27.

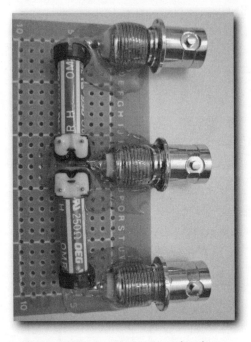

FIGURE 9-26: BNC connectors secured with epoxy

FIGURE 9-27: Epoxy securing relay and BNC connector

Securing Components

You don't have to do things in this order, but I like to secure IC components first since you have to solder everything to the board. Solder the 555 timer IC in place. Then solder the 7473 J-K flip-flop IC to the board. Solder the 7805 5V regulator to the board, and then find a good place to put the two PNP transistors.

Once the ICs and components are in place, find a home for the indicator LEDs and accompanying 330-ohm resistors. Take a long stripped piece of wire and connect all three BNC shields, and then solder both LED cathodes to the grounding strip you just created between BNC connectors. Then solder the 330-ohm resistors to the LED anodes.

With the board facing the same direction as was shown previously in Figure 9-24 (BNC connectors to the right), the right coil lead of each relay will be connected to ground, so solder those coil leads to the grounding strip. Now connect the free ends of those 330-ohm resistors to the other coil lead on the relay. That will put the relay coils and resistor/LED pairs in parallel with each other, so when the relay is powered up, the LED will light as well.

Now you can connect the two protection diodes across each relay's coil leads. Connect each of the protection diode's anode leads (the end opposite of the stripe/band end) to the grounded coil leads on the relays. Connect each diode's other lead (the striped end) to each relay's other coil lead.

Now solder a jumper wire connecting the grounding strip to the center pin on the voltage regulator and you will have finished the mechanical switching portion of the board.

Control Circuit

Now that you've got your switching relays and indicator lights done, you need to build the circuit that will control them. The circuit itself consists of two parts. The first part is a standard 555 timer that sends a pulse out approximately every 5 seconds with the resistor and capacitor values given. If you want to speed or slow the switch rate, change the values of the capacitor, resistors, or both. More capacitance will mean more time between antenna switches. Less capacitance (or less resistance) will give less time between antenna switches, but make sure you don't go below 3 seconds. If the antenna is only active for 3 seconds or less, you'll likely miss some tag transmissions.

The pulse from the 555-timer circuit will trigger the flip-flop to switch. When the 7473 IC is powered up, one output will be turned on by default. When the first pulse comes from the 555 timer, that output will switch off and the other output will switch on. When an output on the 7473 is switched on, it goes low, which triggers the PNP transistor and allows current to flow through the relay, switching it on and connecting the antenna.

Connect It

Starting with the 555 timer circuit, you can connect the 100mF electrolytic capacitor first. The negative side will connect to pin 1 on the 555 IC, while the positive side will connect to pin 2. With the capacitor in place, solder the 45K ohm resistor between pins 6 and 7. Then solder the 1K ohm resistor between pins 7 and 8. Connect a jumper wire between pin 6 and pin 2, and another jumper wire between pins 8 and 4. Now the only thing left to do is connect the timer IC to the voltage regulator. Connect a jumper from pin 1 to ground, and another from pin 4 to the +5V output pin on the regulator.

With the timer circuit finished, you can concentrate on the flip-flop IC. Connect pin 11 to ground, and pin 4 to the +5V output on the voltage regulator. Pins 12 and 13 are the toggled output pins, so connect the base pin from one of the PNP transistors to pin 12, and the other base pin on the other transistor to pin 13. Connect both emitter pins on the transistors to the +5V output on the regulator and you're almost done. The last thing to do is connect the collector pins of the PNP transistors to the relay coil leads and you're finished.

Power the Antenna Switcher

There are a few options for powering the antenna switcher. You can use an AC power adaptor, or you can catch a ride on the nearby reader's power bus. The right port of the reader should be empty, meaning pins 3 and 4 on that port are free to distribute power to your switchboard. Grab an RJ45 modular connector and a crimper. Get two wires long enough to reach from the reader to the switchboard and crimp them into pins 3 and 4 in the modular connector, as shown in Figure 9-28. Now connect the wire from pin 3 to the voltage input pin on the regulator and solder the wire from pin 4 to ground.

Figure 9-28: Crimp wire to pin 3 and pin 4

With everything done, you can put it into a project box or leave it hanging.

Connect More Antennas

Now that you've got a functional antenna switch, it's time to connect some antennas to the thing. The first thing you'll need to do is get a short run of RG-58 or other suitable 50 ohm coax cable to run from the reader to the center BNC connector on the switch. I cut a length of a pre-existing cable and used threaded BNC connector to make a short patch cable, as shown in Figure 9-29.

FIGURE 9-29: Making your own short patch cable

If you need to do the same, cut your cable and strip the inner and outer shielding as shown in Figure 9-30. Use a threaded connector or better yet, get one you can solder. I use threaded connectors because they are easy, but they tend to have more loss due to electrically poor connection between the center conductor and the center pin in the connector. If you want to use a threaded connector, get some solder paste and coat the end of the center conductor before you thread the connector on. Once the connector is on, you can use a soldering iron to heat up the center pin of the connector and melt the solder paste, securing the conductor and making good electrical contact.

FIGURE 9-30: RG-58 coax with stripped housing

It might make sense for you to cover the area where the reader is mounted, so you can place the reader's original antenna on one of the antenna switch's BNC connectors, as shown in Figure 9-31. You can mount the second antenna in another location and run 50-ohm cabling back to your antenna switchboard.

Note   Remember, the longer the run, the less coverage range the antenna at the other end will have due to loss introduced by the cable itself. There is also the possibility of picking up noise along the cable, reducing the effectiveness of the reader. When you run cable, be aware of possible sources of noise. For example, don't run it parallel with AC power wiring.

If you have two Wavetrend whip antennas, you can easily use a BNC female barrel connector to join the male end on the antenna to the male end on the cable (see Figure 9-32).

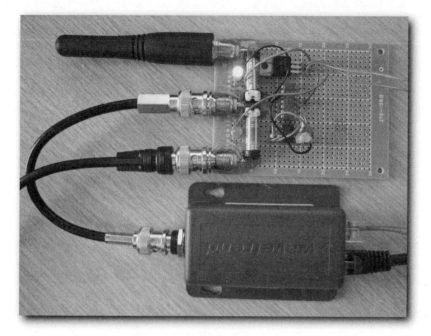

FIGURE 9-31: Antenna switchboard with two antennas connected

FIGURE 9-32: Barrel connector joining whip antenna and cable

Troubleshooting

If you have problems with your flip-flop not switching properly or erratically, you may have to add a 1pF capacitor across the 5V output and ground pins of the voltage regulator. Some noise from the RFID reader might be present if you use it as your power source. You might also try connecting an LED between the LM555 timer-circuit output pin and ground to see if the timer circuit is actually sending pulses to the flip-flop. The LED should blink every few seconds, at which point the flip-flop should change state. If it doesn't, check your wiring. You might also have a bad flip-flop IC.

Step 5: Control Antenna Switching

If you want to use an antenna switch with a location tracking system, like the one featured in Chapter 8, then you're going to need to be able to control which antenna is switched on and when. There are a few different ways to do it, but the simplest way would be to use a BASIC Stamp 2 microprocessor to do the switching. With a BS2, you could switch up to 15 different antennas. More antennas will be possible if you use an I/O extender.

The idea is simple: take I/O pin 0 and make that your control interface pin. It will receive serial commands from the host PC and switch off whatever antenna is currently on, and then switch on the desired antenna. Your PC would need two serial ports available: one for the RFID reader and one for the antenna switch.

 Since you're going to connect your PC's RS-232 serial port to I/O pin 0 on the Stamp, you'll need a resistor. The Stamp requires TTL voltage levels, but the RS-232 voltage levels from your PC's serial port are too high, so make sure you put a 22k resistor in-line between the RS-232 TX pin (pin 3 on a DB9 connector) and the Stamp's I/O pin.

To avoid the potentially damaging scenario of no antennas being connected, the Stamp code instructs the microcontroller to connect antenna 1 by making I/O pin 1 go high. That way, as soon as the Stamp gets power or is reset, antenna 1 is connected by default.

By getting tag events from the reader and knowing what antenna is connected at the time the event occurs, you can determine what location the tag is in. It might be a good idea to take advantage of RSSI information to fine-tune your location derivations. You might also consider coding your PC application so that it ignores any tags reported just before and just after an antenna switch, since delays in communications and/or antenna switching might cause your code to derive an erroneous location for the tag.

You can download the following code from www.rfidtoys.net, but its really only here to give you a conceptual example. Feel free to use it, modify it, update it, and enhance it any way you want.

Basic Stamp 2 Code

```
' ============================================================================
'
'   File....... RFID_AntennaController.BS2
'   Purpose.... Control which antenna is connected to RFID reader
'   Author..... Jon Williams -- Parallax, Inc.
'   E-mail..... jwilliams@parallax.com
'   Started....
'   Updated.... 07 FEB 2005
'
' ============================================================================
'   Updated.... 02 JULY 2005
'   Purpose.... Update code to suit antenna switch project
'   Author..... Amal Graafstra -- RFID Toys
' ============================================================================
'
'   {$STAMP BS2}
'   {$PBASIC 2.5}
'
' ============================================================================


' -----[ Program Description ]----------------------------------------------
'
'   This code waits for serial commands from a host, telling it which
'   antenna to switch on, connecting that antenna to an RFID reader.
'
'   When an antenna number is received, the code will switch off all
'   possible antenna connections, then switch on the requested antenna.
'
' -----[ Revision History ]--------------------------------------------------
'
'   Updated.... 02 JULY 2005
'   Purpose.... Control which antenna is connected to RFID reader
'   Author..... Amal Graafstra -- RFID Toys
'
' -----[ I/O Definitions ]---------------------------------------------------

RX          PIN     0               ' Serial RX to reader
ANT1        PIN     1               ' Antenna 1
ANT2        PIN     2               ' Antenna 2
ANT3        PIN     3               ' Antenna 3
ANT4        PIN     4               ' Antenna 4
ANT5        PIN     5               ' Antenna 5
ANT6        PIN     6               ' Antenna 6
ANT7        PIN     7               ' Antenna 7
ANT8        PIN     8               ' Antenna 8
```

Continued

Basic Stamp 2 Code *(continued)*

```
'More antennas are possible, but unlikely. If you would like to
'control more than 8 antennas, you must modify the code to suit
'your application.

' -----[ Constants ]-------------------------------------------------

#SELECT $STAMP
  #CASE BS2, BS2E, BS2PE
    T1200       CON     813
    T2400       CON     396
    T4800       CON     188
    T9600       CON     84
    T19K2       CON     32
    TMidi       CON     12
    T38K4       CON     6
  #CASE BS2SX, BS2P
    T1200       CON     2063
    T2400       CON     1021
    T4800       CON     500
    T9600       CON     240
    T19K2       CON     110
    TMidi       CON     60
    T38K4       CON     45
#ENDSELECT

SevenBit      CON     $2000
Inverted      CON     $4000
Open          CON     $8000
Baud          CON     T2400


#SELECT $STAMP
  #CASE BS2, BS2E
    TmAdj       CON     $100              ' x 1.0 (time adjust)
    FrAdj       CON     $100              ' x 1.0 (freq adjust)
  #CASE BS2SX
    TmAdj       CON     $280              ' x 2.5
    FrAdj       CON     $066              ' x 0.4
  #CASE BS2P
    TmAdj       CON     $3C5              ' x 3.77
    FrAdj       CON     $044              ' x 0.265
  #CASE BS2PE
    TmAdj       CON     $100              ' x 1.0
    FrAdj       CON     $0AA              ' x 0.665
#ENDSELECT


' -----[ Variables ]-------------------------------------------------
```

```
CommandBuf    VAR    Byte                         ' cmd buffer from PC


' -----[ EEPROM Data ]-------------------------------------------------


' -----[ Initialization ]----------------------------------------------

Reset:
  HIGH ANT1                                       ' connect antenna 1
  LOW ANT2                                        ' disconnect antenna 2
  LOW ANT3                                        ' disconnect antenna 3
  LOW ANT4                                        ' disconnect antenna 4
  LOW ANT5                                        ' disconnect antenna 5
  LOW ANT6                                        ' disconnect antenna 6
  LOW ANT7                                        ' disconnect antenna 7
  LOW ANT8                                        ' disconnect antenna 8


' -----[ Program Code ]------------------------------------------------

Main:
  'The only job of this code is to sit and wait for commands and take
  'action only when the command received is valid.

  'wait for command from PC
  SERIN RX, T2400, [CommandBuf]

  'check for valid command from PC
  IF CommandBuf >= 49 AND CommandBuf <= 56 THEN
    GOTO Process_Command                          ' process the PC command
  END IF

  GOTO Main                                       ' go back to listening

Process_Command:
  'disconnect all antennas first
  LOW ANT1                                        ' disconnect antenna 1
  LOW ANT2                                        ' disconnect antenna 2
  LOW ANT3                                        ' disconnect antenna 3
  LOW ANT4                                        ' disconnect antenna 4
  LOW ANT5                                        ' disconnect antenna 5
  LOW ANT6                                        ' disconnect antenna 6
  LOW ANT7                                        ' disconnect antenna 7
  LOW ANT8                                        ' disconnect antenna 8

  'now process the command
  SELECT CASE CommandBuf
    CASE 49                                        ' PC sent "1" (ASCII 49)
      HIGH ANT1                                    ' turn on antenna 1
    CASE 50                                        ' PC sent "2" (ASCII 50)
      HIGH ANT2                                    ' turn on antenna 2
```

Continued

Basic Stamp 2 Code *(continued)*

```
     CASE 51                                     ' etc...
        HIGH ANT3
     CASE 52
        HIGH ANT4
     CASE 53
        HIGH ANT5
     CASE 54
        HIGH ANT6
     CASE 55
        HIGH ANT7
     CASE 56
        HIGH ANT8
  END select


  GOTO Main


  END
```

Summing Up

Active RFID systems have an advantage over passive designs when you're dealing with asset monitoring because active tags cannot be shielded or snuck out through an unprotected passageway. Shielding an active tag does nothing but alert the system that the tagged item has gone missing. However, because active RFID tags are much more expensive, it's a solution geared toward more-expensive items like computers and perhaps even vehicles in a car lot. A system could be developed to alert lot owners and maybe even police the second a vehicle tag goes missing. By linking vehicle information with the tag, the system could alert police of the car make, model, color, and license place information (if it had one) before the thief made it off the lot.

You can extend the range of active systems or even shape it in a single direction using specialized antennas like the patch antenna previously shown in Figure 9-13. You could also use just about any other high-gain antennas designed for 433 MHz.

Because the system only monitors the presence or absence of tags, you can use an automatic antenna switcher to extend the range by switching between two or more antennas in different coverage zones. This would allow tags in each coverage zone to report their presence to a single reader instead of requiring readers for each zone. However, if you want location information, you could build a controlled antenna switch using a BASIC Stamp microprocessor so the monitoring system is in control of which zone is actively being covered. By controlling the active zone, the system knows that tag transmissions received are coming from a particular zone, and therefore it can derive the location.

The Three R's— Reading, wRiting, and RFID

chapter

10

in this chapter

- ☑ Dealing with binary data and number systems

- ☑ Learning to use bit-level data storage techniques

- ☑ Building a handheld RFID device

- ☑ Writing data to RFID tags

Many uses of RFID require a reader to identify a unique ID and connect this tag to a database. The database then cross-references that ID with relevant data. But what if the tag needs to be read at two or more locations where access to the same database or data is not possible? That's where read/write tags come in.

Breweries often store their products in barrels and kegs. These barrels and kegs are generic looking, without any product labels or defining characteristics. How does a distribution house know the difference between barrel A and barrel B? Often the barrels are labeled with a barcode, but that doesn't tell the distribution house anything until they access a central database. Sharing data between brewery and distribution house requires a mammoth investment in time and money. First off, both companies need to set up a database server and the network infrastructure to handle the data. Then they need to implement a secure method to allow each other access to only the relevant data, and not the rest of the company network. Using read/write RFID tags would allow relevant data to move with the barrel or keg, and could alleviate the need for shared database access all together. Empty barrels and kegs wouldn't need to be relabeled or retagged when recycled either, the data on the tag could just be updated to indicate "clean empty keg."

Writable tags are available with a variety of data storage systems. They also have different levels of access depending on a feature set. Most tags are open read/write, letting anyone read and write data to the tag. Some tags are write once/read many, allowing data be stored in a specific memory block. Once written, it cannot be overwritten with new data. Still other tags allow as many reads and writes to a specific block until that block is locked. Once locked, the contents can be read, but not updated or overwritten. Some more expensive tags employ crypto-security features, allowing only readers that present the correct key to decrypt and read the data and/or modify it.

Different storage capacities exist as well. Some tags can contain as little as a few bytes, while others allow up to several kilobytes of data to be stored. With constant advances in RFID technology, I'm sure we'll be seeing some form of RFID-based personal storage in the not so distant future, allowing important data to be kept on passive, contactless external storage devices. There are a few hurdles to overcome still, mostly involving security and access speed issues. At this point though, writable tags offer a way to mark changes or provide an autonomous audit trail, allowing relevant data to move with the tag itself rather than rely completely on back-end data sources for everything. Decision-making and business logic could be performed based solely on tag data, without interacting with any central data store. Imagine the money that could be saved by not needing to connect every RFID scan point to a network or data source! Autonomous readers with built-in logic could route packages or stamp dates on crates or boxes, all based on updatable tag data. Once the autonomous unit has completed the task, the tag could then be updated to reflect the change.

In this chapter, you'll be building a handheld RFID reader/writer that reads a tag ID, and then updates the tag's writable memory area with specific data. Your handheld scanner will update the tag as a product ID, allowing the next scanner to know what product is in the barrel.

You'll be using the SkyeTek M1 reader module, first seen in Chapter 7, and shown in Figure 10-1. This reader module is a perfect candidate for a handheld application because it's very small, has an on-board antenna, and can interface directly with TTL serial devices.

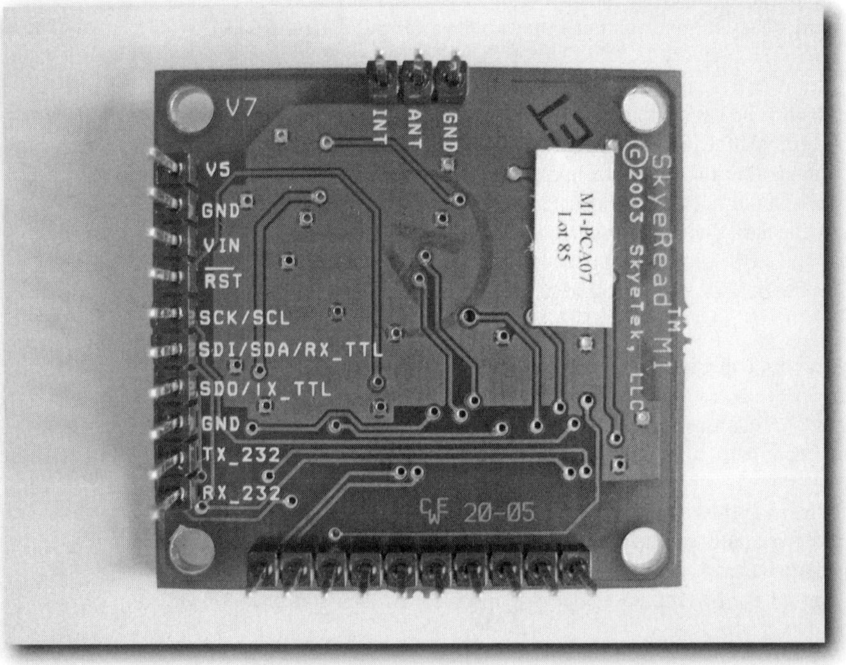

FIGURE 10-1: The SkyeTek M1 reader/writer module

Parts and Tools

You need the following parts for this project:

- SkyeTek M1 RFID reader module
- RSB509B serial buffer IC and 4 MHz crystal kit from www.proteanlogic.com
- Parallax BASIC Stamp 2 (BS2) from www.parallax.com
- A 7805 +5V voltage regulator, Radio Shack part number 276-1770
- A 24-pin IC socket, Radio Shack part number 276-1996
- An 8-pin IC socket, Radio Shack part number 276-1995
- Three 4.7k-ohm resistors (yellow / violet / red color code)
- A 9V battery and battery clip with leads
- A piezoelectric element, Radio Shack part number 273-073
- Plastic project box 4.3" × 2.2" × 0.8" from www.web-tronics.com, part number PB-2P

And you need the following tools:

- Philips screwdriver
- Soldering iron and solder

Working with Data

Before you get into building hardware, I'd like to discuss the data-storage aspect. Since most tags only have enough storage space for a very limited number of bytes, an efficient method for storing data must be thought out and agreed upon by everyone that will be reading or writing to your tags. This common method of making sense of the data that's stored is called a schema.

Data Schema — A Brewery Application

A *schema* defines the structure of data — what data fields exist, where they are placed, how large each field is, and so on. Depending on the type of data that needs to be stored and updated, it might require byte-level or even bit-level data manipulation to effectively store the data required.

Assume you're developing a quality assurance system for a brewery company and a distribution company. Tags affixed to barrels will need to store data on them that give some kind of audit trail that both companies can use, even though they won't be able to access a shared data source.

Both companies have agreed to use ISO-15693 type read/write tags that have four writable memory blocks. As shown in Figure 10-2, each block can store 32 bits (4 bytes), for a total of 16 bytes of storage space per tag.

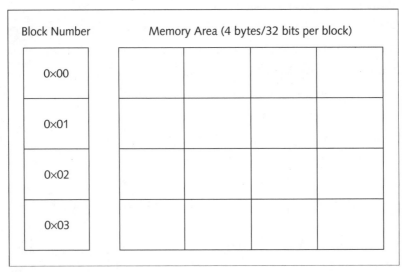

Fɪɢᴜʀᴇ 10-2: Memory block layout

Your job is to build an RFID unit that will scan and update barrels after they are filled with a particular product. You are only allowed to write data to the first memory block (0x00). The other blocks will be reserved for different data used elsewhere in the supply chain. The data you need to convey includes what dispenser station filled the barrel, what product was put into the barrel, and whether the barrel has been sealed or not. To store all that data using only 4 bytes means you'll have to come up with an agreed-upon schema that details what byte values in which positions mean what kind of information.

Byte-Level Data Mapping

A single character stored in a specific place could mean any number of things. When dealing with modern desktop PCs, we're used to thinking of "data" as being a string of characters that we can read and make sense of, much like this sentence you're reading now. If you want to let someone know a barrel has been sealed, you could type the word "sealed" or "done" or any word or set of words you choose to describe the condition "sealed." Communicating information in this way works great for people, but it's very wasteful for computers. This information could be stored as a single character. Using the character Y could mean "yes, this barrel is sealed," while the character N could mean "no, the barrel has not been sealed yet." While Y and N make sense to us humans, it could easily be any two characters. The only thing that matters now is figuring out which byte out of the 4 bytes available represents "sealed" or "not sealed." Figure 10-3 shows a simple schema that accommodates your data-storage requirements.

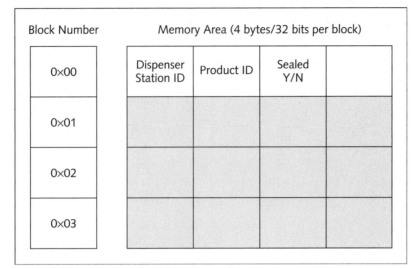

Block Number	Memory Area (4 bytes/32 bits per block)			
0×00	Dispenser Station ID	Product ID	Sealed Y/N	
0×01				
0×02				
0×03				

FIGURE 10-3: Byte positions and their meanings

Now that you know where various pieces of information are supposed to be located, you can easily store the dispenser ID and product ID the same way you stored the sealed status. Because each byte is made up of 8 bits, and 8 bits can represent up to 256 unique combinations, you can store a value between 0 and 255 using a single byte. Let's assume a brewery has 140 different dispensing stations. You can store the value 82 using 8 bits. The 8 bits that represent a value of 82 are 01010010. Now, in the standard ASCII code table used by most microcontrollers and personal computers worldwide, the character R represents those same 8 bits. So, you could easily store the value of 82 on the tag by writing an uppercase R to the first byte in memory block 0.

Note Each character in the ASCII table represents a different set of bits. A decimal value of 82 represents an uppercase R, while a decimal value of 114 represents a lowercase r. For more information on the ASCII table, you can look it up online. Tons of resources online contain the entire ASCII and Extended ASCII tables.

As long as the number of station IDs does not exceed 256, the data schema set up in Figure 10-3 will work just fine. The same process used for station IDs goes for product IDs as well. But what if there are more than 256 products? Well, you could rearrange the data schema to something like Figure 10-4 and use two bytes to represent the product ID.

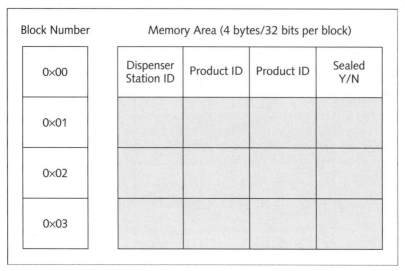

FIGURE 10-4: Two-byte data storage

Using two bytes to store product ID, you could easily combine the values of each byte to store up to 512 different IDs. If you want to store product ID 312, the first byte could represent a value of 255, while the second byte could represent a value of 57. Add those values and you get 312.

Shaking Things Up

Now I'm going to shake things up a bit. What if you had to store up to 65,536 different product IDs? Or what if you were dealing with a small number of dispenser stations and products, but only had one byte of storage space to cram all that data into? My friend, you'll have to dive into sub-byte data manipulation. You'll need to look at data as a collection of bits rather than a collection of bytes or characters.

Bit-Level Data Manipulation

Anyone who has used computers is probably accustomed to byte-level data manipulation. You press the C key on your keyboard and you get a C on the screen. Your single keystroke represents a byte of data, a single character. But in reality, you've actually manipulated 8 bits of data with that keystroke. Change that C to a D and to you, you've only changed a single character. To the computer though, you've changed 8 bits.

Okay, so now you're faced with a brewery that maybe has 6 different dispensing stations and 16 different products. You have one byte to store data in, but you still have to store the station ID, product ID, and whether the barrel is sealed or not. To get a handle on how this can be done at the bit level, you first have to get a basic idea of what bits are and how they work.

Bits, Nibbles, and Bytes

Everyone knows that computers run off 1s and 0s. A single bit can represent only one out of two possible values: 1 or 0. They are the smallest units that make up data. Group 4 bits together and you get a nibble. Group 8 bits together (or two nibbles) and you get a byte. It's kind of like 2 pints to a quart, 4 quarts to a gallon (or like 1000 milliliters to a liter, 10 liters to a deciliter for all you metric folks).

Grouping bits increases the number of unique combinations (or values) that can be represented. A single bit can only represent two different values: 1 or 0. Two bits grouped together can represent four different values based on the simple idea that 2 bits, each with two possible values equals four possible values. This can be represented mathematically with $2 \times 2 = 4$. To get the number of combinations, just multiply by 2 for each bit you're throwing in the group. A nibble or group of 4 bits can store up to 16 different values, as shown by $2 \times 2 \times 2 \times 2 = 16$. You can use a calculator to find out how many combinations a certain number of bits will get you by raising 2 to the power of the number of bits; so 2 to the power of 4 bits, or 2^4, equals 16. If you try 2^8, you'll see it equals 256.

A New Data Schema

To split your byte up into groups of bits, each group with its own significance, you must create a new data schema. The first step in creating a new schema is to assess your needs. You have to store up to 6 different station IDs and 16 different product IDs, and indicate if the barrel has been sealed. Because you only need to communicate two possible states a barrel can be in, sealed or unsealed, a single bit can easily represent this. If the bit value is 0, then the barrel is not sealed. If the bit value is 1, then the barrel is sealed. This is the basic idea behind bit mapping, or assigning specific meaning to individual bits or groups of bits.

If you break a byte down into its 8 bits and look at each bit as a separate entity, you can start to see the usefulness each one has. You can arrange these 8 bits in various sized groups. For instance, you need to store six station IDs. 1 bit will get you two possible values. Two bits will get you four, and 3 bits will get you eight possible values. Therefore, you can group 3 bits to represent any station ID value between 0 and 7.

Note   Keep in mind that 0 is indeed a value that takes up space when stored, just like 1 or 2 or 3. So counting 0, you get eight possible unique values using 3 bits. This is generally referred to as "zero indexing," because you start counting at 0 instead of 1. For example, if you count from 0 up to 255, you've actually counted 256 different values because 0 is the first number counted. If you assign these values to objects like apples, 0 would be the first apple. The apple assigned a value of 255 would actually be the 256th apple in your stockpile of apples.

To represent up to 16 different product IDs, you'll need 4 bits. Figure 10-5 shows these bit arrangements in your new data schema.

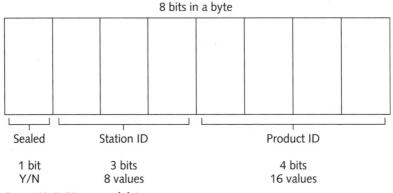

Figure 10-5: Bit-mapped data

Converting to Binary

Assume you have a sealed barrel that was filled at station 5 with product 12. To write that data to the tag, you need to convert each decimal number into binary and place the bits in the correct order based on the agreed-upon schema. Some calculators let you convert numbers between various number systems, making it easy to convert a decimal 12 into a binary 1100, or a decimal 5 into a binary 101.

If you're running a Windows PC, you can use the built-in calculator application to convert these values. When the calculator program starts, it starts in standard mode by default. Click the View menu and select Scientific and you'll see something like Figure 10-6.

Figure 10-6: Scientific calculator view

There should be a lot of new options now, including four different radio buttons in the upper left corner labeled Hex, Dec, Oct, and Bin. Those are number system selectors. The Dec, for decimal, is selected by default. Enter the value **12** into the calculator and simply click Bin to get a binary value.

If you aren't fortunate enough to have a calculator on hand that can do the conversion, you can convert it yourself. I know a couple ways to convert decimal integers to binary, but the easiest way is to simply keep dividing by 2. So, to convert a decimal value of 49 to binary, divide it by 2 and you get 24.5. Because it does not divide evenly, there is a remainder of 0.5, which signifies a binary 1. This 1 goes in the first number column, or the far right side. The binary number will grow right-to-left as you add new numbers. Now drop the remainder and divide 24 by 2, you'll get an even 12, so that's a binary 0, which you add to the left side of your binary number. At this point, your binary number should be 10. Divide 12 by 2 and get 6, which is even. Divide 6 and get 3, another even division. Now when you try to divide 3 by 2, you get 1.5, which means you write down a binary 1. Divide 1 by 2 and you get 0.5, which is both less than 1 and has a remainder, so that is your last division, resulting in a binary 1. Your final binary number should now be 110001, which represents a decimal 49. Figure 10-7 shows this process vertically.

Decimal	Binary
49/2 = 24.5	1
24/2 = 12	0
12/2 = 6	0
6/2 = 3	0
3/2 = 1.5	1
1/2 = 0.5	1
Binary Number: 110001	

FIGURE 10-7: Converting decimal
49 to binary 110001

It's very important to remember columns and number places, and why they are used. Assume you want to store the value 49 as a byte (a full 8 bits of data). Would you store it as 11000100, or 00110001? The answer is 00110001 because 11000100 is a decimal value of 196. Remember to pad your bit spaces with preceding 0s if needed, and not with trailing zeros. Think of it like writing a check to someone—you'd never pad the dollar amount with 0s at the end.

Putting Data into the Schema

To store the fact you have a sealed barrel filled at station ID 5 with product ID 12, you'll need binary values for each piece of data. Because "sealed" can have only two states, yes or no, it can be assumed that yes = binary 1, and no = binary 0. The decimal value 5 is 101 in binary, and decimal 12 is 1100. So put them all together in your schema and you have Figure 10-8.

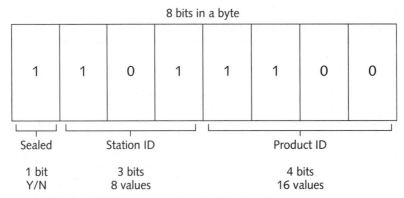

8 bits in a byte

| 1 | 1 | 0 | 1 | 1 | 1 | 0 | 0 |

Sealed   Station ID   Product ID

1 bit   3 bits   4 bits
Y/N   8 values   16 values

FIGURE 10-8: The 8-bit schema populated with relevant data

Converting Back to Decimal

Because most computers and microcontrollers let you work with bytes, not directly with the bits those bytes represent, you'll have to take your bits and combine them to get a byte value. Once you have your byte value, you can do things with it, including write it to an RFID tag memory block location.

Because bytes are represented by decimal values that correspond to characters on the ASCII character table, you'll need to convert the full 8 bits, 11011100 from Figure 10-8, into a decimal number. To convert from binary back to decimal, you can use your calculator or simply reverse the process shown in Figure 10-7. All you do is multiply by 2 and add the binary value as you go. Start on the left side of the binary number, which will always be 1 (leading 0s can be removed from the equation). Multiply that by 2, and then add the next binary value to get your next answer. The next binary value is 1; so your answer will be 3. Now take that and multiply it by 2, then add the next binary value of 0 and you'll be left with 6. Continue down the line until you get to the last binary number and the final answer will be your decimal value, which should be 220. Figure 10-9 shows this process vertically.

Binary Number: 11011100
  0 * 2 + 1 = 1
  1 * 2 + 1 = 3
  3 * 2 + 0 = 6
  6 * 2 + 1 = 13
  13 * 2 + 1 = 27
  27 * 2 + 1 = 55
  55 * 2 + 0 = 110
  110 * 2 + 0 = 220

Decimal Number: 220

FIGURE 10-9: Converting binary
back to decimal

Storing Decimal Values Larger than 255

Okay, so you know the maximum value you can store with 8 bits is 255. Now that you're looking at bits rather than bytes, you can combine bits from more than one byte to store larger numbers. Using 16 bits (2 bytes), you can store values from 0 to 65535. Just add more bits and you can store larger and larger numbers.

The only tricky part is knowing how to handle reading and writing data when your bits cross over byte boundaries. For example, if you want to store the value 3830 it will take at least 12 bits, or about a byte and a half. You could let those extra 4 bits in the second byte just go to waste, or you could use them for some other data. Just keep in mind you'll have to make sure your read and write routines fully read and convert both bytes into binary, process and update the data, and then write both new byte values.

Basically, it comes down to dealing with the differences in how you want to group and deal with data, versus the way the computer system or RFID tag you're working with wants to group and work with data. Case in point, the tag described in the barrel scenario above stores data as single bytes, but only in blocks of four. If the tag and/or reader require all 4 bytes per block to be read or written at a time, then you have to take that into consideration, even if you only want to read and update one bit of one byte in that whole memory block. Likewise, if the data you want to store on the tag is larger, requiring 6 bytes, you will have to add the ability to read two separate memory blocks to get all the data you need, break it all down into binary, and update both memory blocks. Depending on the data access methods and requirements of the equipment you are using, both hardware and software, it can become a pain very quickly. Always consider those other factors when you're designing your data schema, and hopefully you will come up with a schema that works well to organize and categorize the data you're working with, but also works as seamlessly as possible with the equipment that it's being implemented on.

Important Concepts

At this point you should have a basic understanding of data schemas and why they are important. All parties involved in reading from and writing to the tags must agree to a common schema so that everyone understands what data is stored where and what that data means.

Getting to know binary numbers and how to work with bit-level data is also very important. Many read/write RFID applications require storing potentially large amounts of data on a tag with very limited storage capacity. Leveraging the limited data storage capacity of RFID tags to maximize their usefulness in your application will most certainly be a primary design consideration.

The Project

This project shows you how to implement a basic handheld read/write application which will detect a tag, read its ID, and write some data to one of its memory blocks. By getting familiar with the hardware featured in this project, you can expand on the basics shown here to create your own feature-rich read/write solutions, which may or may not even be handheld.

You're going to start building your handheld reader by programming the BASIC Stamp module.

Step 1: Program the BASIC Stamp

The full source code for this project can be downloaded from www.rfidtoys.net.

RFID Read/Write Code

```
' ==========================================================================
'
'   File....... RFID_ReadWrite.BS2
'   Purpose.... RFID Tag Read / Write
'   Author..... Jon Williams -- Parallax, Inc.
'   E-mail..... jwilliams@parallax.com
'   Started....
'   Updated.... 07 FEB 2005
'
' ==========================================================================
'   Updated.... 02 JULY 2005
'   Purpose.... Update code to suit the Read/Write project
'   Author..... Amal Graafstra -- RFID Toys
' ==========================================================================
'
'   {$STAMP BS2}
'   {$PBASIC 2.5}
'
' ==========================================================================
' -----[ Program Description ]-------------------------------------------
'
'   This code issues a SELECT command to the SkyeTek M1 reader module
'   to get a single tag ID. That tag is then written to, storing data
'   in memory block 0.
'
' -----[ Revision History ]---------------------------------------------
'
'   Updated.... 02 JULY 2005
'   Purpose.... Update code to suit the Read/Write project
'   Author..... Amal Graafstra -- RFID Toys
'
```

```
' -----[ I/O Definitions ]--------------------------------------------------

RX              PIN     0                       ' Serial RX from buffer
TX              PIN     1                       ' Serial TX to reader
LED_Status      PIN     2                       ' LED to notify user of status
Buzzer          PIN     8                       ' A buzzer to notify user


' -----[ Constants ]--------------------------------------------------

' -----[ Variables ]--------------------------------------------------

ByteIdx     VAR     Byte                        ' character index in for loop
ByteIn      VAR     Byte                        ' byte var to hold data
ReaderData  VAR     Byte(23)                    ' response buffer from reader

' -----[ EEPROM Data ]--------------------------------------------------


' -----[ Initialization ]--------------------------------------------------

  'show some activity
  HIGH LED_Status

  'configure buffer. Put into config mode with 10ms pulse
  HIGH RX
  PAUSE 10
  INPUT RX
  'output address configuration byte
  SEROUT RX, 49236, [" "] 'empty space is just a placeholder
  'output bitmap configuration
  SEROUT RX, 49236, [%00000000]
  ' wait for RSB509B to reset
  PAUSE 100

Reset:
  ByteIdx=0
  GOSUB DrainBuffer
  LOW LED_Status

' -----[ Program Code ]--------------------------------------------------

Main:
  'Step by step:
  '- First, query for RFID tags. If tag found, proceed. If no tag found,
  'then loop back and check again. The code stores the entire response
  'from the reader, which includes not only tag ID but also the tag type,
  'which is needed to issue a write command.
  '
  '94 = no tags in field
  '
```

Continued

RFID Read/Write Code *(continued)*

```
'- Next, send write command to SkyeTek module to write new data to tag.
'This code will write to block 00 and only write one block worth of data,
'but you can modify it to write to whatever block you want. The data
'written to the tag is simply a well chosen 4 letter word. You could
'update it to write relevant data, you know, if you want.
'
'Possible responses to write command:
'44 = success
'88 = error
'C4 = failed (no tag matching ID given)

'query reader for a tag
SEROUT TX, 84, [13, "001400" ,13]

'pause a bit so full response from reader can enter buffer
PAUSE 50

'get bytes from buffer
GOSUB GetBufferData
HIGH LED_Status

ProcessTagData:
  'check byte 1 for <> LF or byte 4 for CR
  IF ReaderData(0)<>10 OR ReaderData(3)=13 THEN Reset 'no tag found

  'assume tag found. issue WRITE command to write data to the tag.
  'start by sending write command and flags to reader
  SEROUT TX, 84, [13, "4044"]

  'output tag type and tag ID data from buffer to reader
  FOR ByteIdx = 3 TO 20
    'send tag ID character to reader
    SEROUT TX, 84, [ReaderData(ByteIdx)]
  NEXT

  'now that we've output the tag data, drain the hardware
  'buffer (just in case) and init vars
  GOSUB DrainBuffer

  'send block number and number of blocks to write, then send data.
  'write to block 00, and only write 01 block worth of data (4 bytes).
  'Each byte of data is sent TO the reader as two bytes which represent
  'the hex value of the data to store. For example, to store the capital
  'letter U, send "55", which is hex for ASCII code 85, which is U. So,
  'to send 4 bytes of data, 8 characters that represent the hex codes of the
  'data to store will be sent to the reader. Make sense? I don't blame you
  'if you're a little confused but hopefully after reading the SkyeTek M1
  'protocol documentation a bit more a light will come on.
```

```
'send block number to write to (00) and number of blocks to write (01)
SEROUT TX, 84, ["0001"]

'The data being written is "Amal", so the characters being sent are 416D616C

'send the data to be written and end of request character (13)
SEROUT TX, 84, ["416D616C", 13]

'wait for response from reader to fill buffer
PAUSE 50

'get bytes from hardware buffer
GOSUB GetBufferData

'process data from buffer
'possible response data:
'44 = success
'88 = general error
'86 = tag is not writable
'C4 = no tag with that ID in field

'check response from reader
IF ReaderData(1)="4" AND ReaderData(2)="4" THEN Successful_Write

'there was a problem of some kind, so flash LED and do buzzer
FOR ByteIdx=0 TO 3
  HIGH LED_Status
  FREQOUT Buzzer, 150, 3000 'adjust frequency to match buzzer rating
  LOW LED_Status
  FREQOUT Buzzer, 150, 1500 'adjust frequency to match buzzer rating
NEXT

GOTO Reset 'if response is anything else, assume error and forget it.

Successful_Write:
  'now all that needs to be done is buzz the buzzer a bit
  FREQOUT Buzzer, 250, 3000 'adjust frequency to match buzzer rating
  PAUSE 750
  LOW LED_Status
  'nothing more to do, stop processing until next power up
  END

'------------------------- SUB ROUTINES -------------------------
'DrainBuffer is meant to drain any remaining characters from the
'hardware buffer.
DrainBuffer:
  HIGH RX
  SERIN RX, 16468, 100, BufferDrained, [ByteIn]
  GOTO DrainBuffer
```

Continued

RFID Read/Write Code

```
BufferDrained:
  'clear byte array value
  FOR ByteIdx=0 TO 23
    ReaderData(ByteIdx)=0
  NEXT
  'reset index and data vars
  ByteIn=0
  ByteIdx=0
  RETURN 'return to caller

'GetBufferData is used to pull data from the hardware buffer a byte
'at a time and store it in a byte array for processing later.
GetBufferData:
  HIGH RX 'signal hardware buffer to dump a byte
  SERIN RX, 16468, 100, GBDReturn, [ByteIn]
  'check to make sure we're not reading too much data for byte array
  IF ByteIdx>23 THEN GBDReturn
  'add byte to byte array
  ReaderData(ByteIdx)=ByteIn
  'increase index var value
  ByteIdx=ByteIdx+1
  'get next byte from hardware buffer
  GOTO GetBufferData
GBDReturn:
  RETURN 'return to caller
```

Step 2: Prepare the Project Box

The plastic box chosen for this project leaves very little room for extra space. You might consider using a slightly larger box if you don't want to spend a lot of time and effort cramming components together. The reason I chose this box is that it's a good size for handheld applications.

You need to drill only two holes in the box. The first one is for an LED light and the second is for a momentary push button. Pick up the box and figure out where you'd like to put both the LED light and push button. The button will activate the reader, so you'll have to hold the button down a few seconds while the reader does its thing. Once you've found the right places, drill away and mount the switch and LED. I used an LED casing, so my drill hole had to be a little larger than normal. Figure 10-10 shows the button and LED leads and Figure 10-11 shows their placement a little better.

FIGURE 10-10: LED and momentary push button leads

FIGURE 10-11: Button and LED placement

Figure 10-12 shows how the project box fits in my hand, and how the button is placed just right for my thumb to press it.

FIGURE 10-12: Pressing the button

Unless you want to add an elastic hand-strap to the back of the project box cover, you're done. If you do want to add an elastic strap, you might consider one that you'll glue to the back of the project box cover, or one that goes all the way around it. Don't try to cut holes in the project box cover and thread the elastic through the holes because there's absolutely no room in the project box for anything extra.

If you used a larger project box however, then a threaded elastic strap may be required as holding the box might be difficult.

Step 3: Prepare the Microprocessor

For this project I'm back to using my old favorite, the Parallax BASIC Stamp 2 microprocessor. It will be the brains behind the reader/writer, getting tag data from the reader and instructing the reader what to write to the tag's memory block.

There are going to be several components on this tiny little board, so make sure you get things as tight as possible without causing possible shorts. I left a few spaces between components to photograph them more easily, but not much. Figure 10-13 should give you a good idea of how these components are connected.

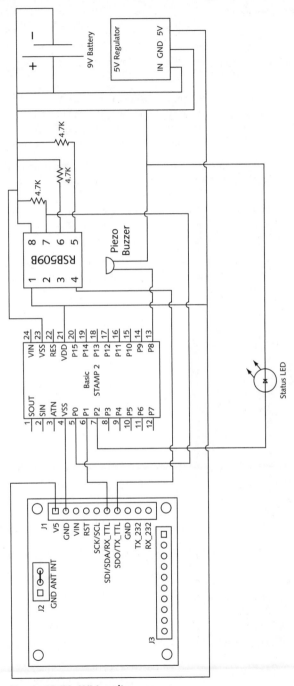

FIGURE 10-13: Wiring diagram

Computing Power and 5V Power

The first thing you'll probably want to put on the board is the microcontroller and 5V regulator. Find a place for your IC socket and solder it in place. Once the socket is in place, you can insert your Stamp microprocessor. Solder the 5V regulator and bend it down so it's not sticking up.

Get your battery clip and solder the leads to the voltage regulator. I do it this way for testing: cut the positive lead later, and solder both cut ends to the pushbutton switch leads. You might not have enough wire length for that in your project box, so you can just solder the positive lead from the battery clip to one of the pushbutton switch leads, and then solder another length of wire to the other pushbutton switch lead that's long enough to get back to the voltage regulator.

Solder a jumper wire from the ground on the 5V regulator to VSS (pin 4) on the Stamp. Then solder another wire from the +5V output of the regulator to VDD (pin 21) on the Stamp. The VDD pin is different from VIN (pin 24) because VDD requires a regulated 5V power source. I figured that as long as I had a nice voltage regulator available, I might as well use it for the Stamp as well. Alternately, you could solder a jumper wire from the input wire on the voltage regulator to VIN (pin 24) on the Stamp and use the Stamp's internal voltage regulator.

When you're finished, you should have something that looks like Figure 10-14. I took the liberty of soldering another jumper wire to the 5V output on the regulator in prep for the next component, so that's what that extra wire is for.

FIGURE 10-14: BASIC Stamp, voltage regulator, and 9V battery clip

The Hardware Serial Data Buffer

Sometimes when working with Stamp microprocessors and high-speed serial data, communications errors occur that software tweaks alone cannot overcome. The Stamp does not have a true serial transceiver. It emulates one using its own internal software and the processor's own computing power. Data rates above 2400 baud sometimes cause problems, especially when trying to receive using the Stamp. The problem is particularly acute when dealing with a cause-and-effect situation.

For example, the SkyeTek reader communicates at 9600 baud. To get a tag ID, you have to issue a serial command and the M1 module will immediately return data. The code running on the Stamp must issue a SEROUT command to send RFID command data to the reader module, and then switch over and process a SERIN command to receive the data coming back from the reader. Many times the data is already on its way by the time the Stamp is ready to listen for it. Because the Stamp's design does not include a serial data buffer, that data is either lost or the data received is garbled because the serial bit timing is off.

Even though you used a SkyeTek module and Stamp together before in Chapter 6, the commands used told the module to look for a specific tag ID. That meant the module had to process a number of things, causing enough delay time for the Stamp to be ready to receive data when the module finally replied. In this project, the commands issued to the reader don't take that long to process so the reader responds immediately. The Stamp will usually miss this data or receive a garbled mess.

To resolve the problem, you can use a cheap and easy hardware buffer from www.protean logic.com. The RSB509B can buffer up to 32 bytes of data and hold it in the buffer until the power goes out. It can even ignore data until a matched byte is received, much like the Stamp's SERIN WAIT command.

Go ahead and solder in an 8 pin IC socket to the board and insert the buffer. Now you should have something like Figure 10-15.

The buffer requires a 4 MHz crystal or resonator and a couple 15 pF capacitors, which can be ordered with the buffer as a crystal kit, There are no polarity issues with the crystal or capacitors, so just solder the crystal leads to pins 2 and 3 on the buffer IC. Then solder one of the leads from both capacitors to a ground. Solder one lead of one of the capacitors to pin 2 on the buffer IC. Solder the other lead from the other capacitor to pin 4. Figure 10-16 shows what this should look like.

FIGURE 10-15: An IC socket and RSB509B hardware serial buffer

FIGURE 10-16: 4 MHz crystal and 15 pF capacitors

Solder a jumper wire from the 5V output on the regulator to pin 1 on the buffer IC. Now you need to connect a few 4.7K resistors to pins 5, 6, and 7. Solder one lead from each of the resistors to each pin. Take all the other leads from those resistors and solder them to pin 8, and then solder a jumper wire from pin 8 to ground. Depending on your style, you might end up with something like Figure 10-17.

FIGURE 10-17: Three 4.7K resistors and ground wire

If you want audio notifications, grab a piezoelectric buzzer and solder it to the board. Some buzzers have polarity, while some don't. Solder one lead to ground, and the other lead to pin 13 on the Stamp (I/O pin 8).

Now it's time to connect the hardware buffer to the Stamp. Solder a jumper wire from pin 8 on the buffer IC to pin 5 on the Stamp (I/O pin 0). You might have something that looks like Figure 10-18 by now.

FIGURE 10-18: Buzzer and buffer IC connected to the Stamp

Step 4: Connect the SkyeTek M1 Module

With your Stamp-based control board done, it's time to connect the RFID reader module. For this application, you'll be using the built-in antenna on the SkyeTek module. For most tags, it has a good 3"– 4" range, which is plenty for this handheld application.

You'll want to jumper the ANT and INT pins on the J2 block. That connects the internal antenna to the signal driver. Figure 10-19 shows the two pins connected with an actual header jumper, but you'll probably be using a short piece of wire.

Note   The M1 module shown in the following figures has headers soldered in place, but you don't need to use headers. You can simply solder lead wires directly to the through-holes.

FIGURE 10-19: The ANT and INT pins jumpered on the M1 module

With the internal antenna connected, now you need to wire the module up for power and communications. Solder a jumper wire from the V5 pin on the M1 module (pin 1 on the J1 block) to the 5V output on the control board regulator. Since you'll be using a shared ground, you can solder another wire from either the power ground or communications ground on the M1's J1 block (pin 2 or pin 8) to the ground on the control board.

Now that power connections are done, solder a jumper wire from the M1's RX_TTL pin (pin 6 on J1 block) to pin 6 on the Stamp (I/O pin 1). Solder a jumper wire from pin 4 on the hardware buffer IC to the M1's TX_TTL pin (pin 7 on J1 block). When you're done, you should have something like Figure 10-20.

FIGURE 10-20: SkyeTek M1 module connected to control board

Step 5: Fit It All In

At this point you should have a functioning reader/writer. You can connect the battery, place a tag within range, and listen for audio queues from the buzzer to know if it's working or not. A successful read/write will result in a short beep. A successful read but a failed write (the tag does not support write or some other write error occurred) will result in a high-low oscillation that sounds like any typical alarm.

Silence means something more serious is wrong. You can connect an LED to ground and pin 7 on the Stamp (I/O pin 2) to get a visual status of what's going on. If the LED is blinking, then at least you're Stamp is functioning. Place a tag over the reader and see if the flashing changes pace or stops. If so, then at least you know there is some kind of communication going on between the reader and Stamp. If the flashing doesn't change at all, then you've probably got a communications issue between Stamp and reader.

Once you have a successful read/write, then you'll need to connect the LED and pushbutton switch already mounted in the project box to your circuit. Solder the LED to ground and pin 7 on the Stamp (I/O pin 2), keeping in mind the proper polarity. Either cut the positive lead between the battery clip and voltage regulator and solder the cut ends to the pushbutton switch leads, or if you already have a lead wire from the switch, solder it to the voltage input pin of the regulator.

With everything connected, it's now time to start squeezing it all into the project box. You can use a pair of cutters to trim every spare millimeter of circuit board off the control board. Don't try to trim the M1 module — there's no way to trim it without cutting the internal antenna loop that makes its way around the board's perimeter. I was able to place a small piece of plastic between the M1 module and stamp control board, and then sandwich the two boards on top of each other.

Figure 10-21 shows the boards on top of each other. Notice there is plenty of room around the boards to cram extra wire into, which is important because the 9V battery just barely fits perfectly in the casing. You can't even have a wire on top of it, or the project box cover won't fit.

Note   You might want to press the pushbutton to test the circuit one final time before gluing things and securing your project box.

FIGURE 10-21: The M1 module and control board sandwiched together

Make sure you secure the boards in place using a tiny dab of hot glue. That way they won't move around inside the box and possibly short out on the pushbutton switch leads. You could also insulate the switch and LED leads if you wanted to.

Close It and Test It

Put the back cover on your project box and give it a test run. Figure 10-22 shows the pushbutton in action with LED lit up.

FIGURE 10-22: Handheld reader/writer in action

Hold your reader over a writable tag and press the button as shown in Figure 10-23. The tag ID will be read and the memory block data will be updated, all in only second or two. You should hear a single beep tone and see the LED go solid for a second, then go dark. Upon a successful write, the Stamp stops processing tags.

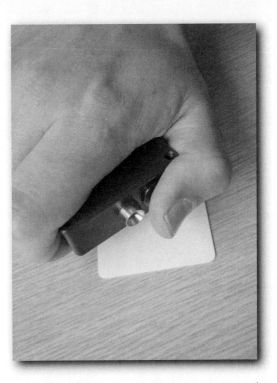

FIGURE 10-23: Hold your reader/writer over a tag and press the button

Battery Life

Because a typical 9V battery has a 500 mAh rating, your handheld reader/writer will function for about 2 hours of constant use. You can calculate this by knowing the power consumption of your components. The BASIC Stamp 2 consumes about 10 mA (worst case) of power when operating. The buffer IC consumes a lot less, but your big power hog is the M1 reader module. It requires around 230 mA when actively reading or writing tags. Just divide 500 mAh by about 250 mA consumption and you get 2 hours. Because the components are only powered when you push the button, you can figure out what the approximate battery life is.

Suppose you could replace the 9V battery with a rechargeable 9V battery pack of about the same physical size. Add some external charge connections to the project box and maybe build a little charge cradle for it. With that setup, an 8-hour workday on a single charge would be ideal. All you have to do is figure out how many tags you could read/write in an 8-hour day, based on the 2-hour limit. If a tag takes 2–5 seconds to read and write to, then just divide 2 hours by 5 seconds (worst case) and you get 1440 tags. Now divide 8 hours by 1440 and you'll see you could read a tag every 20 seconds and still be able to get in a full 8-hour day.

If you need more battery life, you could get a larger project box and use four standard AA cells. A typical AA cell has about a 1.5-volt, 2000-mAh rating, so you could combine four AA cells in series to get 6-volt, 2000-mAh battery pack. Rechargeable AA cells typically have 1.2, 600-mAh ratings. Rechargeable cells have less staying power than alkaline cells do, but they also only get you only 4.8 volts when combined in series, which is not enough to power your components.

Keep in mind, actual battery capacity will always depend on use, ambient temperature, power drain, and manufacturer's specs.

Summing Up

This chapter has covered a few important concepts. This section reviews those concepts just to make sure you have a firm grasp on what you've done here.

Data Schema

One concept covered in this chapter is the design and implementation of a shared data schema. Generally a read/write tag solution is created to address data sharing issues between two or more separate parties where shared access to centralized data is not possible or practical. An agreed-upon schema allows all parties involved to understand the format and organization of data stored on the tag as well as assign agreed-upon write permissions that specify who can write what data to which locations. That way the various parties involved won't be writing over important data.

Binary Data

Most RFID tags contain a very limited amount of data storage capacity. Being able to break data down and store it at the bit level enables you to minimize wasted storage space, efficiently leveraging every single bit available. Understanding binary numbers and how they work within computer systems is key to utilizing this method of data storage and manipulation. If you are interested in learning more about number systems and how they are used, there are numerous resources online that discuss binary and other number systems in great detail.

RFID Read/Write Devices

RFID devices don't have to be portable to be highly effective when used to read and write data to tags. For example, they can be in a fixed location along a production line, making business logic decisions based on the data read from the tag and updating tags as they pass by.

Building a handheld RFID read/write device shows the versatility of RFID in the field by allowing field workers to leverage the technology without being bound to a PC. The concept is the same when dealing with fixed readers, although you can connect a fixed reader to a PC rather than a microprocessor and use more features since the PC may have access to a private and/or shared company database.

All in all, tags with writable storage space can be quite useful in many situations. Hopefully, this chapter gave you a handle of the concepts involved so you can leverage your own creative read/write solutions.

Extreme RFID

What does "extreme" really mean? It's a very subjective term. What might be extreme to one person could be considered normal or even boring to another. In this chapter, I'm going to cover some interesting uses for RFID, which are being implemented by creative types everywhere, as well as some additional projects you can build using RFID technology.

Home Automation

As you saw in Chapters 8 and 9, you can use the Wavetrend active RFID reader with a software package called HomeSeer. This software package is meant for "smart home" automation projects. The software package can interface with many different types of sensory and control mechanisms, including the infamous X10 home control system, which communicates over your home's power wiring to switch on and off different modules.

Interfacing with X10

There are a few different modular home automation technologies out there like X10, however X10 is arguably the oldest and most well known. Even the Parallax BASIC Stamp microprocessors natively support the X10 communication protocol. You could interface an RFID reader directly to a BASIC Stamp, and then interface that Stamp to the home AC power wiring (with appropriate components between) and control X10 modules based on RFID events without a host PC.

In the case of the Wavetrend hardware, you'll need to use the HomeSeer and iAutomate RFID plug-in to be able to interface with the reader. That's all right though, HomeSeer makes taking event-based action as easy as pie. You just need to get your PC to interface with the X10 system. Figure 11-1 shows an X10 CM11A ActiveHome interface module. It plugs into a three-prong (grounded) AC socket and interfaces with your PC through an RS232 serial port.

FIGURE 11-1: An X10 CM11A interface module

Note You can even download an X10 CM11A ActiveX component directly from `www.homeseer`
`.com` that will let you integrate X10 functionality into your own software programs, outside of
the HomeSeer architecture.

There is also an X10 CM15A unit, shown in Figure 11-2, that supports a USB connection to
your PC. However, support for this unit in HomeSeer is lacking. The HomeSeer site does sell
a SmartHome PowerLinc USB X10 Interface (SH1132U) for use with HomeSeer.

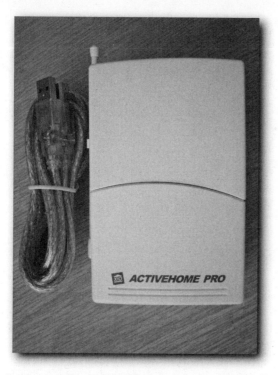

FIGURE 11-2: The X10 CM15A interface module with USB support

X10 Control Modules

There are a few different X10 control modules that you can use to switch devices on and off. There are lighting control modules that also support dimming regular incandescent lights. You can see all these different modules at www.x10.com, but I want to make mention of a couple special ones. Figure 11-3 shows a DC switch module that you can use for controlling DC voltage devices like electronic blinds or gate locks or anything you can think of. It can handle up to 5 amps at 24 volts.

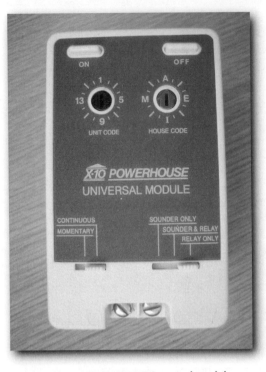

FIGURE 11-3: An X10 UM506 DC control module

It's an X10 controlled relay, but also includes a switch and buzzer that lets you choose between relay, buzzer-and-relay, or buzzer-only action. Another switch lets you set the relay to only close for a moment, or close continuously. The momentary option keeps the contacts closed for about 2 seconds each time the ON code is sent to the unit. If the switch is set for continuous, you'll need to send the OFF code to open the contacts and break the circuit.

Another interesting control module is the X10 XPFM fixture module, shown in Figure 11-4. It goes in-line with appliances like ceiling fans and heaters (up to 15 amps). You can easily wire this unit inside the wall if you need to. If you want to use this type of module with incandescent lighting, you can use the XPDM module that supports dimming.

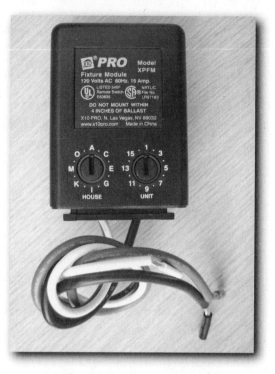

FIGURE 11-4: The XPFM in-line control module

What Others Are Doing

RFID is a popular technology that has finally made it past big business. People are integrating RFID into their own projects and solutions. New businesses and products based on RFID technology are cropping up everywhere. It's an exciting time for RFID.

The power to identify an object without touching it, looking at it, or even repositioning it or disturbing it in any way has sparked the imaginations, as well as fears, of people the world over.

Spime

Spime is a term coined by Bruce Sterling, an accomplished science fiction author, at the 2004 SIGGRAPH conference in Los Angeles.

Spime is a neologism used to name an object which can be identified both in space and time, hence Spime. The concept is that every object made — like plates, cups, forks, earrings, purses, airplanes, televisions and the like — be tagged using RFID, enabling the Spime to be tracked both in space (its location) and time (when it was detected at that location). While this might seem somewhat Orwellian to many, the entirety of his idea makes a lot of sense. The full article is located at www.boingboing.net/images/blobjects.htm, but here's a short excerpt from it:

Scenario: You buy a Spime with a credit card. Your account info is embedded in the transaction, including a special email address set up for your Spimes. After the purchase, a link is sent to you with customer support, relevant product data, history of ownership, geographies, manufacturing origins, ingredients, recipes for customization, and bluebook value. The spime is able to update its data in your database (via radio-frequency ID), to inform you of required service calls, with appropriate links to service centers. This removes guesswork and streamlines recycling.

Like everything in this world, there are pros and cons associated with the idea of Spime. The data matrix that Spime would create could be used for positive purposes, as well as negative purposes.

Producing Spime

Interdisciplinary artist Meghan Trainor (www.meghantrainor.com) has expanded the Spime concept into a reality by embedding RFID tags into the objects of her "With Hidden Numbers" project. Her overall goal is to study the social dynamics of technology within society. She is currently focused on exploring the use of communications networks, databases, and RFID to envision and study the diverse ways these technologies are modified and adopted throughout society.

Each of the items shown in Figure 11-5 contains an RFID tag, which can be used to identify each object in space and time, provided the technological infrastructure and social conditions were in place to do so. Figure 11-6 is closer up, showing the actual RFID tag embedded within one of the objects.

FIGURE 11-5: Various Spimes created by Meghan Trainor

FIGURE 11-6: Close-up of a Spime showing an embedded tag

Interactive Art

Meghan has also used RFID technology as action items in her interactive artwork. One such art piece used Spime objects to invoke audio clips played when a Spime passed through an area. The identification of a Spime also animated a sculpture in a remote location, directly linking motion of an object with the presence of a Spime in a different location.

There are also many artists whose pieces commonly portray RFID as a tool of privacy invasion or indentured servitude used by large corporations as well as others in the society itself. If RFID is to have a place in society, which does not compromise the integrity and security of its members, both supporters and opponents of RFID play an important role in its evolution and acceptance.

Becoming Spime: Implantable RFID Tags

Admittedly, I'm taking this Spime thing a bit far, but I think the concept still applies. Only recently has the FDA approved the VeriChip for human implantation. As of this writing, I think the VeriChip is the only RFID tag approved to be implanted into people. However, there have been implantable tags around for many years, which are put into cats, dogs, livestock, fish, and other various animals for the purpose of tracking and identification. Most implantable tags sold commercially use proprietary chips that require expensive proprietary reader devices, much like the ones shown in Figure 11-7.

FIGURE 11-7: Avid proprietary injectable RFID implant and reader for pets

Animals have been chipped for years now. Unlike pet tags that can easily fall off, become detached accidentally, or purposely removed, an implant chip has little chance of being separated from the pet in question. Tagging wild animals with active RFID transponders allows researchers to easily monitor the animals' movements as they roam their native habitats. Implanting wild animals with passive tags is generally not done, but it's very common practice for livestock and other controlled animal populations.

I have two RFID tags implanted in my own body, one in each hand. For me, the point and purpose of implanting tags into my hands revolves around one thing: access control. I'm the guy you always see searching high and low for his keys, only to find they are locked in my house or my car. Basically, I want to leverage RFID technology without shackling myself with another "key" I can lose or forget to bring. I've personally implemented quite a few of the projects featured in this book, particularly the front door project, the vehicle access project, the computer login project, and the fire-safe project in Chapters 2–5. I can use my hand implants with all of these implementations.

Figure 11-8 shows a few different sizes of implantable tags. The larger the tag, usually the more range can be had when used with appropriately sized reader antennas.

Caution Many glass tags are not meant for any kind of implantation, animal or human. They are meant to be embedded into other products or used in liquid environments. These tags may also contain heavy metals such as lead and might be encased in non-implant grade glass, which could be fragile and more prone to breakage than implantable tags.

FIGURE 11-8: 4×30mm, 3×13mm, and 2×12mm glass tags

My Left Hand

My left hand contains a very simple EM4102 125 KHz tag with a unique ID. The EM4102 chip and its antenna are encased in a glass cylinder 13mm long by 3mm in diameter. You can get them 2mm by 12mm, or even as large as 4mm by 30mm, but I wouldn't recommend implanting something that large and prone to breaking in your body.

The only advantage for getting a larger tag is a slightly increased read range. You can generally get 1" from a small tag and maybe 3"–6" from one of those monster tags. However, there are special 125 KHz passive readers out there that can get read ranges over one foot with even the smallest implantable tag. They cost quite a bit, but in some situations, the cost might be worth it.

EM4102 tags are very common, which many 125 KHz readers support. These tags also work with the Phidgets reader used in some of the projects in this book.

This implant was put in by a cosmetic surgeon using a scalpel. After soaking the tag in a disinfectant and cleaning the implant site, the surgeon cut a very small incision into my skin and slid the tag in-between the dermal layer and the tissue underneath. The process was painless due to a small amount of local anesthesia and I healed in a few days. Figure 11-9 shows the implant site only a couple days after the procedure.

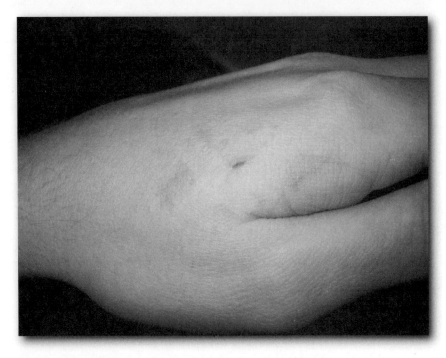

FIGURE 11-9: Tiny cut from scalpel on my still iodine-stained hand

My Right Hand

My right hand contains a 2mm-by-12mm glass Philips HITAG S 2048 134 KHz tag that supports data storage, anti-collision, and crypto-security features. I can store data on the tag, and I can hide that data so it's only accessible if the reader provides the correct passcode. The encryption isn't that great, but it's enough to fend off any momentary attack someone could launch against you while within the 2" range this implant has.

Many glass tags you might find are not designed for implantation at all, into humans or animals. These glass tags are commonly called ampoule tags, which are meant to be used in liquid environments or for embedding into various materials. The 125 KHz radio spectrum these tags use will most often work through liquid and some metal interference, and that's why you don't often see high-frequency glass tags. High frequencies don't generally work well through liquid or metal.

A family doctor performed this implant using an injection needle like the one shown in Figure 11-10. The process was even quicker with less recovery time than my left-hand implant procedure. Many family doctors who are used to implanting time-release birth control implants will be right at home doing this sort of procedure.

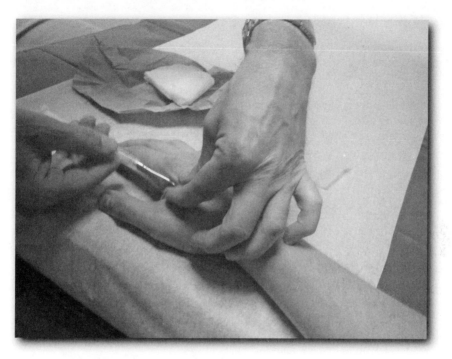

FIGURE 11-10: Injecting the Philips HITAG S tag

Removal and Replacement

If I ever want to remove the tag, I can easily get it removed or even replaced with a different one. A small cut with a scalpel and it would slide right out. If I wanted to replace it, a small cavity would be left, in which a different tag could be easily placed. Otherwise the cavity would close up, just like a pierced earlobe does if you don't keep something in it.

Caution

If you are looking to get a tag implanted somewhere in your body, make sure the tag is not coated with anything. Some glass tags are coated with a material that gives them a translucent look and a slightly rough feel. The coating is porous anti-migration material and is designed to allow flesh to grow into it, locking the implant in place. Migration of a non-coated tag is usually very minimal, so this coating is typically used on tags meant for animal implantation where the implant site cannot be monitored during the healing process. If you ever wanted to or needed to remove one of these coated tags from your own body, you'd be in for a world of hurt—it involves a lot of cutting with a scalpel and is difficult and painful, leaving a lot of scar tissue.

VeriChip Implant

If you fancy getting an implant, you might consider the FDA-approved VeriChip. They are injected into the arm only by doctors certified by VeriChip Corporation to do the procedure. On the plus side, it's approved by the FDA and many doctors are certified. The chip is also an active chip, which contains a power source inside the chip. Active and semi-active chips have much greater range because transmission of information is powered by the internal battery of the tag. Active chips constantly transmit their information, making it possible for event-driven actions to take place rather than having the reader constantly poll for tag presence.

On the down side, the chip is proprietary. If you want to use the VeriChip, you'll have to buy an expensive reader and hack it up for your own uses, or if you have the capability, hack together your own reader. Because the chip contains a power source, it has a finite lifespan, which could be seen as a good or a bad thing depending on how you look at it. Probably the biggest downside to this chip is when you get the implant, your chip ID is linked to VeriChip Corp's global database.

Better than a Toe-tag — RFID for the Dead

Universities such as UCLA are considering using RFID tags hidden inside cadavers to help curb theft. While I don't personally see any good reason to steal dead bodies, I guess they can be sold whole, or in parts, on the black market. The idea is that the tags will be hidden in various places, so it would take quite a lot of digging to find and remove the tag, hence rendering the product worthless to the would-be thief.

Either active or passive tags could be used. Active tags could report the cadaver's presences within authorized rooms. Removal of the cadaver would mean the ID no longer shows up on the real-time inventory and an alarm would be triggered. Semi-active or passive tags could be used with doorway readers that would log the cadaver's movement through the doorway, triggering an alarm if the body was not scheduled to be removed from storage.

During the aftermath of Hurricane Katrina, officials implanted corpses with VeriChip tags in order to speed the process of identification and information exchange with families. The Lafayette County Medical Examiner's office said it would stock RFID chips and scanners for future disaster relief. At the time of this writing, the entire state of Louisiana is currently planning to implement the system to help officials cope with the estimated 500 unidentified bodies in the state. If they don't exist already, it probably won't be long before traditional toe-tags become RFID enabled labels, allowing morgues and other non-disaster-related cadaver management facilities to benefit from RFID without the somewhat gruesome aspect of actually implanting anything.

Other Implant Resources

Slowly, various online communities are forming that connect people who have RFID implants, who are looking to get an implant, or who are just curious about it. Chris Rigby of New Zealand set up one such community, which is simply called "tagged." The URL for this online forum is http://tagged.kaos.gen.nz. There you can ask questions and find resources for various OEM readers, sources of tags, project ideas, software packages, and so on.

Creative Uses for RFID

There are several uses for RFID that make complete sense but are quite innovative. Florida expressway officials have implemented one such innovation. Cars there use in-vehicle RFID tags to pay for tolls as they drive through. Drivers expect the RFID tag to be used for that purpose alone. But, in an effort to automate commuter traffic reports, the traffic authority has taken to installing road-side readers every half-mile or so along both toll and non-toll state highways to pick up vehicle travel times. One might ask, "What's to stop them from using travel times to detect speeders, or to report more accurate real-time locations of individual vehicles, or to compile travel histories for specific vehicles?" The fact is, nothing is stopping them from doing so.

The company that makes the technology states that privacy concerns are not an issue because the unique IDs reported to the traffic server are deleted once travel time has been computed. While that might be true now, that is a software feature on the server and a simple change to the way the software works could easily be implemented. What if the FBI wants a real-time location on your vehicle? I'm sure they could get it. What if the average speed calculated was over the legal limit for that stretch of highway? Would the unique ID be thrown out, or would it be flagged for further logging while an automated ticket was printed and mailed to the vehicle's registered owner as is done with speed-trap cameras?

Other states, such as California and Colorado, are considering systems like this. In my opinion, this creative use of RFID technology crosses the privacy line because the 1 million plus drivers in Florida who linked their personal information to those in-vehicle RFID transponder IDs never directly agreed to allow those transponders to be used for anything but toll payment at specified tollways, and certainly not for use on non-tollways. This is a perfect example of how RFID acceptance needs to be tempered by alert consumers as the infrastructure supporting its use grows.

Chipping Chips

Casinos are now tagging poker chips so they can be tracked both on the tables and in the cashier's office. Security teams can more easily monitor the betting table and detect if bets are placed after wave-off, or if chips are being stolen right out from under a player. Casino owners and managers can get a real-time view of how many dollars are resting on betting tables throughout the facility. Inside the cashier's office, chips can be tracked and automatically counted using RFID technology. I think it's just a matter of time before cash itself will have embedded RFID tags that report back the bill's printed serial number and perhaps the face value, making cash counting as simple as waving a magic wand over the stack.

RFID Used for Positioning Systems

The Port of Singapore has embedded thousands of RFID tags into the asphalt, beams, and flooring all over the shipping yard, creating a multidimensional grid. A centralized system manages the placement and location of containers as they are offloaded and ferried around the shipyard. The forklifts, trucks, cranes, and other moving equipment report container information, as well as the grid tag IDs surrounding them. This allows the system to track a container based on X, Y, Z coordinates anywhere in the shipping yard.

A U.S. observatory found a way to use 36 disc tags positioned around the observation dome as part of their rotation system. By using a Phidgets USB reader, the observatory was able to receive rotation and position data based on which tag ID was read by the reader as the dome rotated.

Binding Physical Mediums to Relational Data

Another Phidgets-related story comes out of the GroupLab department of the University of Calgary, the birthplace of Phidgets devices. Created by Tony Tang and Eric Pattison, DartMail ties tag IDs to content in a database and stored on a file server. The tag is scanned at a DartMail station and a message and/or files are attached to that tag. The message and attached files are then stored in a central database much like a typical e-mail server. The tag is affixed to a rubber dart and shot out of a dart gun toward the intended recipient. When that person removes the dart from their forehead and scans the tag, the message and/or files are retrieved from the server and displayed for them. It's a simple yet effective example of how digital data can be attached to a physical medium and exchanged between people, however silly the exchange method may be.

Advances in RFID Tag Technology

Advances are being made in chipless RFID tags that don't actually use any microchips, but use various chemicals chained together in a specific way to uniquely modulate a radio carrier wave, creating an identifiable "tag" without need for any actual chip. The characteristics of the antenna itself would be the identification mechanism. Current chipless technologies use reflective fibers, or "RF fibers," to reflect back a semi-unique return signal, which can be very useful in certain controlled environments.

Implantable tags are being developed that contain various types of sensors. These sensors could report temperature, or even test the blood for specific substance levels such as insulin or alcohol. Apparently Applied Digital Solutions, the parent company of VeriChip Corp, is working on a sub-dermal implantable GPS chip that could report GPS location.

Tags are also being developed with very large storage capacities in an attempt to make contactless storage a reality. Imagine an RFID tag on your keychain that could store a gig or two of pictures, data, and music and be accessible without needing to remove it from your pocket? One of the many barriers to this possible reality is a poor data transfer rate between tag and reader. To overcome this problem, active compression and ultra-high frequencies need to be used, which increases production costs.

I think it's apparent that RFID is here to stay. It's up to people like you to have a hand in its progression.

The Bottom Line

I hope this book has given you enough insight and inspiration to forge ahead with your own RFID project and creations. With all the different ways various technologies can be interconnected and made to work cooperatively, it seems to me there's no limit to what can be done.

Hardware Overview

So many times when I get a project book in my hands, I wish there was a simple index of the hardware covered in the book that tells me where I can get it and where it was used in the book. I know I would hit that section first thing. Now that I find myself writing such a book, I've included just that.

While there are many different types of hardware utilized in this book, this appendix only covers RFID hardware.

Readers

This section describes the types of RFID readers used in this book and where to get them.

Parallax RFID Reader Module

The Parallax RFID reader module (shown in Figure A-1 and detailed in Table A-1) is a great candidate for microcontroller-based projects. The TTL level output at 2400 bps is perfect for bufferless controllers such as the Parallax BASIC Stamp and various PIC controllers. You can also enable and disable the reader at-will through a control pin, allowing you to control exactly when the reader is actively scanning for tags and outputting data.

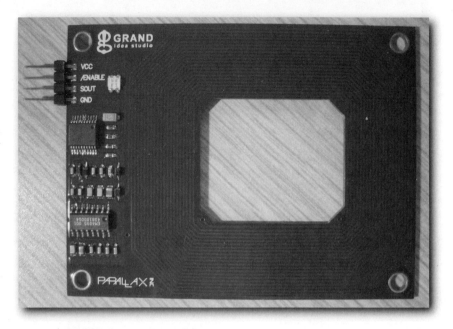

FIGURE A-1: Parallax RFID reader module

Table A-1   Parallax RFID Reader Module Details

Type	Passive RFID
Frequency	125 KHz (LF, low frequency)
Tags supported	EM4102
Interface	2400 bps TTL serial
Where to get it	www.parallax.com
Cost	$39.00
Used in	Chapter 5

Phidgets RFID Reader

The Phidgets RFID reader (shown in Figure A-2 and detailed in Table A-2) is a cheap USB device that works elegantly with Windows PCs. At the time of this writing, work is being done to support Apple computers running OS X. One unexpected advantage of the Phidgets driver and COM object is that the interface is nonexclusive. That means you can have multiple software packages on the same PC all receiving data from the reader at the same time.

FIGURE A-2: Phidgets RFID reader

Table A-2   Phidgets RFID Reader Details

Type	Passive RFID
Frequency	125 KHz (LF, low frequency)
Tags supported	EM4102
Interface	USB to PC
Where to get it	www.phidgetsusa.com
Cost	$50.00
Used in	Chapter 2, Chapter 4

The reader also has an on-board LED, a +5V output, and another LED output. All of these on-board outputs are software controllable, but cannot be queried for state. So, if you have multiple pieces of software interacting with the reader, you'll have to figure out your own way to save and share output state between applications.

I did stumble upon something interesting about these readers. If you are using them with implantable or glass type tags, the reader will lose considerable range if you don't use a properly shielded USB cable or you remove the USB header from the board (even if you shield the wiring). I believe it has something to do with antenna tuning and the removal of components, which were taken into consideration when the antenna was designed and tuned. Range doesn't seem to be affected that much with other types of tags, however.

QKITS RFID Access Card Controller

The QKITS RFID Access Card Controller kit (shown in Figure A-3 and detailed in Table A-3) comes completely disassembled. It includes a board, all the parts, a square coil loop antenna tuned to 125 KHz, and two access cards. This kit can support up to 42 different "allowed" cards. Once programmed, swiping an allowed card across the antenna will result in the relay closing. There is a header block included on the board that makes connecting to the relay's NO (normally open) and NC (normally closed) terminals a snap.

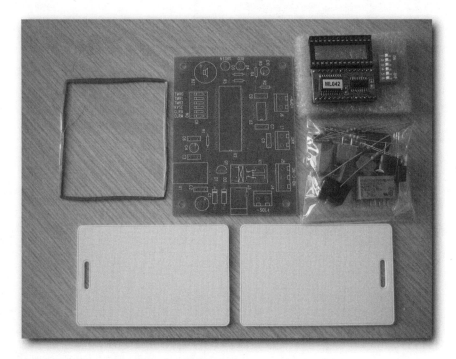

FIGURE A-3: QKITS RFID access card controller kit

Table A-3 QKITS RFID Access Card Controller Details

Type	Passive RFID
Frequency	125 KHz (LF, low frequency)
Tags supported	EM4102
Interface	None
Where to get it	www.qkits.com
Cost	$50.00
Used in	Chapter 3

The range of the antenna isn't that great, mostly due to the low output power of the reader itself. Don't even think about using a glass tag with this kit, it flat out won't read. Because of the low output power, connecting a better and/or larger antenna won't result in better range. For what it is, though, the QKITS access card kit is a neat, compact, autonomous access control solution. They also sell kit readers that output RS232 data and other access control kits, which support more than 42 cards.

SkyeTek M1 RFID Module

As if I haven't raved about this module enough already, I still have to say this very cheap and very small module (shown in Figure A-4 and detailed in Table A-4) is packed with more features than you'll know what to do with.

Table A-4 SkyeTek M1 RFID Module Details

Type	Passive RFID
Frequency	13.56 MHz (HF, high frequency)
Tags supported	Infineon: my-d SRF55C02P, my-d SRF55V02S, my-d SRF55V10P, my-d SRF55V10S
	Inside Contactless: PicoTag 2K, PicoTag 2KS, PicoTag 16K, PicoTag 16KS
	Philips: I-Code1 (SL1), I-Code SLI (SL2), Mifare, Mifare Ultra-Lite
	ST Microelectronics: LR512
	TagSys: GemWave C210, GemWave C220, GemWave C240
	Texas Instruments: Tag-It HF, Tag-It HF-I
Interface	I2C, RS232, SPI, TTL
Where to get it	www.skyetek.com
Cost	$115.00
Used in	Chapter 6, Chapter 7, Chapter 10

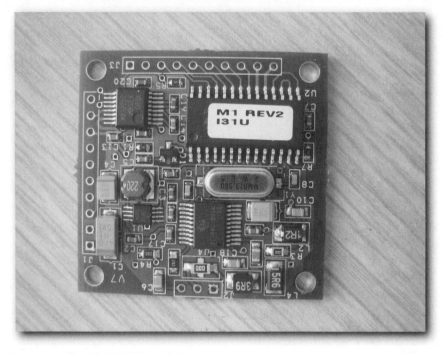

FIGURE A-4: SkyeTek M1 RFID module

This module supports quite a few different types of tags. What's not listed in the table is the fact the unit also has I/O outputs, which you can activate via the SkyeTek command protocol. The module also has a built-in LCD panel interface, letting you connect the I/O outputs to an LCD panel and send special LCD commands to the unit to output data on the LCD screen.

Finally, this module also has 256 bytes of nondestructive memory storage, which could be used to store application data or just about anything you need to. Having 256 bytes of storage doesn't seem like much, but when this module is used with a microprocessor, having 256 bytes of external storage is significant.

SkyeTek M1-Mini

Even though I didn't use this module in the book, I figured it was worth an honorary mention. Figure A-5 shows the M1-Mini, an ultra-small reader module that still manages to pack most of the M1's features into a board no bigger than a quarter. It still has an on-board antenna and manages to feature two pushbuttons to use in your application. This module would work great for handheld applications such as the one featured in Chapter 10.

FIGURE A-5: SkyeTek M1-Mini module

Wavetrend L-RX501 Reader

The Wavetrend reader (shown in Figure A-6 and detailed in Table A-5) is a UHF device, functioning at 433 MHz. This RFID reader is not passive — it's meant to listen for active RFID tags. Because it's an active device, it can use an antenna system completely different from the resonant loops that passive systems require. That opens the door for more typical antenna designs and placements, including the use of directional antennas.

Table A-5   Wavetrend L-RX501 Reader Details

Type	*Active RFID*
Frequency	433 MHz (UHF, ultra high frequency)
Tags supported	Wavetrend L-series tags: L-TG100, L-TG501, L-TG700, L-TG800, L-800IH, L-TG1000, L-TG1200
Interface	RS232, TTL (unsupported), RS485 (between multiple readers only)
Where to get it	www.wavetrend.net, www.iautomate.com, www.auto accessid.com
Cost	Ranges from $250–$500 depending on the source or vendor.
Used in	Chapter 8, Chapter 9

FIGURE A-6: Wavetrend L-RX501 433 MHz active RFID reader

The fact that the company keeps the hardware communications protocol shrouded in secrecy and even requires a signed NDA before they will let you buy their SDK kind of rains on what is basically a great product. Another thing about these devices is you can't purchase them directly from Wavetrend, who makes you buy them from partners and integrators who get to re-label the devices using their own part numbers before selling them. All in all, even with some vendors selling at inflated prices, it still opens the door on active RFID to your average hobbyist. Normally active RFID systems are priced way too high for anyone to consider unless they were rolling out a huge business case. With the introduction of iAutomate's RFID plug-in for the HomeSeer automation software application, leveraging the power of active RFID becomes a snap, even without buying Wavetrend's super-secret SDK.

RFID Tags

Tags come in many shapes, sizes, frequencies, and air interfaces. In this book, you've seen and/or dealt with various tags. Some of them were EM4102 low-frequency tags, some were ISO-15693 13.56 MHz tags, and some were active 433 MHz UHF tags. Since you can't really see the difference between a 13.56 MHz high-frequency tag and a 125 KHz low-frequency tag, I'll show you some of the different types of form factors available. Figure A-7 shows some of the tag form factors I'm talking about.

FIGURE A-7: Various RFID tags

The only regret I have is not being able to show you some 800–900 MHz UHF readers and tags. Not because the technology isn't available, but because the extremely high cost of such technology renders it totally irrelevant and outside the point of this book, which is getting hobbyists, power users, and hacker-types playing with RFID.

The Clamshell Card

This type of tag is usually used for low-frequency applications. It's about the size of a credit card, but it's thick. That's usually to accommodate a larger wire coil antenna, which is required by low-frequency tags. Clamshell cards usually have the best range out of all tags due to the large antenna size and the several turns or windings the antenna wire is able to make with all that extra space.

Like most clamshell tags, the (very dirty) tag shown in Figure A-8 has a hole on one end so it can be used with neck-straps or label clips like a personnel badge.

FIGURE A-8: The clamshell card tag

The ISO Card (Credit Card) Tag

An ISO card, sometimes called a credit card tag, is the size of a (you guessed it) credit card. When used in low frequency, passive situations, it has slightly less range than the clamshell card. That's because the wire coil antenna can't make as many turns, so it's slightly more difficult for the tag to induct the energy needed to power itself.

When a 13.56 MHz high-frequency tag is embedded in this form factor, the ISO card has very good range. Higher frequency energy doesn't need a wire-coil antenna; it can get by using conductive inks printed on various substrates. The point being that a high-frequency tag antenna is not limited by the physical space requirements of using solid wire.

In Figure A-9, the tag on the left is a 125 KHz EM4102 tag. The tag on the right is a 13.56 MHz ISO-15693 tag. As you can see, they look the same and I had to label the 13.56 MHz tag so I wouldn't mix them up while taking the picture.

FIGURE A-9: "ISO" (credit card) tags

Keyfobs and Various Other Shapes

Keyfobs are usually just circular shaped tags embedded in various plastic casings, as shown in Figure A-10. Everything else is usually a circle or square of some kind. Some come encased in clear plastic, and some are encased in rubber with adhesive backing. There are wristband tags and even industrial tags, which have very resilient plastic mounts. Basically, you can find just about any kind of tag imaginable — and if you can't find it, you can even get custom tags manufactured.

Glass Tags

Glass RFID tags are generally low frequency tags that consist of a very small microchip connected to a tightly wound wire coil antenna. The coil is longer than it is wide, which is a unique configuration for an RFID antenna. The entire circuit is encased in glass and can come in a variety of sizes, as shown in Figure A-11.

FIGURE A-10: Various RFID tags

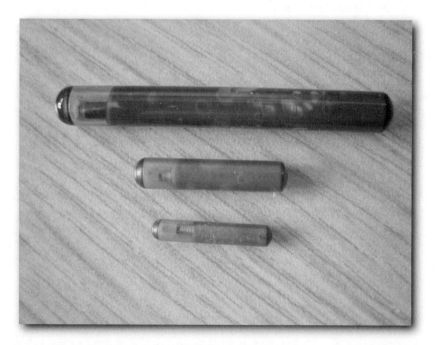

FIGURE A-11: 4×30mm, 3×13mm, and 2×12mm glass tags

Some glass tags are meant to be used for implantation into animals. Tags like the VeriChip are meant for human implantation. Other glass tags are not meant for any kind of implantation — they are embedded into other products or used in liquid environments. One example of this is the ExxonMobile SpeedPass RFID-based gasoline purchasing system. It uses a glass tag embedded inside a plastic casing for its keyfobs.

Wavetrend 433 MHz Active RFID Tags

Wavetrend sells their own active RFID tags to be used with their reader hardware. There are several types available, but probably the most commonly used are the L-TG100 Domino tag, the L-TG800 metallic asset tag, and the L-TG501 personnel tag (see Figure A-12).

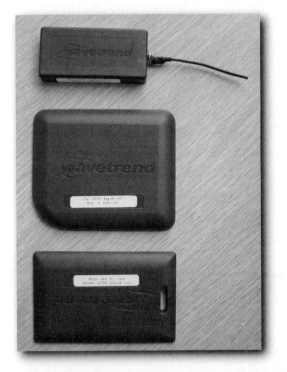

FIGURE A-12: Wavetrend L-TG100, L-TG800, and L-TG501 tags

The metallic asset tag is designed to be affixed to a metal surface (not inside a metallic asset, but on the side of it). The L-TG501 personnel tag resembles a typical clamshell card tag, but it's much thicker due to the need to accommodate the internal battery. You can affix the L-TG100 tag to non-metallic assets like wooden pallets or plastic containers.

Almost all the tags Wavetrend makes support tamper detection by utilizing a tiny yet powerful magnet placed directly over a specific area of the tag. The magnet closes an internal reed switch. Any status change of this switch (closing or opening) triggers an alarm bit to be sent on the tag's next few transmissions.

Antennas

This section describes the passive and active RFID antennas, where they were used in this book, and the pros and cons of each.

Passive RFID Antennas

Passive RFID systems use resonant loop antennas that facilitate magnetic coupling between reader and tag, which allows energy and data to flow between them. Resonant loops are difficult to build and tune. Thankfully, many of the cheaper passive RFID readers come with built-in antennas.

In some cases however, the built-in antenna is not sufficient to fulfill project requirements. External passive RFID antennas are available to fill that need. Also, many high-power passive RFID readers don't come with their own antennas, you have to purchase them separately.

The Feid 13.56 MHz antenna shown in Figure A-13 antenna was used in Chapter 6 and Chapter 7 of this book.

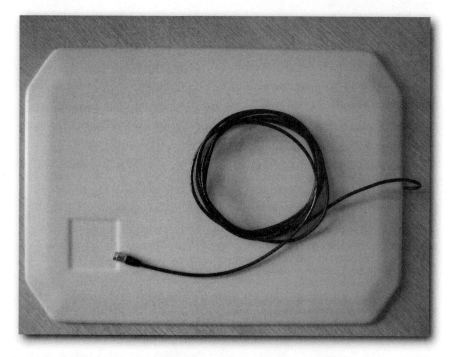

FIGURE A-13: Feig 13.56 MHz pad antenna with a male SMA connector

Active RFID Antennas

Active RFID uses more typical antenna systems, allowing you to utilize the directional capabilities of patch antennas. Figure A-14 shows a typical 433 MHz directional patch antenna with a female BNC connector on the back, perfect for connecting directly to various RFID reader devices. This particular type of patch antenna was featured in Chapter 9 of this book.

FIGURE A-14: Typical 433 MHz patch antenna with a BNC connector

Frequencies, Uses, and Typical Range

Table A-6 lists the common antenna frequencies, how each type of antenna is used for RFD, the pros and cons of each, and their ranges.

Table A-6   Antenna Details

Frequency	Use	Pro/Con	Range
125 KHz –148 KHz			
Type: Passive	Animal tracking (ISO 11784/ 11785), access control, and OEM applications.	Signal negotiates liquids and metals fairly well. Higher tag cost due to long length solid copper antennas.	1/2"– 4" is typical. 6"–12" or more may be possible with specialized equipment.
13.56 MHz			
Type: Passive	EAS (anti-theft), book and document management, access control, and OEM applications	Antennas can be printed on substrate or labels, lowering tag costs. Serious interference from metals.	Can range from inches to several feet depending on reader hardware and tag type.
433 MHz (and 2.5 GHz)			
Type: Active	Highway toll payment systems, vehicle/fleet management, asset tracking, and so on.	Very long range. Very high tag cost. Uses a battery, so tags have a finite lifespan (typically 5 years).	Typically around 30', but can range up to hundreds of feet.
915 MHz			
Type: Passive	Supply chain tracking and OEM applications	Very low-cost tag. Long range. Anti-collision capabilities allowing simultaneous tag reads. Serious interference from liquids and the human body.	About 10' from a single antenna and 20' between two antennas. Longer ranges can be realized with special hardware.

Index

Continued

Continued

Continued